Learning Resource Centre

New Road
Havant
Hants PO9 1QL

Tel: 023 9271 4045
Email: LRC@havant.ac.uk

D1324011

SKILLS-BASED SOCIOLOGY

Series Editors: Tim Heaton and Tony Lawson

The *Skills-based Sociology* series is designed to cover the Core Skills for Sociology A level (and equivalent courses) and to bring students up to date with recent sociological thought in all the key areas. Students are given the opportunity to develop their skills through exercises which they can carry out themselves or in groups, as well as given practice in answering exam questions. The series also emphasises contemporary developments in sociological knowledge, with a focus on recent social theories such as postmodernism and the New Right.

Published

THEORY AND METHOD
Mel Churton

EDUCATION AND TRAINING
Tim Heaton and Tony Lawson

MASS MEDIA
Marsha Jones and Emma Jones

CULTURE AND IDENTITY
Warren kidd

STRATIFICATION AND DIFFERENTIATION
Mark Kirby

CRIME AND DEVIANCE
Tony Lawson and Tim Heaton

HEALTH AND ILLNESS
Michael Senior with Bruce Viveash

THE FAMILY
Liz Steel and Warren Kidd

Forthcoming

POLITICS
Warren Kidd and Karen Legge

RELIGION
Joan Garrod

WEALTH, POVERTY AND WELFARE
Sharon Kane and Mark Kirby

Further titles are in preparation

Skills-based Sociology
Series Standing Order ISBN 0–333–69350–7
(*outside North America only*)

You can receive future titles in this series as they are published. To place a standing order please contact your bookseller or, in the case of difficulty, write to us at the address below with your name and address, the title of the series and the ISBN quoted above.

Customer Services Department, Macmillan Distribution Ltd
Houndmills, Basingstoke, Hampshire RG21 6XS, England

MASS MEDIA

Marsha Jones
and
Emma Jones

palgrave

Published by
PALGRAVE
Houndmills, Basingstoke, Hampshire RG21 6XS and
175 Fifth Avenue, New York, N.Y. 10010
Companies and representatives throughout the world

PALGRAVE is the new global academic imprint of
St. Martin's Press LLC Scholarly and Reference Division and
Palgrave Publishers Ltd (formerly Macmillan Press Ltd).

ISBN 0–333–67206–2

This book is printed on paper suitable for recycling and made from fully managed and sustained forest sources.

A catalogue record for this book is available from the British Library.

10   9   8   7   6   5   4
07   06   05   04   03   02   01

Printed in Malaysia

To our **Joneses** with love

Contents

Acknowledgements   x

Chapter 1: Introduction   1

- Philosophy/rationale behind the book   1
- Subject content   2
- An introductory exercise   2

Chapter 2: Media Use   4

- Media use at home   5
- Television and its audience   5
- Television viewing and age   8
- Newspapers and their readers   10
- Magazines   11
- New technology   12
- Gender and computer use   13
- Young people and film   14

Chapter 3: Histories of the Media   16

- Media processes   16
- The British newspaper industry   17
- Broadcasting in Britain – BBC radio   25
- Independent radio   26
- Breakfast radio   28
- Television   29
- Television and the future (satellite television and
  digital television)   33

Chapter 4: Marxist and Pluralist Theories of the Media   36

- The instrumentalist-Marxist approach   36
- The hegemonic or structuralist-Marxist theory   42
- Pluralism and the media   45
- The ownership and control debate – applying the theories   48
- Examination focus   59

**Chapter 5: Feminism, Postmodernism and the
Mass Culture Debate**   **64**

- Feminist perspectives on the media   64
- Postmodernism   73
- Mass media, mass culture?   78
- Pessimistic views: radicals and romantics   81
- Mass culture or popular culture? Optimism at last?   84
- Examination focus   85

**Chapter 6: Making the News: Selection and Presentation
(Is the Truth Out There?)**   **87**

- Newspapers and audiences   88
- News production   89
- News values   90
- Bias and the media   91
- Television news   92
- Inferential structures of news production   94
- Examination focus   101

Chapter 7: Representation   **104**

- Stereotypes   105
- Representation of gender   107
- Representation of ethnicity   121
- Representation of sexuality in the media   133
- Representation of age in the media   135
- Examination focus   138

Chapter 8: Deviancy Amplification and Moral Panic   **142**

- Characteristics of a moral panic   143
- Mass hysteria and collective delusion   146
- Child sexual abuse   147
- Satanic child abuse   147
- 'Back to basics': the single parent family   148
- The US drug panic of the late 1980s   152
- Theories of moral panics   153
- Examination focus   156

Chapter 9: Audiences and the Effects of the Media   **157**

- Media strong, audience weak: the hypodermic syringe model 158
- The two-step flow hypothesis   161
- Audience needs and satisfactions: the uses and gratifications
  approach   162
- Reinforcement theory   163

- Structuring reality: towards the active audience – cultivation analysis   164
- Reception analysis: media weak, audience active   167
- Semiology   170
- Media, violence and children: a special case?   172
- Examination focus   186

Chapter 10: Politics and the Media   **188**

- The role of the media in a democracy   189
- Elections, voting behaviour and the media   191
- Political bias in the media   202
- New media, new politics? Packaging politics   207
- The state and the media   212
- Examination focus   216

Chapter 11: Globalisation, New Technologies, New Futures   **218**

- What is globalisation?   219
- The development of globalisation   220
- Cultural dimensions of globalisation   221
- Globalisation and cultural imperialism   223
- Globalisation and local empowerment   227
- Case studies of globalisation   228
- Conclusions: is there a global media culture?   231
- New technologies: where do we go from here?   233
- The social impact of new technology   237
- Examination focus   240

References   241

Author Index   253

Subject Index   256

Acknowledgements

The authors and publishers wish to thank the following for granting permission to reproduce copyright material in the form of extracts, figures and tables: Blackwell Publishers, Carel Press, Ewan Macnaughton Associates for The Telegraph Group Ltd (© 1996), Guardian Media Group plc (Guardian Newspaper Ltd: The Guardian ©), HarperCollins Publishers, Her Majesty's Stationery Office, Manchester University Press, Michael Winner, Milton Schulman, Olympus Books UK, Philip Allan Publishers Ltd, News International Newspaper Ltd (© Times Newspaper, 1992).

We are also grateful to the Associated Examining Board (AEB) for allowing us to use questions from past A Level examination papers. All answers and examination hints are the sole responsibility of the authors and have not been provided or approved by the AEB.

Every effort has been made to trace all the copyright-holders, but if any have been inadvertently overlooked the publishers will be pleased to make the necessary arrangements at the first opportunity.

The authors are most grateful to the series editors Tony Lawson and Tim Heaton and to Frances Arnold, Catherine Gray, Stephen Wagg and Keith Povey for their editorial help. We would also like to extend our personal thanks to Andy Jones and Olga Linné for their continued support and encouragement. Our thanks also go to our students at Beauchamp College and La Sainte Union School, who were so important in shaping this book.

1 Introduction

The philosophy behind the book

The philosophy that underpins this book is similar to that of the other books in the 'Skills-Based Sociology' series. The book focuses on the syllabus areas covered by the sociology of the media and is mainly addressed to A Level sociology students. As with the other books in this series, we expect you as students to engage actively with the text. It is an opportunity for you to practise the skills that all the examination boards for A level sociology expect you to demonstrate. The book is designed so that the skills of interpretation, application and evaluation are tested, and the skills of knowledge and understanding are developed.

Until recently, the sociology of the mass media has not been dealt with in any great depth by any of the major contemporary sociology textbooks, so we hope that this book will help to fill in the gaps missed by others. However, as this is not a textbook you will be expected to refer to other resources. What we have produced is an overview of the major areas outlined in the syllabuses. You will find that some of the newer debates in the field of mass media are referred to, especially postmodernism, and the ongoing controversy over the influence of the media on our lives.

We hope that this will help you to become active learners and that you will enjoy studying the sociology of the media. There are plenty of different kinds of exercise for you to undertake, which will enhance your understanding, analysis and evaluation. Some of the exercises focus specifically on examination techniques so that you will become familiar with what exam questions are really asking you to do. You will be able to identify the skills each exercise is designed to develop by looking out for the following symbols: *i* for interpretation, *a* for application, *e* for evaluation, *k* for knowledge and *u* for understanding.

Our book requires you to think and assess the evidence put in front of you, to challenge some common-sense ideas about the media and to evaluate the contribution of sociologists to this exciting field of study. The studies we refer to are as up to date as they can be (at the time of writing) and we believe that you will find the exercises we have included interesting. The book is intended to engage you actively. If you do not attempt the exercises you will only gain half the benefits!

Overall, we hope that you will find this an enjoyable and informative book and that it will heighten your awareness of the media in all their forms.

Subject content

The subject matter of this book is divided into ten broad areas. In Chapter 2 we consider the patterns of media use by contemporary audiences. Chapter 3 provides an historical overview of British media. Chapter 4 examines the more traditional theories of the media together with the theoretical approaches to the ownership and control debate. Chapter 5 examines the newer theoretical approaches to the role of the media in society, including feminism and postmodernism. Chapter 6 examines the news-making processes, especially agenda setting, gate keeping and news values. Chapter 7 looks at the representation of selected groups in the media, while Chapter 8 examines the role of the media in the creation of moral panic. Chapter 9 concentrates on audiences and audience effects. Chapter 10 examines the relationship between the media and politics. Finally, Chapter 11 looks at the future of the media, including the possible impact of new technology and the process of globalisation.

An introductory exercise

Let's see how far you can apply your existing knowledge in answer to some statements about the mass media. We suggest that you try the exercise below before you read any other chapter. You might like to discuss your views with another member of the class. For each statement, decide whether you agree or disagree with it and then give reasons for your decision. Keep your written responses to hand so that you can check them when you read the relevant sections later in the book.

Statements

1. Individuals, especially children are likely to copy what they see on the screen; they might become aggressive, violent or even commit murder after watching video nasties such as 'Child's Play 3'.
2. The media are biased because of the nature of their personnel. These people are largely middle-class, white men who are opposed to extremism in any form.
3. Minority ethnic groups are only portrayed in a limited and generally negative way on television.
4. The audience for the media have a greater say over the content of the media than do the owners.

5. Television is the most important source of information about the rest of the world; people believe what they see.
6. The portrayal of women in the media has totally changed. They are no longer limited to the stereotypical images of sex object, mother or domestic labourer.
7. Advertising has a powerful influence on the consumption of goods; this proves the power the media have on our behaviour.
8. Some types of deviance are highlighted and exaggerated by the media, for example the use of drugs such as Ecstasy and crack cocaine, while the effects of other drugs such as alcohol and tobacco are ignored.
9. The effects of strikes are more likely to be reported than their causes.
10. Newspaper owners are the single most important group in deciding what goes into our newspapers.

2 Media use

By the end of this chapter you should:

- be more aware of your own media use;
- be aware of the nature of audiences for different contemporary media.

Introduction

This book is about the sociological significance of the mass media, especially as they are experienced in Britain. However, nowadays we cannot separate ourselves from the rest of the world. We live in a media-saturated world, where the media are all around us, where new technology has shrunk the globe and made global communication commonplace. Thirty years ago Marshall McLuhan referred to the creation of a 'global village' as follows:

> After three thousand years of explosion . . . the Western world is imploding. Today, after more than a century of electric technology, we have extended our central nervous system itself in a global embrace, abolishing both time and space as far as our planet is concerned. . . . The globe is no more than a village (McLuhan, 1964, pp. 11–12).

However the globe is not an idyllic, rural village, but one where different individuals and nations have different levels of power and where some of the villagers have louder voices and better technological networks for communicating their voices than the rest. We shall see that the power relationships are shifting considerably, and to discuss the changes simply in relation to the Western world would be at the very least ethnocentric (that is, judging something from our own viewpoint), but ultimately we would be ignoring the emergent power of the 'Pacific Rim' countries, which have become big game-players in the new technological developments.

Media use at home

What does 'media saturation' really mean? Our analysis has to start somewhere, so let's look at our own lives and discover how much of our time is taken up by the mass media. It will be interesting to see just how much time you and/or other family members spend with the media, and you might find the results of the exercise quite surprising!

Exercise 2.1

Media diary

Close your eyes for a moment and imagine your lives without television, radio, newspapers, magazines and music. How would you learn about events? What would you do with all the spare time that became available?

This exercise will help you to guage your own media involvement and how much time you and the rest of your family actually spend with different kinds of media.

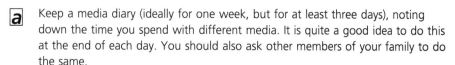

a Keep a media diary (ideally for one week, but for at least three days), noting down the time you spend with different media. It is quite a good idea to do this at the end of each day. You should also ask other members of your family to do the same.

These are the media that you might include: television; videoed programmes/ films, cinema, radio, newspapers, magazines, computer games, music tapes, CDs, records, the Internet.

From your data answer the following questions:

i 1. Which family member spends most time watching television?

i 2. When is the whole family engaged with the same medium, if at all?

i 3. Who spends the most time reading newspapers and/or magazines?

e 4. Write down your general conclusions about your family's use of the media. To what extent is it true to say that, in your family, the time taken up by the media is greater than any other leisure-time activity?

Television and its audience

You might have found that television takes up the greatest proportion of your family's leisure time. This would be typical of families all over Britain, because in general people spend more time watching television than they do on any other single leisure activity. Television has reached virtual saturation point in Britain; 98 per cent of homes possess at least one television and in 1991 36 per cent had two or more sets (see Item C for European comparisons).

Participation[1] in selected home-based leisure activities: by social class, Britain 1993–94[2] (hours per week)[3]

	AB	C1	C2	DE	All persons
Watching TV	13.5	15.4	17.5	20.2	17.1
Listening to the radio	9.2	8.7	11.6	10.9	10.3
Listening to CDs, tapes or records	4.3	4.0	3.4	4.4	4.0
Reading books	5.1	4.3	3.2	3.4	3.8
Reading newspapers	3.6	3.3	3.4	3.2	3.3
Caring for pets	2.6	3.1	3.2	3.5	3.1
Gardening	2.4	2.0	2.2	1.8	2.1
Cooking for pleasure	1.8	1.8	1.8	2.0	1.9
Watching videos of TV programmes	1.6	1.4	1.7	1.9	1.7
DIY or house repair	1.6	1.6	1.7	1.4	1.6
Sewing and knitting	0.9	1.3	1.4	1.5	1.3
Reading specialised magazines	1.2	1.1	1.0	0.8	1.0
Watching other videos	0.7	0.9	0.8	1.3	1.0
Reading other magazines	0.6	0.8	0.7	0.8	0.7
Exercising at home	0.6	0.8	0.4	0.5	0.5
Using games computer or console	0.5	0.4	0.5	0.6	0.5
Car maintenance	0.4	0.4	0.9	0.3	0.5

1. Time spent in an average week in the 3 months prior to interview by persons aged 16 or over.
2. Data relate to the 12 month period ending September 1994.
3. The classifications AB, C1, C2 and DE refer to social classes in Britain.

(Source: Social Trends, Office for National Statistics vol. 25, 1996.)
© Crown Copyright 1998.

ITEM A   *Exercise 2.2*

 1. Using your sociology textbook, give an example of an occupational group for each of the social classifications AB, C1, C2 and DE.

 2. In Item A, which social class spent most time watching television, including watching videos of television programmes?

 3. Suggest three social reasons why this might be the case.

TV-related equipment in the home in 1986

% of viewers who have:	All adults	Adults with children
VCR	38	51
Home computer	18	33
Cable TV	1	2
None of the above	50	68

(Source: Adapted from IBA Yearbooks,1987/1995.)

ITEM B   *Exercise 2.3*

Examine the statistics in Item B.

 1. Describe the differences between homes with and without children.

 2. How would a sociologist account for these differences?

Television and video ownership in Europe

(% of households)	Two TVs	Video
UK	36	58
Italy	36	25
Spain	35	25
Netherlands	31	48
Germany	25	42
France	23	35
Greece	16	40

(Source: M. Denscombe, Sociology Update, Leicester; Olympus Books, 1992.)

Watching television is the single most frequent leisure pursuit of the British public, but it is not simply a time-passing activity. As well as having an entertainment role, television educates and informs – it is a highly credible source of information about the world. Items D and E show the results of various social surveys conducted over a period of twelve years in this country. The graphs illustrate the trends over that period.

Where people said they got their news 'about what is going on in the world today' (first-mentioned source), 1985–96[1]

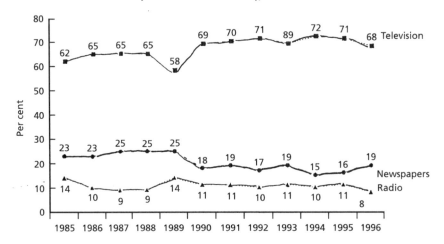

1. Based on surveys of 1000 adults (aged 16 and older) who had a working TV set in their household 'Don't knows' are excluded.

(Source: Television: The Public's View, Carel Press. Fact File 1997.)

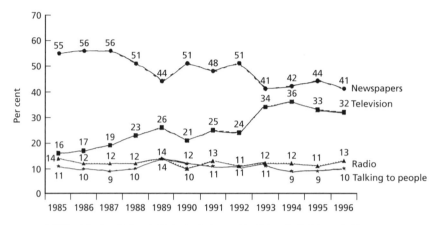

Where people said they got their news about 'your local area' (first-mentioned source), 1985–96[1]

1. Based on surveys of 1000 adults (aged 16 and older) who had a working TV set in their household.

(Source: Television: The Public's View. Carel Press. Fact File 1997.)

ITEMS D AND E   *Exercise 2.4*

Look at Items D and E.

 1. Identify one trend from each graph.

 2. How would you account for the differences between the media sources for world news compared with local news?

 3. What research methods might have been used to collect the data?

 4. Assess the advantages and disadvantages of the kinds of data in Items D and E for sociological research.

TV viewing and age

According to Item F, age and viewing are correlated. The amount of viewing increases with age; although those aged 65 and over watched about two hours less in 1993 than in 1986. It is interesting to note that the age group least likely to watch television is children and young people aged four to fifteen.

Television viewing by age in Britain (hours and minutes per week)

Age groups	1986	1991	1993
4–15	21:06	18:20	19:12
16–34	21:38	22:20	22:42
35–64	27:56	27:38	26:24
65+	37:47	37:27	35:41

(Source: Social Trends, Office for National Statistics, vol. 25, 1996, p. 216,
© Crown Copyright 1998.)

ITEM G ## *Exercise 2.5*

Look at Item G. These are the television ratings for 23 July 1995. Take a current issue of the *Radio Times* or any other weekly television guide.

|i|
1. Check whether these programmes are still broadcast and how regularly they appear.

|i|a|
2. Compare the current ratings against those in Item G. What do you find? (You will find TV ratings weekly in the quality press, for example in the *Guardian*'s media section.)

|k|u|
3. If you were a visitor to this country and had not watched any British television before, how would you describe the current viewing preferences of the television audience? (Complete this question in no more than 150 words.)

|i|a|
4. What might you be able to predict about the tastes of the average viewer from your answer to question 3?

Television viewing figures for week ending 23 July 1995

	Million viewers		Million viewers
BBC 1 Top 10		**ITV Top 10**	
1 East Enders (Tue/Sun)	15.68	1 Coronation Street (Mon/Wed)	17.10
2 National Lottery Live	11.24	2 Emmerdale (Tue/Thur)	11.00
3 Neighbours (Mon)	11.20	3 Home and Away (Tue)	10.58
4 Auntie's Sporting Bloomers	9.17	4 The Bill (Fri)	10.03
5 Casualty	8.35	5 Beaches	8.63
6 Till Murder Do Us Part (Fri)	8.32	6 Wycliffe	8.61
7 Fawlty Towers	8.04	7 The Russ Abbott Show	7.80
8 Birds of a Feather	7.84	8 Heartbeat	7.42
9 News/Sport/Weather (Sat)	7.13	9 World in Action	7.38
10 Nelson's Column	7.05	10 News at Ten (Mon)	6.88
BBC 2 Top 5		**Channel 4 Top 5**	
1 The Outer Limits	5.39	1 Brookside (Fri/Sat)	5.84
2 The Other Side of Love	4.20	2 ER	3.41
3 Golf: the Open (Sun)	3.72	3 Countdown (Tue)	3.26
4 The Travel Show	3.33	4 Ellen	3.20
5 One Foot in the Past	3.06	5 Hairspray	3.15

(Source: Radio Times, 19 August 1995.
Printed in Fact File (1996) Carel Press.)

Newspapers and their readers

On average, in Britain today over 27 million people read at least one daily newspaper. The most popular title is the *Sun*, which has a circulation of approximately 4 000 000 (4 079 559 between January and June 1995) and a readership of approximately three times that figure.

Newspapers are divided into roughly three groups – quality, middle market and mass market (popular tabloids). Examples of the quality press are *The Times*, the *Daily Telegraph* and the *Guardian*: the middle-market includes the *Daily Mail* and the *Daily Express*; and the popular press includes the *Sun* and the *Daily Mirror*. The differences between these papers include the type of news reported, the feature articles, the layout and the nature of the readership.

Exercise 2.6

Take one copy of each of these three types of newspaper on the same day and concentrate on their advertisements.

i 1. Measure the space given over to advertising as a proportion of the whole paper.

i 2. Which products have taken whole pages for their advertisements?

i *a* 3. Choose two products, say cars and furniture, and compare the differences between the advertisements in the three papers in relation to price, luxury, style and 'taste'. What does this tell you about the socioeconomic background of each of the readerships?

ITEM H ### Exercise 2.7

Look closely at the figures in Item H.

i 1. Which is the most popular 'quality' daily newspaper?

i 2. Which social class is most likely to read: (a) the *Sun*, (b) the *Financial Times*, (c) the *Daily Express*?

k *u* 3. Choose three Sunday newspapers and write a profile of their average reader (for example by gender and social class).

a *k* *u* 4. What sociological explanations can you put forward to explain these differences in readership?

Readership of national newspapers by social class and gender[1]

	AB	C1	C2	DE	Males	Females	All adults	Readership[1] (millions)	Readers per copy
			Percentage reading each paper						
Daily newspapers									
Sun	7	18	29	30	25	19	22	9.9	2.5
Daily Mirror	7	13	22	20	18	14	16	7.1	2.8
Daily Mail	14	13	8	6	10	9	10	4.5	2.5
Daily Express	9	10	8	5	8	7	8	3.5	2.5
Daily Telegraph	6	6	2	1	7	5	6	2.6	2.6
Daily Star	1	4	7	7	7	3	5	2.2	2.9
Today	3	4	5	3	4	3	4	1.8	3.1
Guardian	8	3	1	1	3	3	3	1.3	3.4
The Times	8	3	1	1	4	2	3	1.3	2.9
The Independent	6	3	1	1	3	2	2	1.1	3.5
Financial Times	5	2	–	–	2	1	2	7.4	4.2
Sunday newspapers									
News of the World	11	23	36	36	29	26	27	12.4	2.6
Sunday Mirror	9	16	24	21	19	17	18	8.1	3.1
The Mail on Sunday	18	17	11	6	13	13	13	5.9	3.0
The People	6	12	16	15	14	11	12	5.6	2.8
Sunday Express	13	13	9	5	11	10	10	4.6	2.8
The Sunday Times	21	8	3	2	9	7	8	3.7	3.0
Sunday Telegraph	11	4	2	1	5	4	4	1.9	3.1
Observer	9	4	2	1	4	3	4	1.6	3.2
Independent on Sunday	7	3	1	1	3	2	3	1.2	3.5
Sunday Sport	1	2	3	3	3	1	2	9.0	3.5

1. Data relates to the 12 month period ending June 1994.

(Source: Social Trends, Office for National Statistics, vol. 25, 1996.) © Crown Copyright

Magazines

According to the *Media Guide 1997*, there are approximately 6500 magazine titles on sale in Britain at present. Of these, 4377 are professional titles and the rest are consumer magazines, paid for by readers. You might like to do an estimate of the magazines on sale at your local newsagent. Over the last ten years the number of magazines has increased by a third. This increase is the result of several factors:

- Revenue from magazine advertising.
- Desk-top publishing has reduced publishing costs.
- Niche marketing is more and more profitable despite small circulations. 'A Henley Centre report reckoned that magazines are sources of cohesion in an uncertain world ... the traditional structures in society which segmented and distinguished between groups of individuals such as age, gender, class and religion are increasingly being overlaid by smaller groups based on individual taste and interest' (Peak and Fisher, 1996).

- Increases in men's non-porn magazines, emphasising style.
- Spin-off magazines from television programmes, focusing on gardening, antiques and cookery.
- The number of business magazines has doubled in five years.

In the past year the Periodical Publishers Association has acknowledged 548 new titles, with computing, football and magazines for men being among the most common. In February 1997 W. H. Smith decided to withdraw 'soft-porn' magazines from its shelves. This was not the result of a moral agenda, but rather that the sale of these magazines was slumping. In contrast to this decline, the sale of men's style magazines has dramatically increased:

Men's style magazines, number of copies sold, January to June 1996

Title	Publisher	Jan.–June circulation	Year on year %
Loaded	IPC	238 955	+87.2
FHM	EMAP	181 581	+100.4
Men's Health	Rodale	131 887	+14.7
GQ	Conde Nast	131 074	−3.0
Maxim	Dennis	113 264	n/a

Source: Guardian, 5 August 1996.

It is interesting to see how the newer magazines have become so successful so quickly. Three years ago men's titles together accounted for 300 000 sales a month, but today almost one million are sold. This has happened in parallel to the decline of feminist magazines such as *Sparerib* and *Everywoman*. According to Frazer Riddell, assistant editor of The Media Business, a cultural change is underway.... 'Men's magazines used to have their agenda set by women and now it is the kick-back.... The babe-content shot up with *Loaded* and everyone else has followed suit' (*Observer*, 11 August 1996).

New technology

The Internet

How many of you have already surfed the Internet? Some people find it invaluable as a resource while others find it a time-wasting activity. Whatever we think of it, it is likely that the Internet will play an ever increasing role in information technology and communication systems. Those who support it see it as a medium 'which is as revolutionary as the invention of printing. They say that by enabling everybody with a computer modem and phone line to publish to a global audience, the Internet is doing no less than altering media power balances' (Peak and Fisher, 1996, p. 216). Currently, there are about 30 million users world-wide and around one million in Britain. For approximately £12 per month (if you already have a computer, a modem and a telephone) you can be connected. However we have to take into account the fact that we are talking of the 'media-rich'; it is unlikely that many of those with low incomes will be able to participate in this new 'revolution' in the near future.

Trowler (1996) outlines two main arguments about the social significance of the Internet – he refers to them as 'digital liberation' versus 'digital corporatism'. He argues that 'digital liberation' will bring about:

- Decreasing costs of hardware and software; 'tele-working' and 'tele-shopping' from home will become the norm.
- More choice for consumers, who will themselves become interactive producers and directors.
- Interaction that takes place directly and instantaneously: 'synchronously'.
- An end to copyright legislation – information will be freely given and used.
- An increased 'democratisation' of users as information will become freely available.

However the 'digital corporatism' model presents a more pessimistic picture:

- Megacorporations will buy specialised sections of the Internet and charge for access.
- Patterns of conventional media ownership will be replicated on the Internet services as subscriptions will be introduced.
- Individuals will become increasingly socially isolated in front of their computer screens, leading to a decrease in community action.

Gender and computer use

There is some concern that computer technology is less girl-friendly than it could be. You might test out this assumption by checking your school/college computer bases at different times of the day.

Exercise 2.8

[i] Check your computer bases in your school/college at different periods during the day outside lesson times.

1. Count the number of male and female students using the computers. Is there any difference between the ratios at different times of the day?
2. Does one group monopolise the computers, or is there equality of use?

Research undertaken recently (SMRC Childwise Monitor 96/97) found that there is an increasing trend for boys to spend more time in 'the fantasy world of violent computer games, TV and 18 rated films'. The study found that:

- Nine out of ten children had a computer or games machine at home.
- Of 9–10 year olds, 44 per cent of boys had a computer in their own room, compared with 31 per cent of girls.
- Of all those with a computer at home, more boys (34 per cent) than girls (25 per cent) had it in their own room.
- Boys used the computers mainly to play games, the girls often used learning programmes.
- Boys bought more software programmes than did girls.

Young people and film

In December 1996 the Broadcasting Standards Council published its findings on young people's use of the media. Those in the 13–15 age group felt that they were not being taken into account by broadcasters, especially in relation to television programming. A third of those aged 10–12 admitted to having watched a violent, 18-rated film. 'The Silence of the Lambs', which had been broadcast on ITV, had been seen by 34 per cent of those under 12. Quentin Tarantino's 'Pulp Fiction' and 'Reservoir Dogs' had also been seen on video by 23 per cent and 18 per cent respectively of the under-12s. It is clear that the certification of films for cinema and video is not preventing large numbers of underage children and young people from viewing them.

Exercise 2.9

 1. How many cinemas/cinema screens are there in your nearest town/city?

 2. For any given week, list the different films that are being shown, their classification and their country of production. Set out the information you have gathered in a table like the one below.

Name of Film	Classification (PG etc.)	Country of production

 3. From this information, decide which type of audience is most likely to be catered for.

Coursework suggestion

Several of the issues dealt with in this chapter could form the basis of a coursework assignment.

You might like to address the question of media use and gender as a coursework enquiry. It would be interesting to link educational attainment with media consumption by taking a specific year group, possibly pupils who have just completed their SATS tests or GCSE examinations. Using a social survey, you could question them about their media use at home, linking it with the time they spend on homework.

A possible hypothesis would be: 'Pupils with higher levels of media consumption (for play rather than educational use) do less well in public examinations.'

3 Histories of the media

By the end of this chapter you should:

- understand the development of the press and broadcasting in Britain;
- be familiar with the processes of integration, diversification and internationalisation as they relate to this development;
- understand the role of 'media moguls' past and present.

Introduction

The media industries mean big business! This is no simple statement, they are amongst the most profitable enterprises in the world and their close links with national and international politics have considerable implications for their role in democratic societies. A great deal of research has been undertaken into the development of the media industries, especially highlighting the three processes of integration, diversification and internationalisation. Much of this relates to concentration of ownership, which – as we shall see – has been a feature of media businesses over the past century. The focus of this chapter is the British media industry, but inevitably, with the increasingly global nature of media ownership and the introduction of new media technologies, it will be impossible to stay within the confines of the British Isles.

Media processes

There are two kinds of integration that are relevant for a study of the media:

- **Horizontal integration**, where a media company buys up other similar products, so a newspaper proprietor might take over another newspaper company or companies.
- **Vertical integration**, where a media company buys up other aspects of the same industry, so a newspaper proprietor might buy up paper mills and newspaper distribution outlets, hence gaining more power over the whole industry.

Diversification is the process by which media industries do not simply merge, but buy up other interests in diverse media and/or leisure industries.

An example of this process is illustrated by the Granada Group. Not only did it own the second largest television rental chain and the fourth largest publishing group, but it also operated one of the 'Big 5' network television companies and had interests in Bingo clubs, motorway service stations and music publishing (Murdock, 1990).

Internationalisation: there are three aspects to internationalisation – the exportation of media products to other countries; the ownership of foreign media organisations by home companies; and, conversely, the ownership of home media companies by foreign companies (Golding, 1974).

This chapter will examine all these processes in relation to the developments of mass media in Britain.

The British newspaper industry

In order to understand the history of the British press we have to make sense of the complex interweaving and increased concentration of ownership, together with the relationship between powerful proprietors and political processes. Concentration of ownership of the press and other media is by no means a new phenomenon, but what is new is the immensity of the modern media industries.

Even in the late nineteenth century there was evidence of multiple ownership of weekly newspapers; in 1884, for instance, a syndicate headed by an American steel magnate, Carnegie, controlled eight daily and ten weekly newspapers (Curran and Seaton, 1991). Between 1890 and 1920 there was rapid growth in newspaper ownership. In 1921 Lord Northcliffe owned *The Times*, the *Daily Mail*, the *Weekly Dispatch* and the *London Evening News*. His brother, Lord Rothermere, owned the *Daily Mirror*, the *Sunday Pictorial*, the *Daily Record*, the *Glasgow Evening News* and the *Sunday Mail*. Together they owned Amalgamated Press, and their brother, Sir Lester Harmsworth, had a chain of newspapers in the south-west of England. In total the circulation of their newspapers was over six million.

In the 1920s, 1930s and 1940s – the era of the 'press barons' – Rothermere, Northcliffe and Lord Beaverbrooke of the *Daily Express* were not simply the owners of newspapers, they also controlled the political content of their newspapers. On the death of Lord Northcliffe in 1922, four men held the controlling interests of the press, and by 1937 they owned nearly half of the national and local dailies as well as one third of the Sunday newspapers; their combined circulation was 13 million. They espoused strong conservative attitudes, and in 1931

Prime Minister Stanley Baldwin accused them of holding 'power without responsibility'.

Exercise 3.1

What do you think the phrase 'power without responsibility' means? Try to illustrate your answer with examples.

ITEM A

National daily newspapers (selected titles), circulation (thousands)

Title (launch date)	1945	1965	1975	1988	1996
Daily Telegraph (1855)	822	1337	1331	1128	1044
The Times (1785)	195	254	319	436	685
Guardian (1821)	80	270	319	438	398
Independent (1986)	–	–	–	387	279
Daily Express (1900)	3239	3987	2822	1637	1245
Daily Mail (1896)	1752	2464	1726	1759	2058
Daily Mirror (1903)	2000	5019	3968	3157	2474
Sun (1970)	–	–	3446	4219	4049

(Sources: Seymore-Ure, 1991; The Media Guide 1997.)

ITEM A **Exercise 3.2**

With reference to Item A:

 1. Identify the trend in the circulation of the *Daily Telegraph* from 1945 to 1996.

 2. Describe the trends apparent between the circulations of the *Sun* and the *Daily Mirror*.

Gradually, individual proprietorship gave way to corporate ownership (ownership by companies rather than sole proprietors) and this was followed by ownership by conglomerates, although the controlling intenest of some of the main newspaper, here were held by single individuals, such as Rupert Murdoch and the late Robert Maxwell. The processes of concentration and internationalisation attracted a great deal of attention in the 1980s as media of all kinds came under the control of the new international conglomerates (multinational organisations that have been produced as a result of mergers between different enterprises since the mid 1950s). Between 1957 and 1968, over one third of all companies quoted on the London Stock Exchange disappeared through mergers and acquisitions (Murdock, 1990).

As we have seen, horizontal integration was well established before 1945 with the press barons, but what was distinctive in the 1980s was the 'scope, scale, management, balance and volatility' of the new media conglomerates (Seymore-Ure, 1991). The expansion of new media such as cable and satellite television, video recording and personal computers, brought about by new technological developments, played a large part in creating the new era of media ownership.

In the 1940s a media organisation was typically print-based, whereas in the 1980s the process of diversification meant that media conglomerates dealt with television, publishing, music, cinema, travel, international news agencies and satellite broadcasting. A new pattern had emerged whereby non-media conglomerates acquired media interests, as well as media conglomerates acquiring non-media-based interests.

This can be illustrated with a specific example: the Reed International Group. Until the 1960s this was essentially a paper-making company, in which the Mirror Group (IPC) held 44 per cent of the shares. The company then diversified into wallpaper production, and by 1971 Reed was so large that it took over the Mirror Group. In the 1970s and 1980s it changed again. In 1984 it sold the *Daily Mirror* to Maxwell, and by the 1990s it was an international paper, packaging and publishing conglomerate. It was about the fifth largest publishing house in the world, and was especially strong in magazine publishing.

From press baron to media mogul

Tunstall and Palmer (1991, p. 105) define a 'media mogul' as 'a person who owns and operates major media companies, who takes entrepreneurial risks, and who conducts these media businesses in a personal or eccentric way'. They also see other defining characteristics of media moguls as significant, notably that they mainly confine their business activities to the media – although they may have non-media interests, these will be secondary. It is not surprising that media moguls also tend to become involved with politics. In the USA, William Randolph Hearst (an anti-Democrat whose life was dramatised in the film 'Citizen Kane') was accused of delaying the entry of the USA into the Second World War.

Exercise 3.3

It might be interesting for you to see how Hearst's life has been dramatised. Borrow a copy of 'Citizen Kane' from your video library and decide whether the portrayal of this media mogul is sympathetic or not.

Until the general election of 1997, Rupert Murdoch's newspapers were seen as strongly biased towards the political right, and the newspapers owned by Robert Hersant and Axel Springer in France and Germany respectively have also shown very right-wing support in recent elections. Generally, media moguls tend towards support of individual political leaders rather than whole parties. This can be seen in the support the *Sun* gave Margaret Thatcher, whilst picking out other Tory politicians as subjects for their various 'sleaze' campaigns. As we shall see in Chapter 10, Murdoch withdrew his loyalty from John Major's Conservative government to give unqualified support to Tony Blair and New Labour.

The two great moguls of the British newspaper industry, Rupert Murdoch and the late Robert Maxwell, do not really conform to any of the general patterns of ownership. Neither was British by birth, both of them were buyers and sellers of media properties and both were partisan. Murdoch, who inherited an Australian daily newspaper from his father, went to Oxford University and became a journalist on the *Daily Express*. He bought the *News of the World* in 1968 and the *Sun* in 1969. He moved into London Weekend Television, bought *The Times* and *The Sunday Times* and then *Today*. He entered the American market and eventually took US citizenship. After establishing himself as a successful newspaper proprietor in New York, he took a controlling interest in Metromedia (the leading US group of independent television stations) and bought up Twentieth Century Fox for $575 million. He then turned his attention to satellite broadcasting and launched SkY. In 1989 he took over Harper Collins publishing, which included Fontana and Granada Books. As Seymore-Ure (1991) demonstrates, Murdoch's career has been highly individualistic. He still retains some non-media interests, for example part of the TNT trucking company.

Exercise 3.4

 1. Murdoch's involvement in media organisations exemplifies different processes of media development. Which of the following are relevant to his organisations and why – integration, diversification, internationalisation?

 2. Give two reasons why Murdoch would be interested in owning a transportation company.

Although Eddie Shah was the first proprietor to use new computer technology to produce his newspaper, *Today*, Murdoch saw the opportunity to break the unions' power by moving his entire production to a new plant in Wapping and bringing in non-union labour to work it. This was the first step in the modernisation of the industry. Staff levels were reduced dramatically and new newspapers were introduced: the *Independent*, the *Post*, *Sunday Sport*, the *Sunday Correspondent* and the *Independent on Sunday*.

Exercise 3.5

 Using suitable CD-ROMs, look up references to the Wapping dispute of 1986. What does the reporting tell you about the impact of new technology on the print industry as a whole and the print unions in particular?

Purchasing power is crucial to Murdoch's corporation because it allows it to make losses in one product area that can be sustained by profits made in others. For example in 1994 News International lost £45 million in its UK newspaper business, but its profits rose to over £186 million at BSkyB, of which it has a 40 per cent share. 'World-wide, News Corporation saw a general fall in profits from print-based media, but a big rise in film and television profits' (Branston and Stafford, 1996, p. 277).

Murdoch has fought a newspaper 'price war' since 1994, when he dropped the price of *The Times* to 10p. This has had a serious effect on The Independent.

In August 1995 *The Times* was given away free. 'The national newspaper price war ... was estimated to have cost 150m in lost revenues. "We won," said a News International spokesman. "Nobody has won," countered a stockbroker at Smith New Court'. In November the cover price of *The Times* went from 5p to 30p and the *Telegraph* increased to 40p (Peak and Fisher, 1996).

It is interesting to note that the *Guardian* was less affected by this battle because *Guardian* readers were unlikely to leave it for a newspaper that supported the Conservatives.

ITEMS B AND C *Exercise 3.6*

Read Items B and C on the News Corporation and Maxwell's empire.

1. In each of the boxes below, provide three examples of the processes of integration, diversification and internationalisation. The first has been done for you:

Corporation	Vertical integration	Horizontal integration	Diversification	Internationalision
News Corporation	1. West Web printers 2. 3.	1. *The Times* the *Sun* 2. 3.	1. Delphi Internet Services 2. 3.	1. Fox TV 2. 3.
Maxwell Corporation	1. 2. 3.	1. 2. 3.	1. 2. 3.	1. 2. 3.

2. How would a sociologist who holds a Marxist perspective on the media, use Items B and C to illustrate their theory of media ownership?

3. How would a pluralist respond to their argument using the same sources? (You might need to refer to Chapter 4 to help you with these answers.)

News Corporation: the worldwide net

Television

United States
Fox Broadcasting
Company
Fox Television Stations
WNYW – New York, NY
KTTV-Los Angeles, CA
WFLD-Chicago, IL
WTXF-Philadelphia, PA
WFXT-Boston, MA
WTTG-Washington, DC
KRIV-Houston, TX
KDVR-Denver, CO
KSTU-Salt Lake City, UT
WHBQ-TV-Memphis, TN
WBRC-tv-Birmingham,
AL
Aquisition pending
WGHP-TV-Greensboro,
NC
Sale Pending
WATL-Atlanta, GA
Fox News
Australia
Seven Network (10)

Cable and satellite television

United States
fX Networks
fX
fXM: Movies from Fox
Latin America
News Corporation/Globo
Joint Venture (3)
Canal Fox
United Kingdom
British Sky Broadcasting
(7)
Germany
VOX (4)
Australia
FOXTEL (3)

Asia
Star TV
ZEE TV (4)

Filmed entertainment

United States
Fox Filmed Entertainment
Twentienth Century Fox
Fox 2000
Fox Searchlight
Fox Family Films
Fox Animation Studios
Twentienth Century
Fox Television
Twentieth Television
Australia
Fox Studios Australia

Newspapers

United States
New York Post
United Kingdom
The Times
The Sunday Times
Sun
News of the World
Today
Australia & Pacific Basin
National:
The Australian
New South Wales:
The Daily Telegraph
Mirror
The Sunday Telegraph
Sportsman
Cumberland Newspaper
Group
(21 various titles – Sydney
suburbs and regional)
Victoria:
Herald Sun
Sunday Herald Sun
The Times Weekly

The Sporting Globe
Leader Newspaper Group
(31 various titles-
Melbourne
suburbs and regional)
Queensland:
The Courier-Mail (6)
The Sunday Mail (6)
Gold Coast Bulletin
Group (6)
Gold Coast Bulletin
Gold Coast Sun
Hinterland Sun
The Cairns Post Group (6)
The Cairns Post
Tablelands Advertiser
Pyramid News
Douglas Times
Northern Beachcomber
Travel Cairns
Rural Post
North Queensland
Newspaper Group
Townsville Bulletin
(8 various titles – regional)
Quest Community
Newspapers
(17 various titles –
Brisbane
Suburbs and regional).
Northern Territory:
Northern Territory News
Sunday Territorian
Centralian Advocate
The Suburban
Tasmania:
The Mercury
The Sunday Tasmanian
Tasmanian Country
Treasure Islander
Derwent Valley Gazette
South Australia:
The Advertiser
Sunday Mail
Messenger Press Group

(11 various titles –
Adelaide suburbs)
Western Australia:
Sunday Times
New Zealand
Independent Newspapers
(3)
Fiji
The Fiji Times
Nai Lalakai (Fijian
language)
Shanti Dut (Hindi
language)
Papua new Guinea
Post Courier (2)

Magazines and inserts

United States
TV Guide
The Weekly Standard
News America FSI
Canada
News Canada FSI
Coupon Clipper
Pian and Save
United Kingdom & Europe
*The Times Educational
Supplement*
*The Times Higher
Education Supplement*
*The Times Literary
Supplement*
*The Times Scottish
Educational
Supplement*
TV Hits (U.K.) (5)
Hit (Germany) (5)
Inside Soap (U.K.) (5)
Sugar (U.K.) (5)
Australia & Pacific Basin
Brisbane News
Pacific Islands Monthly
Australasian Post (5)
*Australian Home
Beautiful* (5)

Best Bets (50)
Disney Adventures (5)
Girlfriend (5)
Hit Songwords (5)
HM (5)
New idea (5)
Super Models (5)
That's Life (9)
TV Hits (5)
Your Garden (5)
TV Week (9)

Book Publishing

United States,
United Kingdom & Europe,
Australia & Pacific Basin
HarperCollins

Commercial printing

Australia & Pacific
Streetfile (5)
Progress Printers &
Distributors (5)
Keppell Printing (5)
Pac-Rim Direct (5)
Wilke Color (5)
Wilke Directories (5)
Griffin Press (5)
Griffin Paperbacks (5)
Prestige Litho (5)
Mercury Walch (5)
Argus & Australasian (5)
Westernport Printing (5)
West Web Printers (5)
Southweb (5)
Northweb (5)
Pacweb (5)
Swanweb (5)
Asher & Co. (Hong Kong)
(50)
Baskands (Christchurch)
(NZ) (5)

Baskands (Auckland)
(NZ) (50)
Circular Distributors (NZ)
(8)

Other operations

United States
Etak
News Electronic Data
News Corporation MCI
World Wide Joint
Venture (3)
Delphi Internet Services
Kesmai Corporation
United Kingdom
Broadsystem Ltd.
Convoys Group
News DataCom Ltd.
News MultiMedia Ltd.
Sky Radio (1)
Australia & Pacific Basin
Ansett Australia (3)
Australian Newsprint
Mills (6)
Broadsystem (Aust)
Computer Power (B)
Festival Records
FS Faulkner & Sons
Lamray Industries (6)
(Sunshine Plantation)
Mushroom Records (3)
PDN Xinren Information
Technology
Super League

Key:

News Corporation holds

(1)	71%	(6)	41.7%
(2)	63%	(7)	40%
(3)	50%	(8)	26%
(4)	49.9%	(9)	22%
(5)	45%	(10)	15%

(Source: Guardian, 16 July 1996.)

Maxwell's empire

68% of Maxwell Communication Corporation

which owned:
- Que (Macmillan Computer Publishing)
- Berlitz
- Panini
- Nimbus Records
- Maxwell Consumer Publishing
- International Learning Systems
- Official Airline Guides
- Collier
- Molecular Design
- Macmillan/McGraw Hill School Publishing
- Macmillan Inc

Private interests

Through Headington Investments and Robert Maxwell Group
- Maxwell Aviation
- Lady Ghislaine (yacht)
- AGB international
- Property
- Maxwell House, Holborn Circus
- The Independent (6%)
- 50% of Thomas Cook America
- Reading FC (stake)
- Oxford Utd FC
- The European
- Berllner Zeitung (50%)

- Modlin (Israeli newspaper)
- Robert Maxwell Business School – now the Sofia International Management Centre
- New York Daily News

54% stake in Mirror Group Newspapers

which owned
- 26% *Quebecor*
- 26% *Donahue*
- *Daily Mirror*
- *Sunday Mirror*
- *Daily Record*
- *Sunday People*
- *Sporting Life*

(Source: Guardian, 20 January 1996.)

The other 'media mogul', Robert Maxwell, came quite late into newspaper ownership. He made an unsuccessful bid for the *News of the World* in 1968, but it was for his ownership of the Mirror that he is most remembered. As well as the Mirror Group he had investments in Central TV and Border, a cable station and part of the satellite music station MTV. He controlled the Macmillan Incorporated publishing house in the United States and had part-interest in a French TV channel. His death in 1991 left his sons with a conspiracy trial to face, from which charges they were acquitted.

Today in Britain, seven companies account for all national newspaper sales (Item D).

National newspaper owners (approximate circulation percentages)

- News International (35%)
- Mirror Group (26%)
- United News and Media (13%)
- Daily Mail and General Trust (12%)
- The Telegraph (7%)
- Guardian Media Group (3%)
- Pearson (1%)

One of the reasons cited for the high level of concentration of ownership has been the considerable cost of launching a newspaper, although computerised typesetting has reduced the costs. Despite the arguments of pluralists who maintain that it is always possible to challenge the market share of the megacorporations, it is abundantly clear that finance has been the downfall of many a would-be proprietor. For example in 1986, when Eddy Shah set up the only daily tabloid espousing support for the Liberal/Democratic Alliance Party – *Today* – it cost him 18 million pounds in start-up funds and he hoped for a circulation of 800 000. Within four months he sold the newspaper to Lonrho for 20 million pounds, and Lonrho sold it to News International in June 1987 for approximately double that figure. Eventually it too accepted defeat and *Today* ceased operations in November 1995.

In 1988 a new left-wing Sunday newspaper was introduced, the *News on Sunday*, but it was shortlived, as were the *Sunday Correspondent*, the *London Daily News* and the *Post*, which were also set up in the 1980s. The *Post*, also owned by Shah, was abandoned in December 1988 after 33 issues. It achieved a circulation of 100 000 and lost around six million pounds. *The European*, which was set up by Maxwell in 1990, was taken over by the Barclay brothers and is still running at a circulation of around 225 000 (*Guardian*, 28 December 1995).

Golding (1974), Seymour-Ure (1991) and Curran and Seaton (1991) are excellent sources of further information on the historical development of the media industry in Britain.

Broadcasting in Britain – BBC radio

We have come a long way since 1922, when the Crawford Committee recommended a new broadcasting service funded by licence fees paid by owners of radio receivers. John Reith, later Lord Reith, was appointed managing director of the new British Broadcasting Company in 1923 and director general of the new British Broadcasting Corporation, set up in 1927 under royal charter. Today the governors of the BBC still have to maintain its public service responsibility and review it on a regular basis.

Reith's conception of radio broadcasting was a service dedicated to promoting and maintaining the highest possible standards in public taste by providing the best in information, education and entertainment. He wanted to use broadcasting as a kind of social cement to unify the people of Britain. As you read through this chapter you might think about whether broadcasting is now or ever has been capable of being this 'social cement'.

The Second World War emphasised how important light entertainment radio programmes could be to the public morale, and the BBC Home Service was joined in 1946 by the Light Programme (now Radio 2). Very soon the BBC realised that its listening audience was quite diverse, and in 1947 the Third Programme (now Radio 3) was introduced to offer audiences 'broadcasting as art', that is, high-culture serious features, classic music and theatre. Broadcasting at that time could be seen as a parallel institution to the newly introduced tripartite system in education: grammar schools catered for 5 per cent of pupils/ the Third Programme had 6 per cent of radio listeners; technical schools catered for 15 per cent of pupils/the Home Programme had 20 per cent of listeners; modern secondary schools had 80 per cent of pupils and the Light Programme attracted 74 per cent of the listening public. Broadcasting and education together were reinforcing the traditional divisions of culture and class (Seymore-Ure, 1991).

BBC radio broadcasting, promoting as it did the middle-class values of home life and the family, was never really popular with working-class audiences, who tuned into commercial stations as soon as they were launched. When the BBC had a monopoly of listeners, its mode of address was designed to reflect its public service orientation, and it was authoritative and set high standards. The BBC pattern of speech came to be known as 'BBC English' or 'received pronunciation'. It was some time before this was overtaken by regional accents and the more informal language used today.

Exercise 3.7

This exercise will help you to see that different radio stations have very distinct profiles. Take a copy of the BBC radio schedules for any week (you will find these in any radio and television magazine).

Compare the schedules of BBC Radio 1, 2, 3, 4 and 5 for any given day.

 1. What can you discover about the characteristics of each station?

 2. Is each station broadcasting to a different audience?

 3. Take one station and build up a picture of its audience. Now listen to this station at different times of the day; was your earlier audience profile correct?

 4. You could extend this exercise into a coursework enquiry by combining your content analysis with audience surveys. Produce three possible hypotheses that you could investigate in this way.

Independent radio

The potential youth market for radio was hardly considered by the early programmers. Although the Light Programme had some 'youth' programmes, young people were largely ignored, but competition for this new audience was growing from the independent stations, which were broadcasting exactly the kind of music that the new 'teenagers' wanted to listen to. Eventually the independents forced the hand of the BBC. For example 'Radio Caroline', a pirate station broadcast from a ship somewhere in the North Sea, successfully withstood the attempts of the BBC to prevent it from going on air, but in August 1967 the Labour government passed the Marine Broadcasting Offences Bill to prevent British nationals from working on pirate stations. In September the same year the BBC launched its new pop music station, Radio 1. At the same time the Light Programme became Radio 2, the Home Service became Radio 4 and the Third Programme became Radio 3. The BBC started to develop a network of local radio stations, but in 1971 competition arrived in the form of privately owned radio stations funded by advertising (independent local radio, ILR). In the mid 1980s there were around 45 commercial radio stations, now there are nearly two hundred. In August 1995 commercial radio was attracting more than half of all radio listeners. Item E shows the radio audiences for BBC and commercial radio stations in 1993 and 1996.

ITEM E

Radio audiences, 1993 and 1996 (millions)

Station	1993	Listeners 1996
All BBC		29.43*
Radio 1	14.2	11.24
Radio 2	9.0	8.41
Radio 3	2.8	2.28
Radio 4	8.5	8.69
Radio 5 Live	4.0	5.21
All commercial	26.4	28.9**
Atlantic 252	3.8	3.18
Classic FM	4.7	4.94
Virgin 1215	3.0	3.36

* 50.4 per cent.
** 47.6 per cent.

(Source: Media Guide, 1997.)

Since the 1990 Broadcasting Act, independent radio companies have operated under licence to the Radio Authority, which monitors and oversees their programming. Like commercial television and the press, radio ownership is concentrated in just a few hands. Classic FM is owned by a Major consortium that owns Time Warner, GWR, Associated Newspapers, Home Counties Newspapers. GWR also runs local radio stations in Reading, Swindon, Bristol, Bournemouth, Plymouth and Tavistock (O'Sullivan *et al.*, 1994, p. 72).

ITEM F

Radio services: share of listening by age, sex and class, 1986

	BBC R1	BBC R2	BBC R3	BBC R4	BBC local	ALL BBC	ILR
Age							
4–15	54	4	0	2	3	63	33
16–34	56	5	1	5	3	70	27
35–54	20	24	2	14	10	70	26
55+	4	33	2	19	19	77	18
Sex							
Males	33	18	2	10	8	71	25
Females	20	19	1	13	11	73	24
Social class							
AB	20	19	5	31	6	81	16
C1	28	20	2	15	9	74	22
C2	36	17	1	6	10	70	26
DE	27	19	1	7	13	67	28

(Source: Seymour-Ure, 1991.)

ITEM F *Exercise 3.8*

Study Item F.

1. What are the social characteristics of the average listener to Radio 1, Radio 3 and ILR?

2. How might sociologists account for the different profiles you have described in question 1?

3. 'Radio stations broadcast to selected audiences with very specific interests and tastes, rather than to a mass audience.' To what extent does the information in Item F support this statement?

Breakfast radio

According to Steve Barnard (1989), in the 1950s radio adopted 'sequential programming', that is, news, music, features and so on were presented in time blocks – the kind of magazine format that will be familiar to today's daytime television viewers. Sequential programming accepts that listening is casual because it dovetails with our daily lives. This can be seen in early morning radio programming. On breakfast radio the presentations are pacy, active and lively. The presenters are said to be highly professional because radio audiences are relatively loyal, so it is necessary to catch them early and keep them. Morning programmes are feature-packed and fast-paced; it is as if they are keeping pace with our supposedly busy lives. Barnard argues that they act as a bridge between the private, family sphere and the more impersonal, public domain of work.

Exercise 3.9

Listen to BBC Radio 4 and BBC Radio 1 between 7.30 a.m. and 9 a.m. on any two weekday mornings.

[i] 1. Make a list of each of the items dealt with by each station.

[a] 2. How do these differ? (Does one station have more/fewer news items? Where is there more political news? What about music coverage?)

[a][i] 3. How do the presenters address their audiences? (You might think about accents, vocabulary, familiarity, formality and so on)

[a][e] 4. On the basis of this information, produce profiles of the average listener to each station. Now look back at Item F. How accurate are your profiles?

Exercise 3.10

'Radio frames the working day; it reinforces the work ethic' (Barnard, 1989).

[k][u] 1. Explain what is meant by 'the work ethic'. Which sociologist is associated with the concept of the 'work ethic'?

[i][a] 2. What do you think that Barnard means by the above statement? Rewrite it in your own words.

[i][a] 3. Using the radio schedules for one day, show how radio stations may shape our day.

Television

BBC television was introduced to the nation in 1936 – or more accurately, to a small, select, affluent audience in London and the Home Counties – but this was short-lived as television broadcasting was suspended during the Second World War.

It is interesting that commentators at the time foresaw that television was going to have a considerable influence on the social life of the audience: 'Viewing television is a very different activity from listening to sound broadcasts . . . the television set demands your attention; you cannot enjoy television from the next room. You must sit facing the set, with the lights down or shaded, and if you are a normal viewer you will find yourself very reluctant to be disturbed during a programme that you enjoy' (Gorham, head of BBC, 1946). How many families now watch television with the lights down and undisturbed? When television transmission restarted in 1946 it was received by 15 000 households, and by 1956 it could be received throughout Britain. In 1946 9.7 million licences were issued, including 9.6 million radio licences; by 1959 these figures had grown to 14.7 million and 5.4 million respectively. Today there are 19.3 million television licences and radio licences are no longer necessary.

The Independent Television Authority was created by parliament in 1954 as a commercially funded corporate body to inform, educate and entertain. This service presented an immediate threat to the comfortable monopoly of the BBC and forced it to compete for audiences in the new cultural market place. In entering this new competitive market the BBC became more like the commercial channel, but because it was funded by the licence fee it lacked the huge revenues that advertising brought to ITV. The licence fee was increased every third year, and since 1988 has been increased annually.

There were three committees that made significant changes to broadcasting up to the end of the 1980s:

1. In 1960 the Pilkington Committee examined the output of commercial television. The committee was extremely critical of the output and as a consequence the proposed third channel was offered to the BBC – this became BBC2 .

2. In 1977 the Annan Committee was critical of both the BBC and ITV for having become complacent, and of being a 'cosy duopoly'. Annan accused both broadcasting authorities of failing to cater for the wide range of audience tastes. It was recommended that the fourth channel should be managed by an independent open broadcasting authority – a commissioner of programmes, not a producer. This became the new Channel 4, which started broadcasting in 1982.

3. In 1986 the Peacock Committee was set up to review the BBC licence fee with a view to its possible abolition. The committee was in favour of deregulation, with the greatest possible freedom of choice for consumers. The Peacock Report has had a significant impact on broadcasting in the 1990s, influencing as it did the white paper 'Broadcasting in the 1990s'. The report made reference to the 'robust consumer', the audience member who was able to identify and act in her or his own interests. So consumer sovereignty and competition were be the benchmarks of the future.

Exercise 3.11

Look up the following terms in your sociology textbook or a dictionary of sociology and write a definition of each. It would be quite useful to get a friend to test you on your how well you have learned them:

(1) Consumer sovereignty, (2) competitive tendering, (3) deregulation, (4) duopoly.

The Peacock Committee recommended that all restrictions on cable and satellite pay-per-channel and pay-per-programme be lifted. They suggested that competitive tendering for franchises should apply both to ITV and to Direct Broadcasting by Satellite (DBS). The most significant recommendations were for the maintenance of the BBC licence fee and that advertisements should not be allowed on BBC television. The Broadcasting Bill of 1990 set out the government's proposals for a new framework for the deregulation of independent television and radio. The Independent Television Commission (ITC) replaced the Independent Broadcasting Authority and Cable Authority so that it had authority over independent terrestrial television as well as cable and satellite. It was to have a 'lighter touch' than the IBA, which meant that it would be less interventionist in programme content. Other new institutions came into being:

- The Radio Authority, responsible for independent local and national radio and community radio.
- Channel 4 Wales (S4C) the Welsh language channel.
- The Broadcasting Complaints Commission and the Broadcasting Standards Council.

The newly formed ITC was to oversee the franchise bidding for the fifteen independent television companies and Breakfast Television. The private companies had to submit sealed bids to the ITC, which would award the franchise to the highest bidder after a 'quality' threshold was guaranteed. Only in 'exceptional' but unclear circumstances would the bid not go to the highest bidder. Item G shows the new franchises.

ITEM G

The new Channel 3 franchises

Licence area	Applicant (ranked by bid size)	Cash bid	Outcome
Borders and Isle of Man	Border TV	52 000	(a)*
Central Scotland	Scottish TV	2 000	(a)*
Channel Isles	C13 Group	102 000	(f)
	Channel TV	1 000	(b)*
E, W and S Midlands	Central Independent TV	2 000	(a)*
East of England	Anglia TV	17 804 000	(a)*
	Three East TV	14 078 000	(f)
	CPV-TV (East of England)	10 125 000	(g)
London Weekly	CPV-TV (Greater London TV)	45 319 000	(f)
	Carlton TV	43 170 000	(e)*
	Thames TV	32 794 000	(c)(g)
London Weekend	Consortium for IB	35 406 000	(f)
	LWT Holdings	7 585 000	(b)*
North of Scotland	North of Scotland TV	2 709 000	(f)
	C3 Caledonia	1 125 000	(f)
	Grampian TV	720 000	(b)*
N-E England	Tyne-Tees TV	15 057 000	(a)*
	North-East TV	5 010 000	(g)
N-W England	North-West TV	35 303 000	(f)
	Granada TV	9 000 000	(b)*
N Ireland	TVNi	3 100 000	(j)
	Lagan TV	2 712 000	(f)
	Ulster TV	1 027 000	(b)*

Licence area	Applicant (ranked by bid size)	Cash bid	Outcome
S and S-E England	TVS TV	59 758 000	(d)
	Meridian Broadcasting	36 523 000	(e)*
	CPVTV (S of England)	22 105 000	(f)
	Carlton TV	18 080 000	(g)
S-W England	TSW Broadcasting	16 117 000	(d)
	West Country TV	7 815 000	(e)*
	Telewest	7 266 000	(f)
Wales and West of England	HTV Group	20 530 000	(a)*
	Merlin TV	19 367 000	(f)
	Ch 3 Wales & the West	18 289 000	(f)
	C3W	17 760 000	(g)
Yorkshire	Yorkshire TV	37 700 000	(a)*
	Viking TV	30 116 000	(f)
	White Rose TV	17 403 000	(g)
National Break fast Time	Sunrise TV	34 610 000	(e)*
	Daybreak TV	33 261 000	(h)
	TV-am	14 125 000	(c)(h)

Key

* Awarded new franchise.

(a) Licence awarded to incumbent with highest or sole bid.

(b) Licence awarded to incumbent even though not the highest bidder; the others were unacceptable.

(c) Licence lost by incumbent – awarded to higher bidder.

(d) Licence lost by incumbent – awarded to lower-bidding competitor as the incumbent did not satisfy the ITC that it could maintain the proposed service.

(e) Licence awarded to new applicant in place of incumbent.

(f) Applicant did not satisfy the programme quality threshold for Channel 3 regional licences laid down in the Broadcasting Act 1990.

(g) Applicant satisfied the programme quality threshold for Channel 3 regional licences laid down in the Broadcasting Act 1990, but did not submit the highest qualifying bid.

(h) Applicant satisfied the programme quality threshold for Channel 3 national breakfast-time licences laid down in the Broadcasting Act 1990, but did not submit the highest bid.

(i) Applicant satisfied the quality threshold requirements and submitted the highest bid, but did not satisfy the ITC that it would be able to maintain the proposed service throughout the licence period.

(Source: New Channel 3 franchises, Cultural Trends 1993: 17.
© Policy Studies Institute.)

Although the aim of government was to 'open up' broadcasting, it is not clear that this has happened. As O'Sullivan *et al.* (1994, p. 71) argue, there were some disconcerting results:

> Carlton has taken over Central Television (Central owns 20% of Meridian) and has a 20% interest in GMTV, the breakfast contractor. Carlton also owns 18% of, and heads, the consortium that runs ITN. Carlton's head, Michael Green, is also on the board of Reuters which ... provides GMTV with its news service. Carlton shares its news facilities with LWT which also has a 20% share in GMTV. Meridian is owned by a consortium that includes MAI Broadcasting, Central Television and Select TV and is set to take over Anglia TV.

Exercise 3.12

Study Item G.

1. List those franchise 'winners' that had not previously been franchise holders.

2. List the winning incumbents (an incumbent is a company that held the previous franchise).

3. What were the largest and smallest bids? Who made them?

4. Do you think that ownership has become more or less concentrated as a result of the Broadcasting Act? Explain your answer.

Television and the future

Satellite television

In 1986 British Satellite Broadcasting (BSB) was awarded the franchise for satellite broadcasting. It was responsible for its own programming and its audience consisted of class ABC1 (professionals to skilled non-manual workers). At the same time as BSB was launched, Murdoch's News International bought up an existing satellite company based in Luxembourg. This became SkY, and unlike BSB it was aimed at mainly manual audiences.

Neither was initially successful, and in 1991 they merged to become BSkyB, owned by News International, Pearsons and the Granada Group. The new merger seemed to challenge the legal safeguards against cross-media ownership and monopolies. BSkyB has been an aggressive competitor, especially in gaining a monopoly over sports broadcasting. It bought the rights to premier league football matches in 1992, and has created a great deal of controversy by charging subscribers an additional fee for specific sports events (for example subscribers were asked to pay an additional fee to receive the Bruno–Tyson heavyweight championship fight in 1995). It seems likely that pay-per-view will become commonplace.

> The satellite channels seem to appeal mainly to men and young people. Over half (51%) of the adults living in satellite-receiving homes are less than 35 years of age. Satellite-receiving households are larger than average in size. They have an average of 3.3 people compared with a norm for Britain as a whole of around 2 people. . . . In satellite-receiving homes, BBC2's share of the viewing is 38% below that in homes without satellite capability, Channel 4's viewing drops by 41% (Denscombe, 1993, pp. 41–2).

BSkyB has ten channels with over four million subscribers. It owns:

1. Sky One – an entertainment channel. (There were rumours that it planned to bid for Coronation Street from ITV in order to increase the number of women in its audience. However this did not happen.)
2. Sky Movies.
3. The Movie Channel.
4. Sky Movies Gold (numbers 2–4 show 400 films each month).
5. Sky Sports.
6. Sky Sports 2.
7. Sky Sports Gold (numbers 5–7 show 10 000 hours of sport each year).
8. Sky News.
9. Sky Travel.
10. Sky Soap.

BSkyB has recently announced the launch of seven more channels, including European Business News, a history channel, Disney and Playboy channels (*Media Guide 1997*, p. 168). It is estimated that BSkyB will have launched up to 500 new channels by 1998. In April 1996 the number of subscribers had reached 5.35 million.

Exercise 3.13

Take a copy of any publication showing TV schedules for the week and look at the listings for Sky Television.

[i] 1. Which programmes are unavailable on terrestrial channels?

[i] 2. Are any types of programme missing from these schedules?

[i][a] 3. Can you gauge anything about the audiences for Sky that makes them in any way specific as an audience?

[e] 4. Pluralists may argue that Sky Television gives the audience greater choice. How far would you agree with this?

It is important to note that despite Murdoch's News International having a 40 per cent holding in BSkyB, it still only reaches one fifth of the British population. However Whannel and Williams (1993) argue that worse is yet to come. They equate the buy-up by BSkyB of major sporting events, especially football's Premier League matches, with an insidious attack on the basic principles of democracy and citizenship. Their thesis is that satellite television has challenged democratic society's fundamental principle of universal access, because only the media-rich consumer will have access.

Digital television

Television is undergoing an enormous technological change. At present programmes are transmitted by a series of radio waves via an analogue signal. However new technology will allow programmes to be transmitted by a digital signal, which will double the number of scan-lines on screen (at present 625) and the picture quality will be superior to that we have at present. Digital television and radio involves converting sound and images into computer language, which is then transmitted in a compressed form. The signals will have to be decoded by a black box on the television set, and the estimated cost of a decoder is between £300 and £500. A consultative paper from the Heritage Department offered safeguards to the existing terrestrial channels, 'but if they want to expand beyond their existing channels they will have to bid competitively for extra capacity – a process which could cost the BBC, for example, £100 million to £150 million a year' (*Guardian*, 11 August 1995) .

The 1996 Broadcasting Act allowed for 36 digital terrestrial channels on six 'multiplexes' – bunches of channels – that will be capable of delivering three or more channels. Multiplex owners will have to bid to the ITC, they will be licensed by the Department of Trade and regulated by the Office of Telecommunications and the ITC. It appears that digital TV will force the BBC and ITV to compete against cable and satellite operators. The BBC has predicted cuts of £1.8 billion from conventional BBC budgets. The justification is their prediction that by 2005, up to 10 per cent of households will have digital TV services (Peak and Fisher, 1996).

> With more channels there will be more TV, from more points of view. We can then come to see TV as no more sinister than books. My guess is that in 20 years' time people will look back on the impartiality requirements on broadcasting as quaint history, like censorship of the theatre and newspapers in the 18th century. The present rules will wither away.

This statement came from Kelvin Mackenzie, ex-editor of the *Sun* newspaper and now managing director of Live TV (quoted in Peak and Fisher, 1996). It appears at present that Rupert Murdoch has the monopoly in producing black-box signal decoders.

In chapter 11 we will look in more detail at the changes in broadcasting and the likely social impact of these changes.

4 Marxist and pluralist theories of the media

By the end of this chapter you should:

- be familiar with the theories that examine the role of the media in contemporary capitalist society;
- understand the differences between the Marxist and neo-Marxist approaches;
- be able to assess the strengths and limitations of each of the theories;
- be able to apply the theories to different aspects of the media;
- be able to engage in the debate on ownership and control of media industries.

Introduction

In this chapter we will examine theories concerning the relationship between the media and society. Such theories have examined the debate about the role of the media in contemporary capitalist societies, the relationship between ownership and control and the quality of media output.

Our discussion will focus on the established approaches to the media: (1) Marxist, which involves two different positions – instrumentalist or manipulationist, and structuralist or hegemonic; and (2) pluralist. The newer approaches to the media are dealt with in Chapter 5.

We will outline each theoretical position in turn, and then examine their relative strengths and weaknesses as they apply to a sociological understanding of the role of the media in contemporary society.

The instrumentalist-Marxist approach

Marxist theoretical approaches to the role of the media vary, although they all share the basic assumption that the media are inextricably linked to the economic base of society. Theorists who take an instrumentalist position maintain that the owners of communications companies or corporations use their control over cultural production to maintain the *status quo*, and in this way manage to retain their own power. It is a very deterministic approach, in the sense that the economic base is seen as responsible for shaping all the other social institutions. We can illustrate this with a simple diagram (Item A).

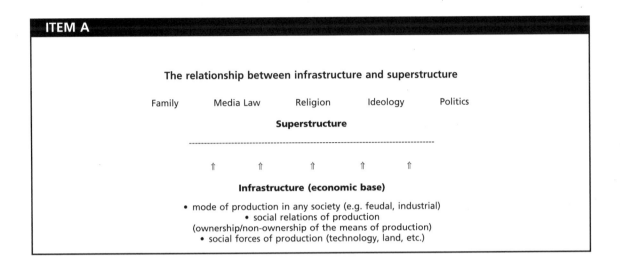

ITEM A

The relationship between infrastructure and superstructure

| Family | Media Law | Religion | Ideology | Politics |

Superstructure

⇑   ⇑   ⇑   ⇑   ⇑

Infrastructure (economic base)

- mode of production in any society (e.g. feudal, industrial)
- social relations of production (ownership/non-ownership of the means of production)
- social forces of production (technology, land, etc.)

ITEM A · **Exercise 4.1**

Using Item A and other sources, explain what is meant by:

1. Infrastructure.
2. Superstructure.

The infrastructure determines the form of the institutions in the superstructure, and the latter structures – for example the law, religion and the media – act to legitimate or maintain the power of those who own the means of production. In this way the media, as part of the superstructure, relay messages that help to keep capitalism going. From this perspective, it is assumed that the dominant or ruling ideas of any historical period are those of the ruling class, and it follows from this that dissemination of the dominant ideas is heavily dependent on the distribution of economic power. Hence ownership of media institutions is essential to the maintenance of capitalist power.

This classical Marxist position is usually associated with the work of Ralph Miliband (1973) and the French philosopher Louis Althusser (1971), although Miliband is credited with having directly examined the relationship between the media and capitalism. In his book *The State in Capitalist Society* he argues that proprietors, especially the owners of newspapers, have used their position to exert a direct influence over their editorial staff, and hence over the actual content of their newspapers. As discussed in Chapter 3, there has been increasing concentration of media ownership, and it is a small step to argue that media owners exert direct control over output.

Marx maintained that those who own the means of economic production (the bourgeoisie) also take ownership of mental production. This means they have control over the dominant ideas of the time, and these ideas support their position of social power. In this way the media operate as part of the 'ideological state apparatus' (ISA) to produce messages reinforcing the ideology of the bourgeoisie (Althusser, 1972). The ISA comprise those institutions in the super-structure – such as the family, religion, the mass media, the law and so on – that serve to legitimate the power of the bourgeoisie without the need for force.

At a very general level it could be argued that the media are engaged in the overt encouragement of commodity consumption (that is, the buying of goods) because of the commercial advertising they carry. At a more specific level, the capitalist class manages to maintain its economic power through the advertising revenue collected from those that use the media to promote their products and services, and ideological control is achieved through dissemination of messages espousing the benefits of consumption. As Miliband (1973) says: 'The direct political influence of large advertisers upon the commercial media need not be exaggerated. . . . Their custom is nevertheless of crucial importance to . . . financial viability, which means the existence of newspapers and, in some, but not all instances, of magazines, commercial radio and television.'

Exercise 4.2

Using one edition of your local newspaper:

1. Work out roughly how much space is given over to advertising.

2. Contact the advertising sales department of your local newspaper and find out the cost of advertising space (per quarter, half and full page advertisements).

3. Make a rough estimate of how much revenue was collected by the paper by selling quarter-page, half-page or whole-page spaces to advertisers for that edition.

3. Check the cover price of the newspaper and multiply it by the circulation figures. How does the amount compare with your advertising revenue estimate?

4. From your research, would you conclude that consumers of the newspaper are more important than advertisers in keeping it in existence?

Commercial advertising is ubiquitous, it is all around us. We may start the day by listening to adverts on our commercial radio station, see them in our daily newspapers and watch them on our commercial breakfast television programmes – all this without even having left home for work or school.

Exercise 4.3

On any 'normal' morning before leaving for school or college, count the number of advertisements you encounter on the radio, television and/or your daily newspaper(s) – don't forget that there are often adverts on food packaging for other types of product. How many did you count?

There are several other kinds of advertising. What about sponsorship? This is relatively new to Britain, but it has crept up on us and we are no longer surprised to find that our weather comes to us with the compliments of Powergen, which brings electricity to us 'whatever the weather'. Sponsorship has grown with the introduction of satellite television channels because it provides a convenient means of increasing revenue. It is of special interest to 'thematic' channels that are devoted to single interests such as music and sport.

'The sales strategy of Eurosport was always to offer programmes specific to our clients', this from Marcus Tellenbach, the joint managing director of Eurosales, which sells airtime on behalf of the European sports channel. He was not, of course, referring to the viewers of Eurosport as 'clients'. Between one half and two thirds of Eurosport's £8 million annual advertising revenue comes from sponsorship, and often the programme sponsor is also the company sponsoring the event.

MTV is another example of a channel that carries sponsorship and is seen as delivering its audiences to the advertisers. Bruce Steinberg, MTV Europe's director of advertising sales, says that 'Sponsorship is simply a more subtle way of advertising . . . it associates the product with MTV; in the eyes of the viewer MTV is at the cutting edge – it follows that the product must be too' (*Cable and Satellite Europe*, no. 106, 1992).

However there are rules and regulations that control sponsorship in Britain and Europe. For example in Britain:

- Any programme may be sponsored except news and current affairs.
- ITV companies and Channel 4 cannot use a sponsor's name in a programme title.
- No product placement is allowed.
- No promotional reference is allowed during the programme (however, when Inspector Morse reaches for his pint in the local bar, we are drawn to believe that it is a pint of Beamish Stout as this product sponsors the series).

---

[i] Look out for programme sponsorship when watching commercial television and count the number of programmes in one evening that are sponsored by companies other than television companies.

There is some evidence that we are getting used to sponsors. The name of the sponsor and its association is recalled by many viewers long after the series run is over (Television Omnibus Monitor, cited in Clover, 1992). Marxists would interpret this as further evidence that we are being manipulated by powerful capitalist forces that are urging us to consume their products. There are other examples from the media that we could apply to demonstrate the power of the dominant ideology. The presentation of game shows on television has been seen as another way in which greed and consumption are encouraged. Also, we find that our daily news comes largely from official news agencies or other official sources, therefore little space is given over to alternative or radical voices. Item B illustrates the instrumentalist – Marxist position in a simplified form.

ITEM B

Instrumentalist analysis – who controls the media corporations?

Owners/proprietors

⇓ ⇓

(a) Specifically:
control of individual
capitalists to advance
their own interests

(b) Generally:
communications
industries operate as a whole
to maintain capitalist power

In summary, the main premises of this position are as follows:

- Control over the production and distribution of ideas is concentrated in the hands of those who own the means of production.
- The views of this group are given a privileged position over other viewpoints and they come to dominate the thinking of the subject groups.
- These dominant ideas play a significant role in maintaining the *status quo*, that is, they help to reproduce class inequalities (Murdock, 1982, 1990).

However, as we shall see later in this chapter, a major debate among media sociologists centres on whether ownership automatically means that media proprietors have control over the products and content of the media. This debate is also linked to the role of the media in a democratic society (see Chapter 10). The strengths and weaknesses of the instrumentalist approach are dealt with later in this chapter in relation to the ownership and control debate.

Case study: televised quiz shows

Finding illustrative material of the ways in which the dominant ideology operates is not an easy task. Although the work of John Fiske (1987) is usually associated with a hegemonic approach to the media, it is possible to adapt his work in this instance to view it from a more instrumentalist position because these quiz programmes reinforce the status given to commodities and subtly reinforce the power of capitalism.

Fiske uses the example of the televised quiz show to demonstrate the potential these shows have to reinforce the *status quo*. He points to a parallel between knowledge and power; he maintains that quiz shows use knowledge in the same way that capitalist culture operates, that is, in order to separate the winners from the losers, based on naturalistic assumptions of individual intellectual differences.

There are different forms of knowledge so we ought to refer to 'knowledges' rather than simply 'knowledge'. The type most frequently used in relation to power and cultural capital is 'factual' or 'academic' knowledge, that is, knowledge that is open to empirical testing. This was at its elitist height in the television programme 'Mastermind', which examined contestants' general knowledge and their subject specialisms, which were very specific and even esoteric. The set was quiet, solemn and in darkness, apart from contestant's chair, which was lit as if an interrogation was taking place. (This programme has recently been transferred to BBC Radio 4.)

Other quiz shows also examine factual knowledge, but the atmosphere is more glittery with a strong sense of fun. Here the presenter is a TV personality who often combines the role of genial host with the stern schoolmaster/examiner. Let's look at some examples:

- 'The Price is Right' trades on everyday knowledge of consumption, not school knowledge, but common social knowledge that appears to be democratic.
- 'Mr and Mrs' was a show that demonstrated the lowest form of knowledge: it was a couple's knowledge of each other that was tested. We as viewers could not join in, only watch to see how well or otherwise they knew each other.
- 'Play Your Cards Right' uses luck and risk taking. 'Luck plays a vital role in the hegemonic structure of societies that are both competitive and democratic' (Fiske, 1987, p. 270).

The structure of these societies is essentially hierarchical and elitist, yet the dominant ideology insists that all of us can make it up the ladder. The ideology of equal opportunities in education is based on the assumption that ours is a meritocratic society and those who are naturally talented and motivated to work will rise above the others. By providing an ideologically acceptable explanation for failure and success, luck works to mitigate the harshness of personal failure. At the same time luck demonstrates that it is possible to win, for example jackpot lottery winners become new millionaires. 'While knowledge may be the socially validated way to power, influence, and material rewards, the elitism that is entailed by the competitiveness which both produces and proves its unequal distribution is given a democratic alibi by luck' (ibid., p. 271).

It is interesting to look at the prizes that are offered on these programmes. They are typically consumer goods, but occasionally they are more subtle, such as respect and status. The Mastermind prize was an engraved glass bowl, not a foreign holiday or a big cash prize. However the prize was only symbolised by the bowl, the real prize was the winner's superior intellect. On other quiz shows the star prizes are held in awe by the audience. They are often presented like star performers on a podium lit by flashing lights and demonstrated by beautiful, scantily clad young women.

So in general quiz shows reinforce the hierarchy of knowledge and, at the same time, commodity capitalism.

Exercise 4.5

Watch a selection of quiz shows that are 'hierarchical' in Fiske's sense.

1. To what extent do you agree with him that these programmes reinforce either the ideology of equal opportunity or the ideology of luck as a democratic force?

2. How would a pluralist explain the popularity of quiz shows? (You will be able to answer this question after reading the rest of this chapter.)

The hegemonic or structuralist–Marxist theory

To understand the relationship between hegemonic theory and media analysis, we should first place it in its historical context as a challenge to orthodox Marxism. The hegemonic theory was developed by Antonio Gramsci (1891–1937) as a critique of classical Marxism. His aim was to unify social theory and practice and to challenge what he saw as the *economic determinism* of orthodox Marxism, which involved no active or autonomous role for the social actor in social life. Gramsci believed that Marxism was an empowering and liberating doctrine, but as it stood, it assumed a fundamentally passive role for the working class.

For Gramsci, Marxist theory largely ignored the relationship of ideas and ideology to revolutionary class action. When analysing the political history of Italy, he became aware that economic crises by themselves were insufficient to bring about the downfall of capitalism – there had to be a hegemonic struggle as well.

Hegemony, for him, was a moral and philosophical leadership that was able to rule by winning the active consent of those over whom it rules. Hegemonic control was ideological control; workers would only accept political leadership through a process of socialisation whereby they came to accept the ideas of the dominant groups as natural and legitimate. This socialisation took place within the family, the education system, the church and, importantly in this context, the mass media. He saw that the subordinate groups would not accept the rule of the dominant groups through force or coercion, they had to be won over so that they would work within a system that they came to accept as fair. To ensure this, the dominant groups had to compromise in order to gain consent. You can see this idea in action in the way that trades unions have gained concessions for their members from employers without challenging the whole structure of capitalism, but by gaining a slightly larger 'piece of the economic cake'.

Gramsci attempted to demonstrate how ruling groups manage to hold on to power once they have achieved it. They do so not by the exercise of force, but by ideological leadership that convinces the proletariat or subject groups of their inherent rightness to rule: It is possible to see this in relation to Mrs Thatcher's Conservative government of Britain in the 1980s. An ideological climate was created in which the values of liberal capitalism were dominant, in which market forces, privatisation and inequality were not only accepted, but promoted, and where even the working classes deserted the Labour Party.

It is interesting that in order to win back the working-class voters and win over the new middle-class voters, in 1997 New Labour had to become a party of the centre and reject all elements that were associated with more left-wing ideas (an example of this may be seen in the association between Prime Minister Tony Blair and Rupert Murdoch).

However the dominant ideas that make sense of the social world are both contested and shifting. They have to take into account new situations, because once they become fixed they are in danger of becoming old-fashioned and losing their power. Nor is complete ideological dominance ever achieved. It is always having to face new crises and new challenges from alternative groups. A clear example of this took place in South Africa. Apartheid was a system based on racist ideology that served to legitimate the white *status quo*. It was a society entirely segregated by skin colour, reinforced by the law, the education system, the church and the media. Few people believed that a black president would ever come to power, unless as a result of a bloody revolution, and yet Nelson Mandela has become an acclaimed world leader and the ideas of apartheid have quietly subsided. So hegemonic ideas have to be flexible enough to face considerable change.

Exercise 4.6

Answer the following questions:

 1. What do you understand by 'economic determinism'?

 2. In what ways does the education system legitimate the power of the dominant groups?

The limitations of Gramsci's approach

Many sociologists and media researchers have adopted a hegemonic approach in their analysis of media texts and some of this work is extremely valuable, as we shall see later. However, as Strinati (1995) argues, Gramsci's arguments can be criticised:

- It is empirically difficult to separate hegemony from coercion. Parliament, for example, sets laws that are coercive, but it is also premised on the idea of democratic freedom, which is hegemonic.
- If culture is always tied to the dominant ideas, there can be no place for autonomy in popular culture. It would be difficult to explain alternative and independent media in this context.
- It is possible to see hegemony simply as another variant of Althusser's analysis of ideological state apparatuses.

Hegemony and research

Many writers have been influenced by Gramsci's ideas and have reworked them when analysing popular culture. Two British academic centres in particular have produced a wealth of evidence on the ideological role of the media: the Glasgow University Media Group (GUMG) and the Centre for Contemporary Cultural Studies (CCCS). They have been especially interested in the processes of news production and the relationship between ideology and representation.

The research of the GUMG has been very controversial since the publication of *Bad News* in 1976, as well as the subject of a great deal of criticism, not least from journalists and broadcasters. *Bad News* was concerned with the television coverage of industrial relations in 1975. The GUMG's analysis of television news led it to conclude that viewers had been given a misleading portrayal of industrial disputes, a portrayal that distorted the 'real' situation. The group's work continued with *More Bad News* in 1980, which examined the language used to describe the two sides in industrial disputes. The descriptions attached to management were such that they persuaded the audience of the rightness of the management position against the demands made by the unions. Their next book, *Really Bad News* (1982), examined the 1984 miners' strike. They have since published *War and Peace News* (1985), and their analysis of the media and the Rwanda crisis is forthcoming. Trowler (1996) has produced an excellent summary of the major findings of their studies, which we have adapted in Item C.

ITEM C

1. The vocabulary of broadcast news is biased against specific groups and this bias structures the listener's perspective.
2. Stories are selectively reported.
3. The effects of strikes are reported more often than the causes of strikes.
4. The 'visuals' used are again selective and help to structure the message being put across.
5. The tactics of protesters are reported more often than their viewpoints, especially when the tactics are deemed 'antisocial'.
6. There is a hierarchy of access to the media, so the voices we mainly get to hear are those of 'experts', specialists and the establishment.
7. News is reported from a particular ideological position.
8. The media set the agenda for debate – they tell us what to think about.
9. They also act as gatekeepers, thus excluding some stories and including others.
10. The news tends to favour of consensus politics, that is, 'middle of the road'. Support is given mainly to centrist viewpoints such as those of the Tory 'wets' and what we would now call 'Blairites'.

(Source: Adapted from Trowler, 1996.)

Exercise 4.7

 At this point it might be useful for you to attempt a short book review in order to familiarise yourselves with these texts. Choose one of the GUMG books mentioned above (see the References section at the end of this book). Read the methodology section carefully. Summarise this and write a criticism of their methodology.

Pluralism and the media

The pluralist view of the media is strongly opposed to the instrumentalist and structuralist Marxist theories. Pluralists reject the Marxist analysis of the nature of power and control in society. For them, power is not concentrated in the hands of a powerful minority who manipulate the media to exert ideological control over the powerless majority. Rather, according to the pluralists, power is held by a wider range of interest groups, and as a result the media reflect the diverse views and opinions of these competing groups.

However the crux of the pluralist argument concerns the relationship between the content of media output and the audience. In contrast to the manipulationist view, which sees the viewer/reader/listener as essentially passive to the media output, pluralists stress the autonomy of the public to choose the media product they want. The media therefore respond to public demand. This argument has frequently been used to defend nudity in national newspapers: if 12 million people read the *Sun* they must enjoy what is in it. Similarly, changes in the media are brought about because the public are no longer satisfied with existing media products, that is, viewing/readership figures decline and therefore programmes are axed and newspapers fold.

Changes to the privacy laws have been instituted since the death in August 1997 of Diana, Princess of Wales. They was a great deal of concern about the harassment of the princess by the paparazzi, who were held in part responsible for the car accident in which she died. (See Chapter 10 for more details of this.)

The pluralist view has clearly been expounded by J. Whale in *The Politics of the Media* (1977), where he cites the history and changing content of the *Sun* as evidence in support of the pluralist argument:

> It is readers who determine the character of newspapers. The Sun illustrates the point in its simplest and saddest form. Until 1964 the Daily Herald, and between 1964 and 1969 the broadsheet Sun had struggled to interest working people principally though their intellect. The paper had declined inexorably. Murdoch gave up the attempt and went for the baser instincts. Sales soared. By May 1978, selling just under 4 million copies, the Sun was reckoned to have overtaken the Mirror . . . as the biggest selling national daily newspaper.

In response to the assertion that the press does not provide a wide range of political opinion, Whale acknowledged that

> the press is . . . predominantly conservative in tone because its readers are. If any substantial number of people seriously wanted the structure of society rebuilt from the bottom, the Morning Star [daily newspaper for the Communist Party of Great Britain] would sell more copies than it does. . . . The broad shape and nature of the press is ultimately determined by no-one but its readers.

It is argued that the wide range of newspapers and magazines available, the differences between the, now five, terrestrial television channels and the wide range of radio broadcasting all go to show that there is considerable consumer choice. There are left-wing journals available on the newstands, and though few people choose to buy them, they are available for purchase. An example of the lack of public interest in alternative voices in the press is seen in the merger of the *New Statesman* with *New Society* in 1995, and the end of the *New Socialist* magazine. Feminist publications have suffered the same fate. If a sufficient number of women were interested in feminist issues, why did *Spare Rib* and *Everywoman* cease publication? It must mean that the majority of women readers are satisfied with those journals and magazines that are popular. With the advent of satellite and digital television, offering a multitude of channels to viewers, the choice will be immense.

However there are dissident voices, and many criticisms can be made of the pluralist position.

Exercise 4.8

 Write a paragraph on how an instrumentalist such as Miliband would challenge Whale's views.

Evaluation of the pluralist approach

Strengths

1. It recognises that audiences are not passive recipients of media messages. (This will become clearer in Chapter 9, 'Audiences'). Audiences are able to make choices about what they watch, read and listen to.
2. It allows us to see that the media do not speak with a single voice. Even taking one medium such as newspapers, we can see that events are given very different treatment by the tabloids and the broadsheet press.
3. It recognises bias in the media, but maintains that audiences are also able to recognise this bias, so the media lose the power to manipulate.

Weaknesses

1. Media diversity does not in reality mean wide-ranging choice. There will be increasing concentration of ownership, especially with Rupert Murdoch taking control of digital television broadcasting.
2. Journalists are closely vetted before recruitment, so very few dissident voices are heard.
3. Newspapers that support more extreme left-of-centre viewpoints are as dependent on advertising revenue as those that support more conservative positions, but as they have a smaller circulation than the other newspapers they are less secure.

4. The question also remains: do we get the media we want, or do we learn to want what we actually get?

In the following section we shall apply the theories we have outlined so far to the debate about ownership and control of the media. This debate has remained highly contentious and is often used as an examination question. There will be an opportunity to test your essay skills at the end of the chapter.

The ownership and control debate – applying the theories

In the previous sections we outlined the Marxist (both instrumentalist and structuralist) and pluralist theories of the media. This section will deal with the very controversial debate about ownership of the media. The debate involves different theoretical positions, and although it is complex it is important to consider it here because it examines the relationship between those who own the media, the production of the texts, and the texts themselves.

Several related questions are raised by the debate and we will address some of them here:

- Does ownership of media enterprises automatically mean control over the production and products?
- Are the media professionals more important than the owners?
- Do those responsible for the day-to-day running of the media have more influence than the shareholders over what is produced?
- What role do the consumers of media products play?

The three major theoretical positions from which we can examine the debate about ownership and control are the classical Marxist or instrumentalist position, the neo-Marxist or hegemonic/structuralist position, and the pluralist or free market position.

As discussed in Chapter 3, concentration of ownership was common before the start of this century, especially with regard to newspapers. More recently we have witnessed the development of cross-media ownership as a result of diversification and internationalisation. This has given rise to considerable anxiety about the possible development of monopolies in ownership. During the earlier decades of this century, concentration of ownership did not generate much public concern. However some concern was expressed by politicians, trade unionists and church leaders that there should be a better spread of media ownership in order to avoid single viewpoints being pressed on to the public (Denscombe, 1996).

It is interesting to examine the reasons why there was general complacency about the earlier forms of concentrated ownership:

- The accepted viewpoint of the general public was that the press was 'free' from political interference, and unlike that of the Eastern Bloc countries, it was a watchdog for the public, scrutinising all governments no matter which party was in office at the time.
- Ideological assumptions about journalism presumed that ownership and control were quite distinct issues and that so-called 'good' journalists could resist the intervention of meddling proprietors.
- The acceptance of what we would call 'pluralist assumptions of consumer sovereignty', that is, it was the readers of a newspaper who dictated its content.
- Overall, because a range of political views were espoused by the various newspapers, there was little need to be concerned about the possibility of propaganda being disseminated over the breakfast table (Wagg, 1992).

Today there is less justification for such arguments. Media ownership has narrowed considerably, and by the 1990s cross-media ownership had become firmly established. As we will demonstrate later, in the past the press also demonstrated an homogeneously Conservative outlook. However, more recently the political affiliations of newspapers have changed alongside the changing profiles of the political parties, notably New Labour.

Let's now look at the theoretical positions. You need to be aware that media sociologists do not fit into neat categories or remain in the boxes that we have made for them, rather there is an inevitable overlap between the approaches, as well as change over time. The descriptions we give of the approaches are necessarily second-order constructs (a second-order construct is a description or label that sociologists apply to the world to help them make sense of it. It is not necessarily the same description or definition that individuals would apply to themselves).

The classical Marxist (or instrumentalist) approach

The classical Marxist approach, sometimes referred to as the instrumentalist position, is based on the assumption that a direct relationship exists between ownership of the media and control over the content of the media. The current pattern of concentration and diversification of media industries means that we could use several media products during the same day without realising that they were all owned by the same corporation.

In 1990 we might have started the day by watching breakfast television on our Granada rental television; decided to watch a Granada video on our rented Granada video recorder (both television and video, incidentally, insured by L'Etoile Insurance – owned by Granada); driven along the M1 to stop for lunch at a Granada service station, where we might have bought a paperback (possibly published by Granada, Paladin or Panther), and then spent the evening at Granada bowling centre or tried our luck at a Granada bingo hall.

ITEM D   *Exercise 4.9*

Read Item D and then think about your own media activities.

 1. Keep a two-day record of all the hours and minutes, roughly, that you and other members of your family spend on any aspect of the media (make one of the two days a Saturday or Sunday). The chart below might help.

Medium	Person	Morning (to 1 p.m.)	Afternoon (to 6 p.m.)	Evening
Radio	Me			
	Parent			
Television	Me			
	Parent			
Newspapers and magazines	Me			
	Parent			
Cinema	Me			
	Parent			
Video	Me			
	Parent			
Music tapes/CDs	Me			
	Parent			

[i] 2. See if you can find out which companies own the media that you have engaged with. (You can obtain this information from sources such as *The Media Guide* and magazines such as *Broadcast* and *Campaign* in libraries.) Have you found a similar pattern to the one in Item D?

 3. Do you think it matters that the media products that take up most of your leisure time are governed by a highly concentrated pattern of ownership? What reasons can you give for your answer?

Instrumentalist Marxists argue that the products of the media serve to legitimate the power of the owners and reinforce the *status*

quo, that is, the system as it is at present. From this perspective, the proprietors of the media are seen as having direct control over their products and this is especially so with the owners of newspapers. Golding and Murdock (1991), despite the fact that they are not instrumental Marxists but political economists of the media, have always maintained that there is a direct relationship between ownership and control of the media. Their approach identifies a socially critical perspective that focuses primarily on the relationship between the economic structure and the ideological content of the media. It directs research towards the structure of ownership of media industries and the way these industries operate within capitalist markets. The characteristics of media production relate to profitability and the need to expand markets.

McQuail (1994) identifies the following key characteristics of media corporations' activities within the capitalist market:

- Controlling the development of independent media enterprises that might challenge their dominance.
- Concentrating on the largest markets for their cultural products.
- Avoiding too many investment risks.
- Reducing investment in less profitable media tasks (for example investigative reporting and documentary film making).
- Neglecting smaller and poorer sectors of the potential audience (for example ethnic minorities).
- Basing their news coverage and reportage on reinforcement of the *status quo*.

Even if we were to engage in a critical political-economic investigation of the media, we would still have to take account of the fact that any sociological investigation of power relationships is fraught with problems, not least because it is very difficult to gain entry to meetings of boards of directors where the important decision-making processes occur. Difficulties also arise because different researchers and theorists use the concept of power differently. However Golding and Murdock (1991), to make the power dimension more accessible to investigation, used the 'ideal types' of 'allocative and operational control' produced by Pahl and Winkler (1974) in their attempt to understand the relationship between ownership and control.

Allocative control means that an individual or group has the power to define the overall goals of the organisation and controls its financial policies. This is the most significant form of control as it allows those who possess it to make crucial decisions for the organisation, such as whether or not to expand or merge, the size of the dividends paid to shareholders and the salaries of the top executives. **Operational control** is a much more a day-to-day form of control. Once funds have been allocated, then media professionals such as editors and producers make decisions about their effective use. However they do exert considerable control over the production process, and this is apparent in the agenda setting of news in the sense of what makes a good story and what makes for a successful television programme.

A contemporary political-economic approach is concerned with the ways the options open to allocative controllers are constrained and limited by the general economic and political environment in which the corporation operates (Murdock, 1982). This approach concentrates on the role of media industries as economic entities operating directly within a capitalist system. Owners, whether individuals or corporations, are driven by the demands of market competition. The media also play a strategic role in reinforcing dominant social norms and values as these perpetuate the capitalist *status quo*.

It is possible to find some evidence of proprietorial interference in the day-to-day running of newspapers. For instance Harold Evans, once editor of *The Times*, was removed by its new proprietor Rupert Murdoch when he refused to accommodate Murdoch's ideas. As Murdoch said, 'I did not come all this way not to interfere.' He did this by 'persistent derision of them [opponents of Mrs Thatcher], at our meetings and on the telephone, by sending me articles marked, "worth reading", which supported right-wing views, by pointing a finger at head-lines which he thought could have been more supportive of Mrs Thatcher' (Evans, 1984).

A more recent case is that of Sue Douglas, the first woman editor of the *Sunday Express*. She had been in post for less than a year when she was dismissed in September 1996 by the newspaper's new proprietors, Lord Hollick's MAI. She had attracted some controversy over the headline 'A Bunch of Shits', an actual quote from John Major. It is not clear exactly why she had to leave, but the circulation of the newspaper had steadily declined over a long period and she was the sixth editor in ten years. As Roy Greenslade said, 'I cannot imagine that gender played a part in the Grabiner–Hollick decision-making. They are more likely to have concluded that her demands for extra investment, and even arrogance, made her unsuitable. . . . Bosses do not like to hear their employees telling them they know better' (*Guardian*, 2 September 1996).

Lord Hollick is an interesting example to use in determining the relationship between ownership and control. He is a Labour peer, a multimillionaire and owns the now ailing *Daily Express* and *Sunday Express*, newspapers renowned for their Tory support. His background is merchant banking and money broking, he launched the Institute of Public Policy Research and took control of the ITV franchise for Meridian in 1993. It seems paradoxical, seen from a manipulationist or instrumentalist position, that this proprietor, who has been a life-long supporter of the Labour Party, should become involved in a newspaper known for its conservatism. However Hollick disagrees:

'Am I uncomfortable with some of the things I read in the Express. Yes. . . . The centre of gravity has already shifted. It changed before I came on the scene. Richard Addis [editor-in-chief of both papers], takes the view that we should not be the slavish follower of the Conservative Party. We need to set our own agenda. That is essentially set by Richard for our readers who are broadly small "c" conservative'. Hollick wants the paper to give the Labour Party a 'fair show', but he says the editor 'has not asked for guidelines, if I gave him some he would probably tell me what to do with them' (*Guardian*, 16 September 1996).

Exercise 4.10

The example of Lord Hollick appears at first to challenge the argument that proprietors have the ultimate say in what goes into their papers. How could you use the example of Lord Hollick to support the instrumentalist position? Write your answer in approximately 150 words.

To summarise, if we are to accept a strict (instrumentalist) Marxist viewpoint on ownership and control we would have to establish these main points:

- Ownership is concentrated in a few hands.
- Concentration of ownership equates with control over production.
- Distribution is also concentrated in capitalist hands.
- Governments have considerable influence, especially as sources for news makers.
- Alternative or radical voices do not get heard.
- More often than not the products of the media are trivial, sensational and act as diversions that disguise the 'real' social issues.

Exercise 4.11

Key concepts: match the concepts with their appropriate meanings.

Key concepts	Meanings
1. Proprietorial control	A. The ideas of the ruling class
2. Legitimation	B. The system as it stands at present
3. *Status quo*	C. The way in which the owner of a media organisation manages to make the important decisions
4. Dominant ideology	D. Having the power to ensure that your ideas are the ones that are accepted by the rest of the population
5. Ownership of the means of mental production	E. The means by which other institutions maintain the position of the ruling class

Evaluation of the instrumentalist-Marxist theory

Strengths

1. It recognises the centrality of the media as important players in capitalist society.
2. It examines the power wielded by proprietors over the content of their media products.
3. It is a structuralist approach that allows us to see the possible relationship between the systems within the infrastructure and the superstructure.

Weaknesses

1. Owners do not exist as an identifiable capitalist class who have recognisable interests in common (Negrine, 1989). If this were so, journalists and broadcasters in the press and commercial broadcasting institutions would be merely transmitting the ideas of the owners. Negrine argues that there is potential for direct and indirect control; proprietors do appoint editors and chief executives, and these people work within predefined structures and processes: 'It is through the setting of objectives and the process of resource allocation that control remains with the proprietors. However, it is unlikely that such proprietorial power will be exercised without reference to commercial considerations or marketing considerations' (ibid., p. 75).
2. The approach assumes that the audience is essentially passive and accepting of media messages (see Chapter 9 for a discussion of reception analysis).

The hegemonic (neo-Marxist or structuralist) approach

We shall now investigate the debate from the neo-Marxist perspective. This position has become more popular than the strict instrumentalist position and is referred to as 'structuralist'. This perspective focuses not on proprietors, but on the structures and pressures under which broadcasters and journalists work. It takes its basic assumptions from the work of Gramsci (1971), so rather than simply assuming direct control between the ownership and production of media products, its supporters maintain that the ways in which media production takes place actually produce a set of dominant ideas and taken-for-granted assumptions about the world. The hegemonic approach argues that the media, taken as a whole, portray a loosely interrelated set of ruling ideas that permeate society in such a way as to make the established order of power and values appear to be based on a 'natural' order. Those who support the hegemonic position do not accept that proprietors must also control, nor do they see any ruling ideology being imposed on the audience, but from their perspective a '*Weltanschauung*', or 'world view', is produced, as if by virtue of an unquestioned consensus (McQuail, 1994).

This world view is produced by white, middle-class, middle-aged, politically liberal men. These are the people who write the television scripts, collect and report the news and direct the cameras, or commission others to do these things. It is their ideas that infiltrate the texts of the media and other voices are not given space or are set aside to be subjected to ridicule.

Rather than the owners having direct control, the actual structures within which these professionals operate force them to produce a set of dominant ideas. The production process, especially where it concerns news and current affairs, involves agenda setting, gatekeeping and news values that, taken together, constrain the nature of the final product. These concepts are explained in detail in Chapter 10.

> One had to see that dominance was accomplished at the unconscious as well as at the conscious level: to see it as a property of the system of relations involved, rather than as the overt and intentional biases of individuals in the very activity of regulation and exclusion which functioned through language and discourse (Hall, 1982, p. 95).

It is very important to note that this approach actually directs our attention to the ways in which capitalist relations are maintained by gaining the consent of the working class itself, so that the power relations and inequalities that characterise capitalism appear to be natural elements of society.

Exercise 4.12

Key concepts: using your sociology textbook or any dictionary of sociology, look up the following terms and write a brief description of each: hegemony, agenda setting, gate keeping, marginalisation, dominant ideologies.

The pluralist approach

Those who adopt the pluralist position do not really engage in the debate about ownership and control, because for them the consumer is sovereign – they see the consumer of the media as having sovereignty. They accept that there is concentration of ownership, and this brings with it an inevitable bias and distortion in media products. However this is irrelevant because the most significant factor is the ability of the audience to make its own needs and desires felt. The audience, therefore, is active and this disables the debate about audiences being manipulated into acceptance of the dominant ideology or being lulled into a sense of false consciousness by the media so that they cannot see the true nature of capitalist society. According to the pluralist position, the audience is engaged in three processes: selective exposure, selective perception and selective retention. Selective exposure means that audiences decide which papers to read, which television programmes to watch, which radio stations to listen to; selective perception means that they interpret the messages from the media according to their own social characteristics; and selective retention means that they are only able to remember a small part of what they see, read and so on. As a result of these processes of selection the audience is able to be discriminating, and thus there is no need for concern.

Pluralists reject the Marxist position and argue that it cannot be applied to all media because not all media are owned by private enterprises. In Britain we have public broadcasting financed by the licence fee, so that, theoretically at least, the BBC is free from the need to be profitable and keep its shareholders happy. Also, since the Broadcasting Bill of 1990 boundaries have been set on cross-media ownership. Newspaper groups are allowed no more than a 20 per cent share in terrestrial television companies, and local newspapers may not own more than 20 per cent of local radio or cable television. These measures are meant to prevent monopolies of media ownership (Denscombe, 1996).

Exercise 4.13

The following exercise requires you to link the appropriate statements with the corresponding theory.

Differences between the Marxist and pluralist approaches

Element	Marxist	Pluralist
News source	Ruling class/dominant elite	Competing political, social and cultural interests
Media	Concentration of ownership/uniformity of product	
Production		Creative, free, original
Content/world view		
Audience		
Effects		

Insert the following into the appropriate spaces:

1. Many, and independent of each other.
2. Standardised, routinised, controlled.
3. Selective, uniform, top-down.
4. Diverse, competing, responsive to audience demands.
5. Strong, confirms *status quo*.
6. Numerous, inconsistent, unpredictable, no effect.
7. Fragmented, selective, active.
8. Dependent, passive, mass, reactive.

Postscript to the ownership and control debate

The debate has been clouded by more recent patterns of ownership that challenge our assumptions about any simplistic relationship between ownership and control. The major difference in recent media history is the fact that modern media corporations are effectively owned by shareholders, the most powerful of which seem to be institutional; that is, rather than being owned by individuals or families they are owned by insurance companies and pension funds. It therefore becomes more difficult to analyse the relationship between ownership and the production processes because financial advisers and accountants are more important than shareholders, especially when it comes to decisions about cross-media ownership. So the evidence of owners having direct control is not clear-cut. As we have already stated, there are impersonal shareholders such as pension funds and insurance companies, and it is difficult to see them as determining the content of specific media. These organisations are also international and subject to greater economic constraints than those from just one country. Branston and Stafford (1996) have identified some of the important European media corporations that they see as major international media players. Details of the top six in 1995 are presented in Item F.

ITEM F

Corporation	Country	Sector	Turnover ($m)
Bertelsmann	Germany	Music, TV, publishing	8684
ARD	Germany	TV	5953
Havas	France	Advertising, publishing, TV	5621
Fininvest	Italy	TV, publishing, sports	5178
Reed Elsevier	Britain	Publishing	4484
BBC	Britain	Broadcasting	3416

There are also significant differences between the European media corporations and those in the USA:

- Public sector broadcasting is more important in Europe.
- Filmed entertainment is more significant for the US market, whereas broadcasting and publishing are more important for the European corporations.
- Until recently, expansion by the Europeans has been within Europe, however US corporations are searching for cable and satellite markets in Europe.

Revision guide to the ownership and control debate

You may have to answer an essay question on this debate, and therefore you need to have a clear understanding of the differences between the three main theoretical positions: instrumentalist Marxist, structuralist Marxist and pluralist. The following is a very brief summary of their respective positions.

Instrumentalist Marxist

- Ownership of the media has become increasingly concentrated and the views expressed are essentially conservative. The key concepts are concentration and conglomeration.
- The media simply serve to legitimate ruling interest groups, they maintain the power of the owners of the means of production.
- Managers only have discretion within the framework set by owners and therefore have limited power.
- Owners share similar social backgrounds and therefore similar interests. They are typically members of a privileged ruling class and run their organisations according to their perceived interests.

Structuralist Marxist (hegemonic)

- Structuralist Marxists disagree with the instrumentalists because they argue it would be physically impossible for owners to have direct hands-on control of the day-to-day running of the organisations.
- Media professionals control the output of media industries. As they are media professionals they have acquired a 'nose' for a good story and know what makes good television.
- They are a privileged group in themselves; they are white, middle-class, middle-aged men with a consensual view of the world. The ideologies that underpin the media messages are essentially theirs.
- This viewpoint is still Marxist because the prevailing ideas are seen as pro-capitalist, pro-consumerist and against minority interests.
- However structuralist theorists do not see audiences as being easily manipulated, but as actively engaged in making sense of media communication.

Pluralist

- Pluralists do not see ownership and control as necessarily or inevitably connected. For them, power is not held by a small ruling elite group, but is dispersed among many different groups in society. Despite there being concentration of ownership, large shareholders simply do not have the time to be involved in the day-to-day running of the production process.

- Pluralists also see the possibility of any number of people being able to control media enterprises, and ultimately the consumer is in the 'driving seat'.
- Consumer sovereignty reigns supreme. Audiences are active and make their own decisions about what to watch, read or listen to. Therefore pluralists argue that it makes no difference who owns the media: 'we' as audiences make the most important decisions.

Examination focus

Exam question and student's answer

This exercise is designed to help you to order an essay logically. The essay question is taken from the AEB's A Level Paper 2, summer 1993. There follows an essay written by a student under examination conditions. However we have jumbled the paragraphs and your task is to reorder them. When you have done that, highlight the sentences that demonstrate interpretation and application skills. How many marks out of nine would you give for these skills?

Question

'Newspapers may appear to be run by professional managers and journalists, but, in reality, it is the owners who wield ultimate power'. Discuss this statement with reference to sociological evidence and arguments. (*25 marks*)

Student's answer

Paragraph 1: This instrumentalist view has, however, been criticised, both from within the conflict perspective, and also from interactionist and liberal perspectives as well. The interactionist view goes against the idea in the question, as it claims that the content of the media is influenced by society as a whole. This is shown by the work of Hartmann and Husband on the content of the media. They state that the content of papers/media is only a reflection of society as a whole. This is the view favoured by owners and editors and 'Fleet Street' in general. In this view, the papers merely reflect the agenda 'out there in society', and that there is no conspiracy theory of sinister owners manipulating the agenda.

Paragraph 2: However, there are a number of criticisms of this view. Firstly, it is claimed that the consensual view in society is influenced by the ruling classes because of the way that their ideology is institutionalised by the rest of society through the education system and the media as a whole. This view supposes that the ultimate power in the media does indeed lie with the owners as their ideals are already instilled in the editors and journalists because of professional socialisation. A second criticism is that it ignores economic factors which can affect the content of the media because if papers fail to sell, they fold. Thus economic factors are important.

Paragraph 3: This view is also supported by the evidence of the growth of the 'human interest story' provided by Whannel, Douglas and Curran, which has led to the polarisation of the British press. This has developed because of human necessity, and the need to survive – in order to achieve the maximum readership, 'human interest' stories are run, but they do not challenge the *status quo*. This type of content means that although the owners have the power over what goes in papers, they do not have to exercise it.

Paragraph 4: Other constraints such as the production of news, can also have an effect. This is shown by Schlesinger in 'Putting Reality Together'. In this he demonstrated how factors such as the available space affects the length of the article, and also the fact that a certain amount of space is allocated to each type of news regardless of events. So this evidence would also seem to go against the statement because it suggests that the practical constraints of newspapers puts power in the hands of editor/journalists not owners.

Paragraph 5: So to conclude, the evidence seems to show that the owners do not wield ultimate power because of the other factors mentioned. However, the recent reorganisation of the newspaper industry in Britain, and the introduction of computers would seem to indicate that owners do have the power and do select editors who will 'fit in'. The editors in turn pick journalists 'fit in' (or in Paul Foot's case to 'fit out' at the *Daily Mirror*), and all of this leads to a situation where conformist journalism is encouraged. Yes, the editors and the journalists use their professional values in writing and editing stories so long as these conform to the owners' values and politics; when they do not do this, they can be removed by the owners (Evans at *The Sunday Times*). In a market economy, the owners ultimately wield power.

Paragraph 6: This statement is put forward from an instrumentalist perspective, which is the view held by Ralph Miliband. It is a conflict view which is from a Marxist perspective, and is indicating how the power and influence of the owners of newspapers influence the content of news, for example. This instrumentalist approach to the control of the newspapers says that ultimate power is in the hands of the owners of the mass media, and that managers only have a certain degree of control, which Miliband calls 'operational control'.

Paragraph 7: This view claims that as the present consensual agenda in society is one that is pro-capital, pro-sensationalism, pro-sex/sin etc., and the papers merely reflect these rather than determining them. The fact that this view supports the ruling class ideology is coincidental, and they claim that this will not always be the case as views in society may change, and this will be reflected in the content of the media – editors and journalists, being part of the new consensus, will be responsible for this.

Paragraph 8: This view is also supported by Murdock and Golding who adopt a structuralist approach. They criticise the pluralist view for not seeing the effect of economic factors resulting in owners having ultimate control and power. They show this by the fact that 88% of British newspapers are produced by seven companies, and five of these are controlled by families and individuals. For example, Rupert Murdoch's 'News International' is a massive international media conglomerate with massive influence. They claim that because of this, the papers have the same viewpoint because the controllers have the same lifestyle and are from the same class. This has led to a concentration of the press around right-wing ideas and the dominant ideology. When alternative newspapers are produced, the high costs of production and the criticisms of the consensual press usually means they have to close. They criticise the instrumentalist approach because the owners do not necessarily have to directly influence the content of the papers, since there views are transmitted via socialisation and the economic factors of paper production.

Paragraph 9: The statement is also supported by the work on journalists' professional values and how this affects the contents of the papers. Firstly, the gatekeeper approach states that the editors have ultimate power because they can choose whether or not a story is included. This view is criticised by a number of sociologists who state that whether a story is included or not is already decided before it reaches the editor's desk. This is shown by the work of Galtung and Ruge in the 1960s on news values, where they state that journalists themselves, because of their professional ideology and cultural and bureaucratic news values, decide what the content of the paper is likely to be. Chibnell, in his work on crime reporters, showed that they had specific news values and professional ideologies, which meant that they favoured certain types of crimes rather than others, and that their contacts with the police distorted the information that they were provided with. So these pieces of evidence would seem to go against the view in the question, as it seems that it is the journalists who wield ultimate power.

Paragraph 10: He claims that the owners directly control the newspapers, and the media in general, in the following ways. He claims that editors and journalists are affected, and accept the ruling class ideology, because of the system. Thus, although papers may appear to be run by managers and journalists, instrumentalists would claim that the function of papers and other media is to support and maintain the existing patterns of power and privilege in society. So instrumentalists argue that the media, and newspapers in particular, are instruments of ruling class domination, and because editors and journalists accept this ideology, newspapers play a role in the manipulation of the public. The link between ownership and control of the papers is direct, even though the public may not be aware of it.

This student scored full marks for interpretation and application. The essay always focuses on the question, which has been interpreted well, and the student has consistently applied evidence and relevant studies to the argument. She or he also scored full marks in the other skill domains; an excellent piece of work!

Further essays on this section

1. 'Evaluate the contributions of the pluralist and Marxist theories to an understanding of the role of the mass media in modern society' (AEB, summer 1995). (Hint: our brief revision of the theories may be used as a framework for the essay. Try this essay under examination conditions, that is, within 45 minutes.)
2. 'Assess the claim made by some sociologists that the mass media operate in ways that support the ideology of the dominant groups' (AEB, winter 1995). (Hint: It is important to make clear what is meant by 'dominant groups' in your answer. These may be class or political groupings, but they may also be dominant gender or ethnic groups. You might wish to question the idea of the existence of a single 'dominant ideology', which is essentially an instrumentalist approach, and challenge this with a hegemonic position that sees different sets of ideologies operating. Application skills can be demonstrated by referring to the work of the following: the Glasgow University Media Group, Althusser, Gramsci and Hall *et al.* – see References.)
3. 'Assess the extent to which it is possible to argue that the mass media reflect the culture of a ruling class' (AEB, summer 1994). (Hint: this is very similar to question 2 and you could use the same material, but this time focus more upon the 'culture' of a ruling class. You could make reference to a potentially wide

variety of sources such as news reporting, the ownership and control debate, and crime reporting. You should read Chapter 5 on the 'mass culture debate' before you attempt this question as the information provided there is also relevant.)

5 Feminism, postmodernism and the mass culture debate

By the end of this chapter you should:

- be familiar with the newer theoretical approaches to the media;
- be able to apply these approaches to current media debates;
- be able to assess the strengths and limitations of each theory;
- be able to engage in the debate about the effect of mass media on mass culture;
- have practised an exam question yourself.

Introduction

In Chapter 4 we examined the more traditional sociological theories as they relate to the media. This chapter examines the 'newer' approaches of feminism and postmodernism. The latter approach plays an important part in the debate on whether the mass media have created a 'mass culture' in our society. Critics of the media often refer to a decline in the quality of television programmes and the way media producers pander to the lowest common denominator of taste. Some would argue that our culture has suffered from a 'dumbing down' of taste. This debate will be addressed after we have discussed the feminist and postmodernist approaches.

Feminist perspectives on the media

As with other substantive areas in sociology, the media can be analysed according to feminist theories. As you may be aware, feminism has several faces and a considerable amount of literature has been recently produced by various feminist writers, so in this section we shall merely provide a general overview of the major issues.

Despite the fact that there are many different brands of feminism, it is possible to distinguish feminist analysis from other contemporary sociological perspectives such as neo-Marxism and postmodernism.

Feminism focuses upon *gender* as the key factor, whereby social reality and mediated reality (that is, as presented to us by the media) is structured for us and experienced by us. The early feminist researchers in media sociology concentrated on 'numbers', that is the percentages and ratios of men and women appearing in the media. Using the content analysis method (see p. 107) the number of female characters and roles were added up and compared with those of men. Very little critical work was undertaken in the 1970s and early 1980s. Whilst the work edited by Tuchman *et al.* (1978) was interesting in its examination of the way in which women were made invisible by the media – the 'symbolic annihilation' of women – it nevertheless provided few analytical tools with which to produce a theoretical feminist critique.

Let's look at the different strands of feminist work undertaken by media researchers. It is accepted that there are three major dimensions within feminist thought: liberal, radical and socialist. Although there are problems with these fairly arbitrary classifications, we shall use them here as ideal types. (An *ideal type* is a device first used by Weber as an aid to the examination of social reality. It is a construction of the essential criteria of a phenomenon; a kind of yardstick, which is held against actual social reality to see how close it comes to the defining criteria.)

Liberal feminism and the media

This is essentially a reformist approach, which sees more equal gender relations being brought about by equal opportunities policies and affirmative action programmes. Significantly, it does not question the power dimensions in society that maintain male superiority of status and female inferiority. As we shall see in Chapter 7, research into gender representation in the media has been mainly carried out by liberal feminists who have undertaken a great number of content analyses. 'Sex role stereotypes, prescriptions of sex-appropriate behaviour, appearance, interests, skills and self perceptions are at the core of liberal feminist media analyses' (Van Zoonen, 1991, p. 35).

Many of the content analyses are quantitative and largely focus on advertisements, soap operas and dramas. Typically, the major finding is that there are fewer roles for women than for men, that women appear less often in main dramatic roles (although there are variations across genres, with soaps being an important arena for women's characterisations) and in limited roles. The general finding is that sex-role stereotyping remains a major feature of television programming, both here and in the USA, and women actors are confined to roles that centre on domesticity and personal, familial relationships. The mediated reality of television – that is, the world as revealed to us by television – seems to be suffering a cultural lag. Women's lives have undergone significant social changes and these are only partially reflected and represented by the media.

The strategies suggested by this approach to improve the position of women and the media include the teaching of women's studies as part of courses for journalists and broadcasters, and disseminating information to journalists and broadcasters about the nature and impact of gender stereotyping.

The liberal feminist position maintains that over time the media representation of women will catch up with their actual social position and the media will present a more accurate view. As Van Zoonen (1991) points out, one of the consequences of their awareness strategies has been the development of a new stereotype – the 'superwoman'. It is interesting to see that magazines for women have taken into account the working woman, and many of the 'glossy' magazines have introduced the superwoman who adeptly 'juggles' her family and her successful work life.

Exercise 5.1

[i] 1. Compare two women's style magazines (for example *Elle*, *Vogue* or *Cosmopolitan*) with two men's magazines (such as *FHM*, *GQ* or *Esquire*). Count the number of articles in each that refer to coping with the strains of combining work and home life.

[a] 2. Think of a suitable hypothesis to use if you were to investigate the differences these magazines reveal between the lives of men and women.

Radical feminism and the media

This approach is very different from the first. Radical feminist analysis investigates the effect of patriarchy on women. Patriarchy is the system whereby all men directly or indirectly dominate and oppress all women. If they are not involved in this directly, then it is assumed that they at least benefit from the system that allows patriarchy to rule.

Exercise 5.2

[a] Patriarchy is supported by ideological assumptions about the differences between men and women. Make up three statements that illustrate a patriarchal position, for example 'Women are unable to take on command roles in management as they are too emotional.'

1.
2.
3.

Research carried out by radical feminists has revealed the darker side of family life, for example domestic and sexual violence. They have also exposed the exploitation of women by the pornography industry and, more recently, examined the increasingly popular international 'sex tourism' and sex trafficking. At its extreme, radical feminism rejects all male society and considers that the only way for women to be liberated is through segregation, usually in the form of lesbian separatism. There are relatively few studies of the media from this perspective, but there have been some studies on pornography, notably that by Dworkin (1980).

Strategies for media occupations suggested by this approach include women-only communication productions. Women are encouraged to produce their own media products, essentially by setting up collective community organisations. However thus far they have made few inroads into the male-dominated media industries. There are notable exceptions, though, where women's collectives have produced successful media products, especially in publishing, for example. The Women's Press, Virago, Hidden From History, *Spare Rib* and *Everywoman*. However changes have taken place recently: Virago has been bought out, *Spare Rib* and *Everywoman* have ceased publication, and London's women-only radio station 'Viva' has been searching hard for an audience.

Louise Saunders, the former editor of *Everywoman* magazine (which ceased publication in August 1996), said that 'Feminists are now in the mainstream'. She meant that as other women's magazines now dealt routinely with feminist issues, it was less of a loss that *Everywoman* had folded. She also maintained, somewhat paradoxically, that the influence of feminism at a general level has operated as a threat to men, provoking them into behaving so badly in their new glossy magazines (*Observer*, 11 August 1996).

Socialist (Marxist) feminism and the media

This approach does not focus exclusively upon gender, but incorporates analyses of social class, ethnicity, sexual preference, age and disability into the discourse. Some analyses also privilege ideology as the focus of debate. The work of Gramsci has been of particular influence here. The theory remains grounded in socioeconomic conditions, to which other factors take second place.

So the media are generally perceived as ideological apparatuses that represent the essential rightness of capitalism as a social system; within this framework socialist feminists focus upon the ways in which gender is constructed through language and imagery.

Research in this area has tended to be semiological (see page 170) and the strategies for change involve reforming mainstream media whilst concentrating on the construction of a separatist feminist media system.

Now that we have examined the three perspectives within feminism, complete Exercise 5.3 by listing the strengths and limitations of each perspective. You could complete the table provided.

 Exercise 5.3

Perspective	Strengths	Limitations
Liberal feminism	1. Based mainly on evidence collected from content analyses 2. 3.	1. Changes will be slow and minimal 2. 3.
Radical feminism	1. Locates the media within a theoretical framework 2. 3.	1. Little concrete evidence for their work 2. 3.
Socialist feminist	1. Locates the media within a Marxist frame of reference (manipulative model) 2. 3.	1. What about non-capitalist societies? 2. 3.

Postmodern feminism

By the mid 1980s the mainstream feminist approaches were losing cultural and political credibility, challenged as they were for being white, middle-class and mainly heterosexual. The new challenge has come from postmodern feminists. Central to their approach is the 'decentring of women'. They propose replacing the unitary image of women with a concept of fractured, multiple identities (Seidman, 1994).

As Haraway has argued, 'Identities seem contradictory, partial, and strategic. . . . There is nothing about "being" female that naturally binds women. . . . Painful fragmentation among feminists along every possible fault line [e.g. race, class, sexuality] has made the concept of women elusive.'

Postmodern feminists reject the idea that there is one truth, and argue that there are many truths, none of which is privileged along gender lines. So feminist knowledge is no better than 'malestream' knowledge. One of the major problems with this position is that, as Abbott and Wallace (1997, p. 298) argue, 'It abolishes both sociology and feminism as academic modes of research – if there are no general categories, then there can be no study of structured inequalities or power relations and no attempt to understand women's oppression.'

A case study: feminists looking at women's and girls' magazines

We shall use girls' and women's magazines as a case study of the way in which different feminist approaches have been utilised in media analysis. You will find many more references to the portrayal of women and men in Chapter 7.

As far as women's magazines are concerned, there is a clear distinction between analyses conducted in the 1970s and those of more contemporary feminism.

For liberal and socialist feminists looking at women's magazines in the mid 1970s, female oppression was perpetuated through romance and advocacy of submission and feminine consumerism. In what they viewed as almost a male conspiracy, the magazines were aimed at keeping women in their place, that is, as decorative objects for men or domestic home makers and carers.

One of the problems with this approach is that it assumes a passive audience, that the readers soaked up the messages of the magazines unquestioningly. This view of the relationship between media texts and their audiences assumes direct effects. If the media, in this instance women's magazines, were so powerful, what was it that protected the early feminists from the messages disseminated by the magazines? What defences did they possess that enabled them to reject the influence of the magazines, given that they assumed that the magazines were such powerful tools in the subjugation of *other* women. As with the various moral entrepreneurs against media violence, these feminist writers must have assumed that their readings were the 'correct' ones and that being academics they were able to debunk the system. However it seems less than 'sisterly' to attribute such gullibility or extreme naiveté to all those non-academic women who were unable to understand the 'true' nature of the ideological oppression offered by these magazines.

As feminist analysis developed, so did the construction of femininity. More attention came to be paid to different meanings of femininity, but underlined by the dominant understanding of what it was to be a 'real woman'. Women's magazines have been considered an important aspect of popular culture for women. They have often been seen as the pivot around which women's personal and social identities have been created. Several feminist researchers have used magazines to demonstrate changes in the lives of women.

McRobbie (1991) examined the codes of romance in the magazine *Jackie*. She maintained that teenage magazines such as *Jackie* encouraged girls to focus exclusively on romance and boyfriends at the expense of female solidarity and independence.

Janice Winship (1987) analysed the way different magazines viewed the interests and desires of the women who constituted their readership and the ways in which these interests and desires changed over time. Rosalind Coward (1987) considered that women were portrayed as subordinate, passive and sexually desirable. Marjorie Ferguson (1983) examined the 'cult of femininity'. In 1978 Judith Williamson decoded advertisements and argued that they had a critical role to perform in the 'production of femininity'.

However there are several problems with the approaches we have outlined above:

- They assumed passive audiences, that is, they assumed that female readers unquestioningly accepted everything that was offered to them.
- They took a mediacentric approach, that is, they assumed that the messages given out by the magazines and advertisements were more important to the gender socialisation process than other influences such as family and friends.
- They assumed that femininity was white and heterosexual.

During the 1980s the focus moved from a sociological approach to a more psychoanalytical approach. This became especially popular with cultural theorists who wanted to explain the 'pleasures' of reading magazines. It was understood that the glossy pages, colourful visuals, glamorous imagery and romantic fantasies associated with the construction of conventional femininity enticed readers to buy. Psychoanalytical analysis tended to see feminine identity as being unlike male identity in the sense that it remained undeveloped until it was linked to an adult male identity. It was also assumed that women's magazines would be able to do the 'cultural work' necessary to help women gain an appropriate female identity, by pointing them in the appropriate gendered directions.

Eventually, however, some researchers became uneasy about the assumption that women readers were victims of ideology, seeing this as both demeaning and naive. So during the 1980s a gradual acknowledgement of the diversity of representations of women developed, together with acceptance of a more active readership. Women were given more credit as readers able to counter the ideological influence of the magazines, and the relationship between reader and magazine was viewed as less mechanistic. There was an end to the censorious feminist analysis and a move towards building a more fruitful relationship between feminism and femininity.

Postmodern feminism: sex and magazines

McRobbie (1996) has examined the tremendous success of the recent crop of glossy magazines aimed at young women, such as *More!*, *Bliss* and *Marie Claire*. What is postmodern about these magazines is their irony, exaggeration and breaking of sexual taboos. Sex has been given a privileged position in this aspect of popular culture. It has become 'up-front'; sex covers the front pages and it is selling magazines. Sex now provides the framework for the magazines.

Exercise 5.4

Scan the women's magazine section in your local newsagent. Count the number of times the word 'sex' appears on front covers.

It is possible to argue that the postmodern age has taken a hold on women's magazines, especially those aimed at younger women who have been less directly involved in the feminist struggle. These younger women have enjoyed equal opportunities in the educational and occupational stakes and are doing very well in both. This attitude towards freedom and independence is reflected in their magazines, but there are other factors at work too.

Why sex, why now?

- Sex clearly sells magazines.
- It suggests new forms of sexual conduct for young women.
- It proposes boldness and brazenness in behaviour.
- It enhances sexual confidence and 'knowingness'.
- It suggests an 'ironic distance' from the 'old rules of sexual behaviour'.
- It uses an intimate, girls' club mode of address and thus extends the possibilities of what it is to be a woman/girl.

Exercise 5.5

Obtain two popular magazines for young women (for example *More!* and *Marie Claire*.) See if you can locate their distribution figures, and then give examples from each of the magazines that confirm the characteristics listed in the bullet points above. You could cut out pictures, photographs, features, letters and so on and use them as illustrations for a class seminar presentation.

McRobbie (1996) has recently researched the production of magazines, especially of the most popular young women's magazines – *More!* and *Marie Claire.* She found that many of the editorial staff were young women who were graduates of media courses and themselves avid magazine readers.

The readers had come to represent an extended community of the producer's own circle of friends and acquaintances.

The emphasis on sexuality is a newer way of drawing the boundaries of a fixed gender identity, of what it is to be female. Though this idea changes over time, the focus remains essentially on women as feminine, white and heterosexual. Others, such as black, Asian and lesbian women, remain marginalised but are given token acknowledgement in the form of 'interesting' features about them. The very popular magazine *Marie Claire* has a regular feature on women in other countries – a quasi-anthropological look at the world of women. These women are categorised as non-mainstream, as somehow 'exotic'.

For those women who have not succeeded in achieving complete femininity, there are important DIY makeovers, self-improvement and agony columns.

What about the readership?

McRobbie (ibid.) argues that being a magazine reader is not itself a defining category (that is, women do not define themselves as 'a *Marie-Claire* reader'), even though publishers may like to think it is. Readers of magazines, as well as being readers, have significant subjectivities influencing their lives – education, family, age, community, social class, ethnicity and other media. They easily 'slip through the net' of the more fixed subjectivities offered by the magazines. Brand loyalty is uncertain, cruising is the order of the day. Magazines have to shout loudly from the shelves in order to be bought – hence sex and more sex.

This new postmodern sexual subjectivity indicates a transition or fluidity in what it is to be a (young) woman today. New sexual movements are being acknowledged, especially feminist and gay politics. These newer magazines have produced a new kind of openness about what it is to be a woman, which is not narrow, prescriptive or traditional. It is interesting to see that sales of *Cosmopolitan* have slipped in relation to other glossy magazines; although it is still a market leader, its appeal rests on a more American style of femininity that involves keeping your man happy while still being successful at work.

Where does this new sexual emphasis come from? McRobbie argues that it is a process of 'denaturalising sex' – we need to learn how to *do* sex properly. Rather than an assumption that, like romance, 'it all comes naturally if you are with the man you love. Both romance and sexual expertise have been revealed as myths and they have been replaced by a much more frank, even mechanical approach to sex, but one which is without the cold, clinical or moralistic language associated with sex education' (McRobbie, 1996, p. 186). The consequences of this change can be summarised as follows:

- Female sexual pleasure is emphasised.
- Romance is demystified.
- Sex is no longer viewed as magical or 'sacred'.
- It is possible that increased awareness of AIDS has also had an impact on casual sexual encounters.

Postmodernists argue that the main emphasis in popular culture is on irony, parody, mockery and a shared knowingness. This is clearly illustrated by the new magazines that trade in shared dreams and fantasies, not 'truths'. So we are faced with complex and contradictory female subjectivities – a postmodern sexuality as the model for contemporary female sexuality and a new framework for young women's self-identities.

In conclusion, there seems to be an increasing focus on strong, frank and explicit sexuality and sexual representation, the topical discourse is around safe sex, sexual subjectivity, self-knowledge and self-reflexivity, all aspects of the postmodern condition. It is to postmodernism that we now turn.

Postmodernism

'Postmodernism is sceptical of any absolute, universal and all-embracing claim to knowledge and argues that theories or doctrines which make such claims are increasingly open to criticism, contestation and doubt' (Strinati, 1992).

We have looked at the main theories used by sociologists to explain the role of media in contemporary society. However there is another way of seeing the media that challenges all the traditional assumptions. This 'new' approach is postmodernism, which 'dismantles foundations, disrupts hierarchy' (Seidman, 1994).

Postmodernism can be seen more as a movement than a theoretical position because, as we shall see, to call it a theory is to challenge its own basic assumptions. We are used to the theories of the founders of sociology – Comte, Durkheim, Marx and Weber – as competing approaches to understanding the development of industrial societies. These theories are now challenged as being little more than metanarratives or 'big stories', and no better than any other story. Writers associated with postmodernism are Jameson (1991), Lyotard (1984) and Baudrillard (1983). The term 'metanarrative' was used by Lyotard to mean 'making an appeal to some grand narrative, such as the emancipation of the rational or working subject, or the creation of wealth' (Lyotard, 1984, p. xxiii). He was referring to the way the metanarrative of science had become fragmented into many disciplines, specialisms and paradigms; however writers such as Strinati are more interested in the postmodern condition as it relates to culture.

The mass media are central to the postmodern condition because what we now take as 'real' is to a large extent what the media tell us is real. We are bombarded from all sides by cultural signs and images in all aspects of our media. According to Baudrillard (1983), we have entered the world of the 'simulacra'. These are 'signs that function as copies or models of real objects or events. In the post-modern era, simulacra no longer present a copy of the world, nor do they produce replicas of reality. Today . . . social reality is structured by codes and models that produce the reality they claim to merely represent' (Seidman, 1994, p. 210).

Before we examine the postmodern condition it may be useful to define what modernism meant, as it is this which is being replaced. Sugrue and Taylor (1996), using the work of Walker (1994), identify five essential characteristics of the modernist movement in art:

1. Modernists rejected the 'blandness, sentimentality and historicism of the academic art of the 19th century'.
2. Experimentation, innovation and novelty were means of challenging tradition.
3. A preference for geometric rather than organic forms – simplicity, clarity and uniformity.
4. They favoured an international style as modernism could be applied universally.
5. An orientation towards the future. A new environment based on new technology and science would produce a better society.

In cultural terms, modernism rejected the traditionally established forms and practices in favour of newness. As modernists believed they were the experts of this new thinking, they imposed modernist art and architecture on the rest of society, who were not really consulted. Hence people were forced to live in high-rise blocks of flats and new town developments, which were often poorly serviced by public transport.

From the 1960s onwards there was a revolt against this imposition of universally applicable criteria of good taste and a validation of popular taste. So we move to the postmodern critique.

In *An Introduction to Theories of Popular Culture*, Strinati (1995) outlines five defining characteristics of postmodern thought that are relevant to the sociology of the media:

1. The breakdown of the distinction between culture and society.
2. An emphasis on style at the expense of substance.
3. The breakdown of the distinction between art and popular culture.
4. Confusion over time and space.
5. The decline of metanarratives.

The breakdown of the distinction between culture and society

Traditional media theories assume that the role of the media is to mirror social reality. In contrast the postmodernists consider it is no longer possible to separate the media from that reality: 'this mirror is now the only reality we have' (Strinati, p. 224). Unlike Marxism, which identifies economic production and its parallel social relations of production, postmodernism focuses on consumption patterns as providers of our identities. Distinctions of class relations based on socioeconomic relations are subsumed by consumption.

Emphasis on style at the expense of substance

'Images dominate reality' (Harvey, 1989). Here the argument is that we increasingly consume images and signs for their own sake rather than for the goods they represent, that is, we buy the labels and packaging rather than the clothes and goods themselves.

Exercise 5.6

We hear of young men in the USA being killed for the latest Nike or Reebok trainers they are wearing.

 1. In pairs, list five products that have status in Britain because of their labels or associated images.

2. In what ways do you think it is possible for young people to avoid this emphasis on style rather than content?

The breakdown of the distinction between art and popular culture

As postmodern culture emphasises playfulness and irony in art and architecture, it is very difficult to separate art from popular culture. The pop art of the 1960s demonstrates this clearly, for example Andy Warhol presented soup tins and cola bottles as art, as well as challenging the uniqueness of Da Vinci's portrait of the Mona Lisa by silk screening her image thirty times – 'Thirty are better than one'.

Art and classical music have been used by advertisers to sell products and opera arias have introduced international sporting events.

Exercise 5.7

1. In pairs, try to identify television advertisements that:
   (a) use classical music as product recognition;
   (b) make reference to other media products, especially films, or use irony to sell their products.

2. Which major sporting events have used classical music as their opening theme?

Confusion over time and space

The old established linear unities of time and space have been undermined; satellite broadcasting has produced instantaneous images and information. In the comfort of our living rooms we watched the Gulf War 'live', we witnessed the Ethiopian famine and we daily receive international news from all parts of the globe. As Harvey (1989, p. 293) argues:

> Mass television coupled with satellite communication makes it possible to experience a rush of images from different spaces almost

simultaneously, collapsing the world's spaces into a series of images on a television screen. The whole world can watch the Olympic Games, the World Cup, the fall of a dictator, a political summit, a deadly tragedy ... while mass tourism, films made in spectacular locations, make a wide range of simulated or vicarious experiences of what the world contains available to many people.

This is McCluhan's (1964) vision of the 'global village' made manifest; whether it is available to all will be questioned later in the book.

We are able instantaneously to communicate world-wide on the Internet, which confuses our sense of time and space.

In the cinema, this confusion can be seen clearly in films that fuse time and space, for example 'Back to the Future', 'Pulp Fiction' and 'Twelve Monkeys'.

Ridley Scott's 'Blade Runner' is an example of a classic postmodern text. The genre of the film is not coherent, it is an amalgam of film noir, fantasy and science fiction. The narrative informs us that we are in Los Angeles in 2019, but this future appears to be remarkably similar to past and present. It is portrayed as a city where 'empty warehouses and abandoned industrial plant drip with leaking rain. Mist swirls, rubbish piles up, infrastructures are in a state of disintegration that makes the pot holes and failing bridges of contemporary New York look mild by comparison' (Harvey, 1989, p. 310).

Exercise 5.8

i Hire a copy of 'Blade Runner' from your local video library (the first version, not the director's cut). If you watch the first ten minutes of the film you will be able to see the confusing of time and space quite clearly.

Its pessimistic portrayal of the future resonates with another premise of postmodernism, that there is no inevitability about progress. Postmodernists challenge the Enlightenment ideal that there is universal movement to human emancipation. This optimism is misguided, because the world is characterised by uncertainty and incoherence.

Can you recognise these characteristics in any other film that you have seen?

The decline of metanarratives

The last characteristic of postmodernism is the one that poses the greatest challenge to sociology as a discipline. It casts doubt on the possibility of any theory being able to explain history or account for power relations in contemporary society. It seems that there are no fixed 'truths' any longer, and we need to recognise the validity of competing narratives to make sense of social reality. If we take Marxism as an example, it becomes a metanarrative through its attempt to explain past societies by using historical materialism and by its emphasis on the linear nature of societal development. The collapse of the

Soviet Union and the subsequent rise of capitalism in Eastern Europe has shaken the foundations of orthodox Marxism. 'What we see and know and, therefore, are, is merely for here and now, and only until another story comes along' (P. Jones, 1993, p. 111).

The strengths and limitations of postmodernism

Strengths

1. Underlying the postmodernist approach is a reluctance to accept that there is one truth. The 'big stories' of history are delusions – the means by which some groups impose their views on the rest of society. Contrary to this, postmodernism celebrates relativism.
2. Postmodernists reject the idea of guaranteed social progress and view society as fragmented, diverse and without clear structures.
3. Postmodernism points to the central position of the media not only in everyday life, but in the very process of constructing our cultural identity.
4. Postmodern images in art and the media are playful, ironic and irreverent.

Limitations

1. Postmodernism ignores current media debates surrounding:
   (a) ownership and control;
   (b) effects of the media;
   (c) bias in the news;
   (d) differential access to the media.
2. Postmodernism is itself in danger of becoming a new metanarrative. It is highly critical of grand theories such as Marxism, yet it offers its own theory of society as a replacement.
3. It does not take sufficient account of the different cultural and economic circumstances of individuals in the creation of identities. We cannot all afford to surf the Internet and adopt different identities simply by changing our patterns of consumption.
4. The audience is credited with the ability to recognise cultural references in media texts. However this 'knowingness' might simply be another form of media literacy that could be understood as a form of cultural capital limited to the economically better-off.

Exercise 5.9

Revision activity on theories of the mass media

Match the following statements with their corresponding theoretical position. Put the appropriate letter in the boxes provided.

Theoretical positions

(a) Manipulative theory
(b) Hegemonic theory
(c) Liberal feminism
(d) Marxist feminism

(e) Radical feminism
(f) Postmodernism
(g) Pluralist theory

Statements

1. The media reflect public demand. ☐
2. Patriarchal ideology dominates media output. ☐
3. As the media industries employ more women a more diverse rather than stereotyped representation of women emerges. ☐
4. Although proprietors are highly influential, it is the day-to-day structures of journalism that are more significant. ☐
5. The media feed the public a constant diet of trivia in order to divert their attention away from the real causes of oppression. ☐
6. Power is concentrated in the media but consumer sovereignty reigns. ☐
7. Women-only media collectives offer the only tenable solution to patriarchy. ☐
8. Images of women are limited. ☐
9. Agenda setters and gatekeepers are more influential in production than the owners of newspapers. ☐
10. The dominant ideas purveyed by the media are always those of the most powerful groups. ☐
11. The media are powerful because the audience is essentially passive and non-discriminating. ☐
12. A consensual view of the media is produced by white, middle-class, professional men. ☐
13. No one theory can explain media production and consumption. ☐
14. Class position is no longer significant in understanding media consumption patterns. ☐

Mass media, mass culture?

In this section we shall examine the arguments about the effect of the mass media on contemporary culture. In order to do this we must first examine another school of Marxist thought that is relevant to the debate – the Frankfurt School.

The founders of this school of Marxism, including Marcuse (1898–1979), Adorno (1903–69) and Horkheimer (1895–1973), were all critical of the development of what they saw as mass culture and mass consumption. Forced to leave Nazi Germany and flee to the USA in the 1930s, they watched with increasing disillusionment the postwar success of capitalism. Taking a critical position, they saw that mass culture seemed to operate to prevent revolution occurring from within the proletariat.

Their analyses focus upon the role of the 'culture industry' in this lack of revolutionary spirit among the working class. The orientation of the school has been towards the linking of modern capitalism with the control exerted by media industries and products over the consumer. Using the concept of 'commodity fetishism', they demonstrate the ways in which cultural forms operate to perpetuate modern capitalism.

Commodity fetishism means that the products of people's labour become commodities or objects for sale; that is, the products become more valued for their exchange value – the money they can command on the market – than their use value – their practical use to the consumer. We can see what has happened with art objects. That a painting of a bowl of flowers by Van Goch can sell for £23 million tells us much more about the exchange value of the painting than it does about its use value.

Strinati (1995) quotes Adorno to illustrate this point more clearly: 'The real secret of success . . . is the mere reflection of what one pays in the market for the product. The consumer is really worshipping the money that he himself has paid for the ticket to the Toscanini concert' (Adorno, 1991, p. 34). We are therefore worshipping the exorbitant price we paid for the concert ticket rather than the performance of the artist.

The commodity is an important concept in the Frankfurt School's critique because they saw art and culture being marketed for profit. Marcuse referred to this mass consumption society as 'one-dimensional' because it generated 'false needs' in the public that could only be met by the culture industry. 'True needs' were freedom, happiness and the new society.

Evaluation

1. The problem is to differentiate between false needs and true needs. For instance if labour-saving machines allow more leisure time in which to watch television, go with friends to the cinema and so on, it becomes difficult for us to recognise where the false needs lie. If washing machines provide more time to watch television or listen to popular music, would a true need emerge from spending the available time not watching the television but hand-washing our clothes instead? It seems that these thinkers adopted a value position over the nature of 'true' needs, as if they had the power to detach themselves from the lives of the rest of society.

2. They asserted that the working class is kept docile and accepting of the *status quo* by the diet they are fed by the daily media. Although their critiques did not address television and video, we would be justified in including these important media today. They focused upon popular music, cinema and radio as the means whereby the public audience accepted their situation.

Marcuse *et al.* saw popular media forms as ultimately debasing the public and reducing culture to the lowest common denominator of taste.

3. It is easy to see how this approach lay itself open to accusations of elitism and of taking the moral high ground. We might ask who they thought they were in telling the public that what they really enjoyed was worthless and degrading.

Adorno's theory of popular music is also bound up with his ideas about capitalism and commodity fetishism. He argues that popular music is characterised by two processes – standardisation and pseudo-individualism. Although these two seem to be opposites, in fact they are part of the same process.

Standardisation refers to the fact that popular songs begin to sound more and more similar, and pseudo-individualism refers to the peripheral additions attached to the songs so that they appear to be different. It is interesting in this context to note that in 1995 a new 'boy-babe' band was 'created' by the industry to fill the gaps about to be left by ageing boy-babes. This new band, 'Upside Down', was formed from respondents to an advertisement for new talent. The members of the band were merchandised, choreographed and reconstructed from there onwards.

Without doubt, Adorno is dismissive of popular music. He is himself a trained musician, composer, music theory expert and champion of avant-garde and non-commercial music (Strinati, 1995, p. 65). It comes as no surprise, then, that he despised the popular songs of the 1950s. He is also an elite intellectual, a person who is seemingly able to withstand the control of the culture industry; he holds a privileged position from where he can look down with disdain at the rest of society. This argument about popular culture and capitalism plays an important part in the debate on whether the mass media have created a mass culture.

Exercise 5.10

1. How would a sociologist define 'culture'? (Check your definition against that in any dictionary of sociology.)

2. If we described a person as 'highly cultured', which of the following activities would you expect them to engage in? Bingo, horse-racing, classical music concerts, dog racing, fox hunting, opera, the novels of Jeffrey Archer, ballet, the novels of Dostoevsky and the music of Stravinsky, the Spice Girls or Andrew Lloyd Webber.

3. What criteria did you use to make your decision?

4. If you have already studied the sociology of education, you will undoubtedly be familiar with the term 'cultural capital' to demonstrate the difference between the backgrounds of working-class and middle-class students. To what extent do you think that this concept relates to 'high culture'?

Mass media, mass culture, mass society?

What is mass culture? According to Sugrue and Taylor (1996) there are several processes that culminate in the production of a mass culture:

- Culture becomes a product to be consumed, like any commodity.
- Culture becomes homogenised, thus dissolving distinctions of taste and quality.
- Technological development produces mass audiences for broadcast media.
- Scope for political change, resistance and individual self-identities is reduced.

If these are the processes that generate mass culture, what exactly is it? Strinati, (1995, p. 10) sees it as 'popular culture which is produced by mass production industrial techniques and is marketed for a profit to a mass public of consumers'. This is a very impartial view of it, however; other writers take a more judgmental view. MacDonald (1957) was far more critical:

> it is a debased, trivial culture that voids both the deep realities (sex, death, failure, tragedy) and also the simple, spontaneous pleasures . . . a narcotized acceptance of Mass Culture and of the commodities it sells as a substitute for the unsettling and unpredictable . . . joy, tragedy, wit, change, originality and beauty of real life.

We need to address the question of whether the concerns of the Frankfurt School were well-founded. In general, the fears of mass culture and mass society revolve around the working classes and the loss of authenticity. According to these writers, traditional working-class culture included brass bands, folk dancing, folk festivals and collectivism. These writers paid little attention to changes in the cultures of the middle, upper-middle or upper classes, so we must be wary of value judgements being made about the working class. Although other writers might adopt several different positions on the 'mass culture debate', they can be divided into two approaches: pessimistic and optimistic.

Pessimistic views: radicals and romantics

It is interesting that the mass culture debate has sometimes united both sides of political opinion. Writers from what may be loosely termed the 'radical right' and 'radical left' have been dismayed by the effect of mass culture on the lives of the working class.

Within the left-wing position there are the views of the Frankfurt School, as outlined above. They viewed the traditional, authentic culture of the working class as being under attack from commodity capitalism, which generated 'false needs' and manipulated the masses with a diet of 'bread and circuses'.

Exercise 5.11

 1. What do you think the phrase 'bread and circuses' means?

 2. Which of today's media products do you think the Frankfurt School might regard in this way?

A similarly pessimistic position was adopted by certain left-wing literary critics, social historians and cultural theorists who mourned the loss of a working-class culture that they had believed to be authentic, vital and spontaneous. This view appeared first in the 1930s in social literary criticisms by F. R. Leavis and D. Thompson (1933) and was later taken up by what we might call the 'romantic left' – Richard Hoggart (1958) and Raymond Williams (1963). Leavis and Thompson (1933, p. 3) argued that:

> Those who in school are offered (perhaps) the beginnings of education in taste are exposed, out of school, to the competing exploitation of the cheapest emotional responses: films, newspapers, publicity in all its forms, commercially catered fiction – all offer satisfaction at the lowest level, and inculcate the choosing of the most immediate pleasures got with the least effort.

This was written many years before television, videos, computer games and pornography on the Internet.

These writers saw education as the key social institution to protect impressionable young people by teaching them to discriminate between what was 'good' and what was 'bad' in cultural products. Implicit in their argument was their belief that the products of high culture – opera, classical music and literature – were unquestionably superior. Therefore a knowledge of these products would enhance the lives of the working class. 'The continuing thrust of these critics has been to attack the commercial roots of "cultural debasement" and to speak up for the working-class consumer of mass culture as the victim rather than the villain of the story' (McQuail, 1994). What McQuail seems to be implying is passivity on the part of the working-class audience, who can do no other than accept this 'cultural debasement.'

Those whom we have called the radical right share many of the assumptions of the theorists of the Frankfurt School, such as the alienation of the working class and a debasement of their authentic culture, the differences lie in their perception of the working class themselves. For the left, the position of the working class derives from socioeconomic inequality. However, for the radical right there is a 'natural' difference between the elite and the masses. This viewpoint is reflected in the elite theory of power propounded by Vilfredo Pareto (1963) and Gaetano Mosca (1939), where the elite are intellectually and culturally superior whilst the masses are necessarily inferior. (For a discussion of elite theory, see Haralambos, 1995, pp. 515–17.)

This essentially paternalistic view sees the masses as having their own valid, if somewhat simple, rough-hewn culture. So we find yet more nostalgia for 'folk festivals', Morris dancing, herbal remedies and story telling – nostalgia for a mythological past as the twin evils of industrialisation and the mass media served to destroy this folk culture and replace it with an artificial culture. This position has reemerged among certain right-wing journalists. The following was Paul Johnson's perception of the teenage television audiences for 'Juke Box Jury' in 1964:

> While the music is performed, the cameras linger savagely over the faces of the audience. What a bottomless chasm of vacuity they reveal. Huge faces bloated with cheap confectionery and smeared with chain-store make-up, the open sagging mouths and glazed eyes . . . a collective generation enslaved by a commercial machine (*New Statesman*, 28 February 1964).

Thirty years on these views are still being voiced. In 1992 Tony Parsons, television critic and journalist, presented in a television documentary called *The Tattooed Jungle* his personal view of the changes that had taken place in working-class culture. This is his view of the working-class today: 'Something has died in the working class: a sense of grace, feelings of community, their intelligence, decency and wit. The salt of the earth have become the scum of the earth, a huge tribe of tattooed white trash. Today the working class are peasants' (*Daily Mail*, 6 October 1992). This is criticism indeed, coming as it does from someone who claims to have had a working-class upbringing. It is interesting to see the reasons Parsons gives for this transformation of the working-class:

> Now the working class are so immersed in the culture of America that they have only their loathing of European nations to remind them of their identity . . . [they] have gained the booty of the material world and lost their souls. Their poverty today is not financial but cultural . . . They are post-literate. They can read. But – apart from a daily dose of tabloid – they don't. They would rather rent a video nasty (ibid).

Although he might not choose to place himself alongside Paul Johnson, the sentiments he expresses seem to reflect Johnson's view thirty years on. He too is extremely critical of mass culture and its effects on working-class life. He takes for granted that the media are powerful influences operating on essentially passive audiences: 'despite their surface aggression, the working class are horribly passive. Afflicted by cultural lethargy, their flabby minds are as undiscerning as blotting paper, willing to soak up any rubbish that prime-time trash culture decides to pump out' (Parsons, 1992).

Mass culture or popular culture? Optimism at last?

So far these positions have been very pessimistic, but it is possible to take a pluralist view of the situation and see a more optimistic picture. 'Mass culture' brings with it heavy value judgements about what is considered to be good and bad taste. If we replace the word 'mass' with 'popular', we may find that it has more positive associations. The term popular culture implies that it is 'much enjoyed by many people' (McQuail, 1994). To accept this is to take a more pluralist position because if cultural products are enjoyed and enjoyable, this presupposes that some choices are being made by an active audience.

This can be seen in the work of John Fiske (1987), who thinks that audiences gain pleasure from television viewing. For him, the importance of popular culture is precisely its popular nature. 'Popularity is here a measure of a cultural form's ability to serve the desires of its customers. . . . For a cultural commodity to become popular it must be able to meet the various interests of the people amongst whom it is popular as well as the interests of its producers' (ibid., p. 310). Fiske rejects the view that cultural capital necessarily flows along economic lines and argues that audiences have the ability to shape media texts themselves, that is, the audience derive meanings that make sense to them. In this way they have 'semiotic power' (see p. 170).

This view of the nature of popular culture is close to that of the postmodernists. As we have seen, postmodernist writers assert that the old distinctions of high and low culture are no longer tenable. Society has become fractured and fragmented, and individuals choose their own identities, freed from the old constraints of socioeconomic status. So the debate on whether the mass media have produced a mass culture is redundant as far as the postmodernist approach is concerned.

Exercise 5.12

In the left-hand column of the chart below, there is a list of cultural products – we would like you to place them in the appropriate columns as you think fit. When you have done this, compare your answers with those of a classmate.

Item	High culture	Mass culture	Popular culture
'The X Files'			
'East Enders'			
'Swan Lake' (the ballet)			
'ER'			
Oasis			
Vanessa Mae (violinist)			

Examination focus

'Evaluate the sociological arguments surrounding the claim that the mass media have created a mass culture in society' (AEB, June 1992, paper 2). (Hint: look at the following diagram – you should use it as a framework for this essay.)

 On the diagram you could highlight in one colour the sections that would give *k* and *u* marks, and then in another colour highlight those that would give *i* and *a* marks.

 The diagram does not provide evaluation marks for the essay. In order to ensure that you are rewarded for evaluation, you could weigh up the pessimistic arguments against the optimistic and say which you find most persuasive.

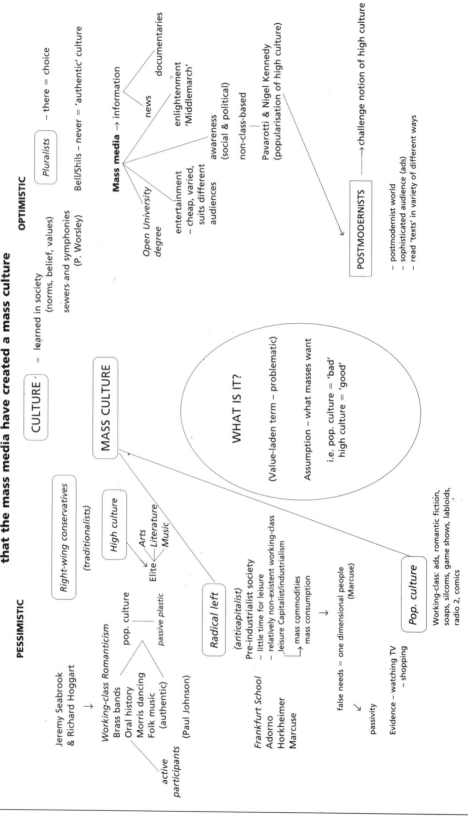

Sociological arguments surrounding the claim
that the mass media have created a mass culture

PESSIMISTIC

OPTIMISTIC

CULTURE = learned in society
(norms, belief, values)

Pluralists – there = choice

Bell/Shils – never = 'authentic' culture

Mass media → information

news   documentaries

enlightenment
'Middlemarch'

awareness
(social & political)

non-class-based

Pavarotti & Nigel Kennedy
(popularisation of high culture)

*Open University
degree*

entertainment
– cheap, varied,
suits different
audiences

Right-wing conservatives

(*traditionalists*)

sewers and symphonies
(P. Worsley)

High culture

Arts
Elite Literature
Music

MASS CULTURE

WHAT IS IT?

(Value-laden term – problematic)

Assumption – what masses want

i.e. pop. culture = 'bad'
high culture = 'good'

POSTMODERNISTS → challenge notion of high culture

– postmodernist world
– sophisticated audience (ads)
– read 'texts' in variety of different ways

Jeremy Seabrook
& Richard Hoggart

→

Working-class Romanticism
Brass bands
Oral history   pop. culture
Morris dancing
Folk music   *passive plastic*
(authentic)

(Paul Johnson)

active
participants

Radical left

(*anticapitalist*)
Pre-industrialist society
– little time for leisure
– relatively non-existent working-class
  leisure Capitalist/industrialism
      → mass commodities
        mass consumption
        →

false needs = one dimensional people
(Marcuse)

↓

passivity

Evidence – watching TV
– shopping

Frankfurt School
Adorno
Horkheimer
Marcuse

Pop. culture

Working-class: ads, romantic fiction,
soaps, silcoms, game shows, labloids,
radio 2, comics

6 Making the news: selection and presentation (is the truth out there?)

By the end of this chapter you should:

- be familiar with the selection processes involved in news production;
- be able to deconstruct the news values inherent in the national press;
- critically assess bias in the media;
- understand agenda setting, gatekeeping and the inferential structures of the media;
- be able to answer an essay question on the topic.

Introduction

> Give us twenty minutes and we'll give you the world
> We bring good things to life
> The news you need from people you can count on
> Doing what we do best.
>
> And in the flickering light and the comforting glow
> You get the world every night as a TV show
> The latest spin on the shit we're in, blow by blow
> And the more you watch the less you know.
>
> (Jackson Browne 'Information Wars,' Elektra
> Entertainment Group, 1996)

This chapter will examine the process of news production, both in print and broadcast. The media are believed to act as potentially powerful agents of secondary socialisation, along with schools, peer groups, work and religion. They provide role models for us by showing us a range of potential behaviours in new situations; importantly, they also provide us with information about the world.

So much of our information comes to us second-hand. We learn about local, national and international affairs from our newspapers, radios and televisions, and, significantly, we seem to believe what we see, read and hear.

This may not be particularly surprising because as individuals we cannot experience the multiplicity of events and phenomena that take place on any given day. However the news is the end product of a very complex process of selection, filtering and editing. In a very important sense the news is socially constructed.

Newspapers and audiences

On average, in 1994 around 27 million people read at least one daily newspaper each day. The most popular newspapers were the tabloids, and of these the most popular was the *Sun*, which was read by around ten million people. To estimate the readership figures, multiply the circulation figures by about three – not all readers buy their own copies.) Now let's have a look at who was reading these newspapers:

Link exercise 6.1

1. Using Item H in Chapter 2 (p. 11), produce a brief audience profile for two tabloid newspapers and two broadsheet/quality newspapers.

2. How might sociologists account for the gender differences apparent in this table?

The *Sun* is the most popular newspaper for all social groups but classes A and B (that is, those in professional, semiprofessional and managerial occupations), but does the readership trust what it says? How do we know which newspaper, television channel or radio station to trust? Let's look at how audiences see it (Item A).

ITEM A

Readership and trust

Most believable source	Any newspaper (%)	Telegraph, Guardian Times or FT (%)	Express, Mail (%)	Mirror, Sun or Star (%)
TV	57	30	59	66
Newspaper	15	35	13	11
Radio	15	20	16	13
Don't Know	12	16	12	11

(Source: British Social Attitudes, 1985; reprinted in Sociology Update, 1986.)

ITEM A   *Exercise 6.2*

Using the data in Item A, answer the following questions:

1. Which news source is considered to be the most believable? How would sociologists explain this?

[i] 2. Which readership believes their newspaper most?

[i][a] 3. Which readership group has least belief in its own newspapers? How would
     you account for this?

News production

Every moment of the day in every society 'news' is being made. Hundreds of thousands of events that are meaningful to groups of people in those societies occur every day. However very few of these events actually make it on to television news programmes or into our newspapers. When you next pass a newsagent run your eyes across the headlines of the daily newspapers on display. What should strike you is the similarity of the front pages, especially, but not exclusively, those of the tabloids.

Exercise 6.3

List the headlines of today's front page stories in each of the following tabloid newspapers: *Sun, Daily Mirror, Daily Mail, Daily Express, Daily Star*.

[i] 1. How many stories are there in total?

[i] 2. How many of the stories are about the same news item?

[i] 3. Which of the following people and events are involved: the royals, sports, cinema, TV and pop celebrities, politicians, 'foreigners'?

   Why is it that these front pages look so alike when they are produced by different journalists, editors and reporters working in different organisations? If we believed in the paranormal we might think that some great supernatural power was at work; but we are sociologists so there must be other reasons.

   Newspapers obtain their stories from many sources, not just from the journalists employed by the papers, and it is these sources that help create the type of news that is conveyed. 'There is more news than a paper has room to print, so all stories have to compete for space and it is the editor and senior journalists' job to decide which stories to focus on' (Crace, 1996). According to Crace, who is explaining the process of making the news, editorial meetings are held throughout the day, and some stories that were to have been published are dropped for more pressing ones – as in the television series 'Drop the Dead Donkey' about a day in the life of a busy television newsroom. News comes from various sources: reporters on the scene, foreign correspondents, other media such as TV satellite and video, computer links to other papers, global news agencies and home news agencies. This still does not explain the nature of the decision-making process to select news items for broadcasting and publication. This is where 'news values' contribute to the process.

News values

In 1973 J. Galtung and M. Ruge analysed the foreign news in a set of daily newspapers. They obtained very interesting results, and although their work took place a long time ago their analysis seems as relevant today in examining news production as it was twenty years ago.

Galtung and Ruge found that for any event to become a 'news item', and therefore considered 'newsworthy', it had to pass through a selection process. If it conformed to a particular set of criteria the news staff judged it to be eligible for entry. This is not to say that the staff were consciously subjecting items to judgement, rather that they used a professional methodology to 'nose' out a good story. This set of criteria Galtung and Ruge called 'news values'. There are both practical and social factors at work in this process. The practical factors include the timing of an event and the amount of space available in the newspaper or TV news broadcast. The social factors form a framework or pattern from which journalists select items that they consider are most appropriate. Item B illustrates the news values that help determine an event's potential newsworthiness.

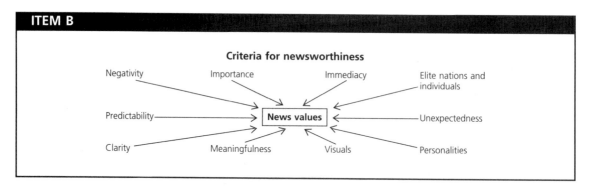

ITEM B

Criteria for newsworthiness

Negativity   Importance   Immediacy   Elite nations and individuals

Predictability ——→ **News values** ←—— Unexpectedness

Clarity   Meaningfulness   Visuals   Personalities

Each of the criteria below are defined:

- **Immediacy or frequency**: this is the time span taken for the event to appear. If the event fits in with the frequency of the news media, then it is more likely to be included.
- **Importance**: this refers to what are seen as elite nations and/or elite people. Events involving national leaders of significant countries will usually make the news.
- **Clarity of events**: this refers to the ease of understanding of an event. The *Daily Mirror*'s headline 'Caged' above a photograph of a young woman behind prison bars conveyed a clear meaning. If stories are complex they are less likely to be covered.

- **Meaningfulness**: this is the cultural relevance and proximity of the event. McLurg's Law is a fairly 'tongue-in-cheek' view of the way foreign news is covered. If a disaster occurs, it will be reported if one of our nationals is involved or if it is seen as having specific relevance to us. McLurg's ratio of relevance is that one Briton is equal in newsworthiness to 1000 Africans and 50 French.
- **Expectedness and unexpectedness**: although these are seemingly contradictory, they are not. An event that is unexpected, such as a disaster of some kind, will be reported; and an event that has gained news value will continue to be reported because we have become familiar with it.
- **Composition**: sometimes an event is reported that seems to have little significance and this happens if there is imbalance in the news. If several major international events have been reported, a small national item will be put in to counterbalance them. Also, you will have noticed the 'and finally' item on television news programmes – this is usually a light-hearted piece to sign off with so that the broadcast does not leave the audience too depressed by bad news.

In addition to the above Galtung and Ruge proposed a further four that they saw as important to the Western media:

- **Reference to elite nations**: Western countries usually receive prominence.
- **Reference to elite people**: usually stars, celebrities and the royals.
- **Personalisation**: this usually occurs in relation to politics where the actions of political leaders are taken to stand for political action.
- **Negativity**: paradoxically, bad news usually makes good news. A disaster, war, famine or a crash where many people are injured will make the news. These unexpected stories will run for a period of time.

If an event has several of these values we are more likely to hear of it.

Exercise 6.4

Return to your work for Exercise 6.3. For each of the stories on your front pages, decide which news values have made the events newsworthy.

Bias and the media

One of the main themes that occupies media researchers is inherent bias in the media. As we saw in Chapter 3, there is a considerable concentration of media ownership, especially of newspapers, and until very recently much of the British press had long supported Conservative politics. Likewise some social groups are given differential treatment by the media. This operates at the level of news values. Some sociologists, notably those with a Marxist perspective, would argue that the media reproduce the views of the ruling class in what they see as a conspiratorial way. From the Marxist perspective, the dominant ideas of any historical period are those of the ruling class, that is, the owners of the means of production, both material (economic) and mental (in relation to ideas and ideology). In this way the media act as legitimating agents for the powerful; and what the media produce is essentially in the interests of ruling groups.

However other sociologists, while maintaining the conflict perspective, see the relationship between capitalists and the media as rather more complex. It is undeniable that the media *reinforce* the position of powerful groups, but not as a result of some conspiracy. Hegemonic theorists, for example, maintain that the significant role of the media is an ideological one.

Television news

Exercise 6.5

Although audiences tend to trust televised news above that printed in newspapers, this does not mean that the news on television is necessarily objective. This exercise tests out possible bias in television news. Record the early evening news bulletins on BBC1 and ITV on the same evening. List the news items on each channel in two grids line the one below (the number of rows in the grids will depend on the number of news items for that bulletin). The nature of the news item might be political, national/international, sport, natural events, entertainment and so on.

Channel: (BBC1 or ITV)

Nature of news item	People interviewed	People referred to	Location (where filmed)	News reporter (male/female)
1.				
2.				

 1. Compare your two charts and answer the following:
  (a) How many news items were there in each of the two bulletins?
  (b) How many items referred to the same news event?
  (c) Did the same events appear in the same running order in each broadcast?
  (d) Were the same people interviewed? If not, how did they differ?
  (e) If so, could you see any differences between the approaches of the two channels?

 2. Write two paragraphs on how (a) hegemonic and (b) pluralist theorists might account for any differences between the two broadcasts.

Two processes have been viewed by media researchers as important in the production of news: agenda-setting and gatekeeping.

Agenda setting is explained by McCombs and Shaw (1993, 1995) as follows: 'In choosing and displaying news, editors, newsroom staff, and broadcasters play an important part in shaping political reality. Readers learn not only about a given issue, but also how much importance to attach to that issue from the amount of information in a news story and its position.' In this way the editors, journalists and producers together decide which items are worthy of making up the television news bulletin on being printed in the national and local press. As Lang and Lang have observed (1966), 'The mass media force attention to certain issues. They build up public images of political figures. They are constantly presenting objects suggesting what individuals in the mass should think about, know about, have feelings about' (quoted in Boyd-Barrett and Newbold (1995, p. 154).

The audience are presented with news items as if they are the most significant news of the day, without a hint that these items are simply those deamed as newsworthy by news personnel. We are not told what to think in a direct sense, but what ought to be on our agenda of what to think about. Hence the news media play a part in shaping public opinion.

The agenda-setting hypothesis is presented by McQuail (1994, p. 357) as follows:

- Public debate is represented by important issues (an agenda for action).
- The agenda derives from a combination of public opinion and political choice.
- Mass media news and information reflect the content and order of priority of issues.
- This representation of issues in the mass media exerts an independent effect on the nature of issue content so that the public comes to believe in their importance.

However, past research on agenda setting has been criticised for not addressing the possible effects on people's thoughts about who is important, where important things happen and why things are important. For instance the public may not necessarily have the same views or put the same value on news events as those of the media: 'media vary in their credibility . . . personal experience and the media picture may diverge' (ibid., p. 356).

Another process closely linked to agenda setting is that of gatekeeping. This term has been used to refer to

the process by which selections are made in media work, especially decisions whether or not to admit a particular news story to pass through the 'gates' of a news medium into the news channels . . . information has to flow along certain channels which contain 'gate areas', where decisions are made, under the influence of various favourable or unfavourable forces (ibid., p. 213).

Gatekeeping is an important process that helps us to understand why some events are presented as news while others may never get on to the news agenda. This is especially significant in times of social crises such as war, when 'bad news' is withheld in case it has a negative effect on public morale (for example the number of casualties of a war or conflict may be withheld if a general election is imminent).

However it is interesting to note that, during their study of the media coverage of child sexual abuse, Kitzinger and Skidmore (1994) did not witness straightforward news management techniques in action or even an agenda-setting pattern that showed news producers as all powerful.

Instead [they] found a significant arena of contestation in the production of news stories . . . It could be argued that ultimately the news editor or individual journalist does have the 'real' power – to edit, non-prioritise, or sensationalise. Yet the research also shows that those who act as sources of information for the media can successfully inform the news agenda through integrated professional PR strategies and on such occasions can have an impact on the audience (Skidmore, 1995; for more details of this research, see Chapter 8).

John Crace, writing in the *Guardian* (Resources section, 17 September 1996), stated that 'there is no such thing as an impartial news story. Even a story that seems to be politically neutral tells you something about the values of the news organisation that produced it by its length and positioning on the page, or its place in the television running order.' This is an interesting statement given that it was made by a journalist employed by a newspaper that was engaged in the very process he described.

As we saw in Chapter 3, the Glasgow University Media Group have long been engaged in investigations of the agenda-setting role of the media.

Inferential structures of news production

Hall *et al.* (1978, p. 60) argue that 'the routine structures and practices of the media in relation to news making serve to "frame" events within dominant interpretations and paradigms'. In *Policing the Crisis*, Hall *et al.* demonstrate the process by which this takes place. Using the assumptions outlined earlier of what makes specific types of event newsworthy, they show how journalists make these events 'intelligible' to the public. This is a very significant part of the process of hegemonic control and it is made possible by specific journalistic practices that involve acceptance of a set of assumptions about the nature of society.

Firstly, the idea of consensus: this means that audiences are assumed to share a common stock of knowledge about the world, and so have access to shared meanings about society. Using what we might recognise as a functionalist approach, journalists work on the basis that there is one set of cultural meanings and this operates as a 'central value system'.

Secondly, the routine structures of news production. Think for a moment about where the news comes from. How do journalists gather news? Are they all engaged in 'investigative journalism'? Trowler (1996) lists the many and varied sources from which journalists actually collect news, depending on the sociological perspective adopted (Item C).

ITEM C

News sources as perceived by the three approaches

Manipulative	Hegemonic	Pluralist
Official sources: parliament, the church, royalty, official 'diary' events, central and local government. Press agencies such as Reuters, United Press International and so on	Official sources: parliament, the church, royalty, official 'diary' events, central and local government. Mainly metropolitan stories.	Casual sources, other media, the public, police and fire services, official sources and journalists themselves
Not 'ordinary' folk, therefore homogeneity	Not 'ordinary' folk, therefore homogeneity	Anyone, therefore heterogeneity

(Source: Adapted from Trowler, 1996.)

Thus if we accept a hegemonic position it is clear that journalists take their news from reliable, usually official news sources and, owing to the increased pressure placed on journalists to meet critical print deadlines, they become increasingly reliant on these sources rather than going out into the field and 'discovering' the news.

There is another significant factor involved in the whole process: the need for news to be seen as impartial, balanced and objective. This is of course formally enforced in television news production, but the press tend to present information from official sources as if it were factual and objective. These 'accredited' sources are essential players in the process of news production. They may be government spokespeople, managers, leaders of industry, police officers and so on – what they have in common is privileged access to the media. Hall refers to them as 'over accessing' the media. They become the *primary definers* of the situation and therefore play a very significant part in how we the audience understand a news event. Let's see how this takes place:

1. An event occurs; the media arrive at the scene.
2. Journalists interview a spokesperson, usually an official.
3. This person becomes the initial definer of the event.
4. All oppositional views are set against this framework.
5. The 'inferential structure' becomes difficult to shift.
6. A limit or boundary has been set for future discussion.

Exercise 6.6

Look in your newspaper for the first report of a specific piece of news.

 1. Who is interviewed/referred to?

 2. Whose voices are not heard?

 3. What reasons would you give for the invisibility of some groups? Follow the event until it ceases to be newsworthy – can you find the primary definition? How are opposing voices dealt with?

After the primary definers have set the framework for the discussion of an event or issue, there is a process of transformation whereby the new 'facts' or arguments are transformed into news form. As we have seen, media professionals are selective about whose statements are reported. This is very important for reinforcing the profiles of particular newspapers. The news criteria that are common to them all are dealt with differently by each newspaper editor because they have to cater to very different readerships. The item is coded into the specific language or mode of address of the paper concerned. (The mode of address is the manner in which the newspaper speaks to its audience, this can be formal or informal, impersonal or as a member of a 'club', simplistic or complex. The mode of address tells us a great deal about the nature of the readership of a newspaper or television programme.)

This transformation into a style that is particular to each medium gives the news item an external public reference and validity. It becomes one of the significant issues of the day – part of the agenda set by that medium. What is also very significant from a sociological point of view is that this very transformation demonstrates what the public 'thinks'. Newspaper editorials often print statements as if they are taken from public opinion – for instance 'The People of Britain want . . .', '*Sun* readers believe . . .' – but these are simply statements by journalists and editors. Once they are published they take on a separate reality, as if they really are public opinion, and are then used as 'impartial evidence' of what the public really does want or believes to be true.

Watching the watchdogs

Sociologists on journalism

The profession of journalism proclaims itself to be the nation's watchdog, but who watches the watchdog? Increasingly, sociologists. Given the growing centrality of the mass media in daily life as a source of images and ideas, a form of social technology and an increasingly privatised practice marking the (temporal) rhythms of modern existence, it is not surprising that the mass media, and the news media especially, should be of interest to sociologists.

There are widespread 'common-sense' views on the news media, but sociologists have not generally sought to account for the output of the news media either in terms of owner intervention and control or political conspiracy and manipulation. . . .

Four general sociological approaches to the study of news currently order discussion and research, each directing its sights at different levels of analysis and each moving well beyond simplistic notions of 'journalist bias'.

Political economy: studies in commercial constraints

Studies in political economy have questioned the popular reliance upon intentional and politically motivated behaviour (instrumentalism) as an explanation of news output. 'The pivotal concept,' explains a leading exponent of the political economy approach, 'is not power but determination. Structural analysis looks beyond intentional action to examine the limits to choice and the pressures on decision making' (Murdock, 1982, p. 124).

The argument here is that it is not necessary to find politically motivated interventions in the news process to explain prevailing forms of news coverage; rather, it is necessary to look at the structural dynamics and constraints compelling the cultural industries within a competitive economy to pursue profits. The search for reduced costs and increased sales inevitably leads to processes of *centralisation* (the tendency to swallow up competitors) and forces of *conglomeration* (the tendency to swallow up related industries and enterprises).

The resultant lack of media diversity is seen to lead to the production of standardised formats and politically safe media products (whether newspapers, television pro-grammes, films or records) aimed at the mass audience. High market entry costs, advertiser pressures and the necessity to pursue the largest audience all conspire to *marginalise* alternative and oppositional media products and voices, tending instead towards the production of the lowest-common-denominator cultural products for mass consumption. Such impersonal market forces are increasingly international in scope and, such is their sphere of influence, they also impact upon public service broadcasters who must 'compete' for audiences and government patronage.

This . . . approach . . . can itself be criticised, however, not least in relation to:

1. its tendency to generalise processes of cultural homogenisation and its consequent underestimation of the extent to which economic forces can produce different products for market niches;
2. its under-theorisation and empirical silence concerning different audiences and processes of reception;
3. its implicit, simplistic notion of a 'dominant ideology'.

The political economy approach . . . continues to provide a broad and necessary underpinning to any serious account of the news media and their news agencies now operating within an increasingly international marketplace. . . .

Organisational studies: contexts and contacts

As every journalist knows, the news watched on the TV or read in the morning daily does not just 'happen'; it is produced as a matter of routine. A newsroom division of labour, editorial hierarchy, news policy and routine news-beats and source contacts are all 'known' by journalists as the means by which a news product is daily produced on time and to the specified requirements. Such mundane professional habits, observing sociologists have maintained, exercise a profound, if unintended, *bureaucratic* impact on the news stories selected and their forms of presentation.

> News is a peculiar form of knowledge: its character derives very much from the sources and contexts of production. With few exceptions, those sources and contexts are bureaucratic, and news is the result of an organised response to routine bureaucratic problems (Rock, 1981, p. 64).

Production is so organised that its basic dynamics emphasise the perishability of stories . . . It is always today's developments which occupy the foreground. The corollary of this point is that there is an inherent tendency for the news to be framed in a discontinuous and a historical way, and this implies a truncation of context, and therefore a reduction of meaningfulness (Schlesinger, 1987, p. 47).

Importantly, such studies have frequently observed how journalist reliance upon routine sources also serves to reproduce the voices of the powerful.

> Broadcasters and their institutions mediate – hold the pass, command the communicative channels – between the élites of power (social, economic, political, cultural) and the mass audience (Hall, 1975, p. 124).

This reflects not only bureaucratic constraints but also the profession's need to be seen to be 'objective' and 'impartial'.

Ironically, by accessing those social, political or military élites who command the authority and knowledge to comment authoritatively on events, journalists can be publicly seen to be *impartial*. As a consequence, the élites of society, via the news media, are granted an opportunity to become the nation's 'primary definers', setting the terms of reference and prescribing courses of political action in relation to newsworthy events.

Studies have provided insights into the way in which news organisation and production impact upon news output, and complement to a large extent the general framework of the political economy approach. Like the political economy approach, though, these studies can also be criticised, not for reducing everything to the impersonal logic of the market place perhaps (*economic reductionism*), but to the bureaucratising imperative (*organisational functionalism*) which explains everything, from the patterns of news access and general news subjects reported to the truncated, ahistorical, decontextualised character of news itself. . . .

Journalist studies

Communicators and their culture

If the social composition of journalists is found to be less than representative of society as a whole, it is tempting to conclude that élite educational backgrounds, class origins or perhaps considerations of ethnicity or gender may have something to do with it. Studies of journalists as 'gatekeepers' of news, however, have tended to conclude that such considerations are of secondary importance when compared to processes of *training* and *professional socialisation*. In any event, journalists have not been found uniformly disposed to any particular political viewpoint (Elliott, 1977). Professional considerations, not personal choices, appear to be implicated in the selection and subsequent treatment of news stories.

Conflict-avoidance

Shared news values and adherence to a news policy, while standardising the selection and style of news output, serve professional and newsroom conflict-avoidance goals as well. . . .

Furthermore, some sociologists have maintained that professional claims to 'objectivity' are a means of conflict-avoidance, though not with the profession's external critics. . . .

Socialisation and identification

Others, observing the interactions between journalists and their sources, have noted a subtle process of increasing socialisation and identification with their source's professional judgements and interests. Once again, according to such studies, it is simply not a question of individual journalist attitudes or personal viewpoints. Rather,

> It is in fact a complex process of socialisation by which the journalist's frame of reference, methods of working and personal system of perceptions and understandings are brought into line with the expectations of his sources (Chibnall, 1981, p. 88).

Such *interactionist* studies, looking at the relationships between journalists and their colleagues, their various sources and their external critics, have provided a major insight into the nature of news production. If such studies at least begin to focus upon the complex nature of journalist interactions – a dimension seemingly lost from view in other approaches – and see this as an important consideration in the production of news and news output, one last strand of theorisation, though also moving beyond simplistic charges of 'news bias', tends once again to *minimise* the active role of news producers.

Culturalist studies: culture as control, contest and ritual

In the main, journalists have tended to be seen as giving expression to deep-seated, often unconscious, cultural values and viewpoints. Of course, news values can themselves be seen to be so professionally entrenched as to be almost 'unconscious', such is their routine contribution to the journalistic selection and framing of stories.

An early study of news values noted how news should fit the *frequency* or time-span of the publication cycle of the news medium itself (so a murder or a battle is more likely to be reported than social trends or the history of a war, for example): it should rise above established news *thresholds* and pertain to *élite persons* and *élite nations* and should involve *personalisation* and *negativity* (Galtung and Ruge, 1981, pp. 52–615).

Others have suggested, however, that news values may serve more particular ideological interests and needs by selecting and interpreting events in accordance with dominant social interests. The controversial series of *Bad News* studies by the Glasgow University Media Group are representative here.

> Television news is a cultural artefact; it is a sequence of socially manufactured messages, which carry many of the culturally dominant assumptions of our society. From the accents of the newscasters to the vocabulary of camera angles; from who gets on and what questions get asked, via selection of stories to presentation of bulletins, the news is a highly mediated product (Glasgow University Media Group [GUMG], 1976, p. 1).

If such studies imply that news broadcasts advance a dominant ideology (though, again, this is not reduced to journalist 'bias'), other studies have suggested that, though offering a 'preferred reading', news may contain more contestation than was formerly thought to be the case (Morley, 1980). Increasingly, other studies point to the different ways in which audiences receive and interpret the news (Philo, 1990). The writings of Stuart Hall, developing upon Antonio Gramsci's idea of 'hegemony', have tended to indicate a more conflictual understanding of ideological engagement with the battle for hearts and minds, given the continuing sources of social and political conflict, never finally won. . . .

If culturalist approaches to news have tended to operate within a Marxist and neo-Marxist framework of analysis, other theorists appear to be closer to a Durkheimian understanding, where bonds of social solidarity expressed and reinforced through collective forms of worship and ritual come to the fore. As one scholar expressed it:

> Ritual cannot simply be reduced to the rational. It draws on what is customary, familiar and traditional in the culture. It tries to add spiritual and emotional

communion to any sense of political unity, though from any single point of view it may not work (Elliott, 1980, p. 146).

One need only ponder those patriotic news appeals unleashed in times of national disaster and war, or the symbolic and emotional appeals of royal weddings and so on, to realise that news can and does 'work' at the level of emotional appeal as much as rational dissemination of information. News may well, in other words, provide a ritualised performance in which the symbolic bonds of 'community' find repeated expression and confirmation.

The creative explosion of interest in cultural studies in recent years has pointed to renewed interest in questions of audience *reception* as well as the interpretation and analysis of news 'texts'. In particular, attention has tended to shift from differing 'interpretive communities' and their different 'decodings' to the domestic contexts of media consumption, its working with gender relationships, the involvement of technological hardware and its wider incorporation into the arrangements of modern societies.

Culturalist studies of news, then, have tended to approach news as a site both simultaneously made up of and making contemporary social relationships and their various contests. The role of journalists and news production tends to become secondary to the contests and engagements granted 'expression' through the news media and its place within the domestic arrangements of consumption. If the approach can be criticised for failing to recognise the importance of *news production* and some of those complexities and constraints indicated earlier, it also cannot be accused of simplistically pursuing news bias.

(Source: Simon Cottle, Sociology Review, September 1996.)

ITEM D **Exercise 6.7**

Read Item D and answer the following questions:

i 1. What approach is least likely to be used by sociologists when accounting for the output of the news media? Which four approaches have been favoured instead?

i *k* *u* 2. Put the following passage into your own words: 'The argument here is that it is not necessary to find politically motivated interventions in the news process to explain prevailing forms of news coverage; rather, it is necessary to look at the structural dynamics and constraints compelling the cultural industries within a competitive economy to pursue profits.'

i 3. Describe the political economy and organisational studies approaches.

e 4. What are their weaknesses?

e 5. What do you see as the strengths of the interactionist approach?

i *a* *k* *u* 6. What is meant by the term 'preferred reading'? What are the two other types of reading?

k *u* *i* 7. What do you understand by the term 'hegemony'?

Exercise 6.9

i *a* This revision exercise will be useful for writing essays on the process of news making. McQuail (1994) has produced a useful summary of what he sees as the most significant and best-documented generalisations of bias in the news. Match each of the following statements with the correct theoretical approach. Some approaches are used more than once. Choose from instrumentalist Marxist, hegemonic, feminist, pluralist.

1. Media news overrepresents the social 'top' and official voices in its sources.
2. News attention is differentially bestowed on members of political and social elites.
3. The social values that are most underlined are consensual and supportive of the *status quo*.
4. Foreign news concentrates on nearer, richer and more powerful nations.
5. News has a nationalistic (patriotic) and ethnocentric bias in the choice of topics and opinions expressed and in the view of the world assumed or portrayed.
6. News reflects the values and power distribution of a male-dominated society.
7. Minorities are differentially marginalised, ignored or stigmatised.
8. News about crime overrepresents violent and personal crime and neglects many of the realities of risk in society.
9. Politically relevant news tends to be neutral or support parties to the right of the spectrum.

Examination focus

Essay

'In presenting the "news", the mass media cannot give an objective account of the world to us because they must select from many events.' To what extent do sociological evidence and arguments support this statement? (AEB, S94). Try this essay under examination conditions.

(Hint: this is an opportunity to demonstrate your understanding of the news-making process – the role of official sources, the selection and filtering process associated with news values, and the agenda setting and gatekeeping aspects of news making. At the theoretical level you could compare the approaches of the instrumentalists, hegemonic theorists and pluralists. You could illustrate your arguments by looking at the marginalisation of particular groups such as women and ethnic groups, the coverage of the royals and the empirical studies undertaken by the GUMG. You might also refer to the recent controversy over press intrusion and the consequent changes in privacy legislation.)

Exam question and student's answer

Exam question

'The selection and presentation of the news depends more on practical issues than on cultural influences.' Critically discuss the arguments for and against this view (AEB, summer 1996).

Student's answer

This essay has been undertaken by a student under exam conditions. Read the essay yourself and mark the appropriate skills in the margin. Compare your marks with those of another student to see whether you agree or disagree on the marks for the skill domains given at the end of the essay. How do you think the essay might be improved?

The selection of the news is a subject that many sociologists disagree on. The ideas of what are 'practical issues' will vary between each sociological perspective.

Pluralists would agree that the news tackles practical issues that concern the cultural influences of the population as a whole. They believe that the presentation of news reflects the interests of society as a whole and as such, would cover a broad range from trivia and gossip to international stories. The selection is fair and just and the media works in the interests of everyone.

Marxists would criticise this view as naive. They see the media as a whole as a manipulative device in the hands of those who own the processes of production. The content of the media is broadcast in their interests, its aim is not to rock the boat. The ideological messages of the media and, therefore, also the news is that of pacification of the working class and the importance of a false consciousness that doesn't challenge the status quo. Regarding the preparation and selection of the news Marxists would say there is more of a cultural influence upon this process, but that this cultural influence is negative and coercive: that of the dominant class. The journalists who work under the rule of the editor would have their stories selected on the basis of the dominant ideology. Stories that show the dominant class or ruling government in a critical light are omitted, and this ability for non-decision making sets an agenda that keeps its audience in the dark about real political and social issues. The media are supposed to be impartial and as such, news selection and presentation should reflect this impartiality, but who determines 'practical issues' and even when due partiality is claimed, does it really happen?

The Glasgow Media Group carried out several studies – *Bad News, More Bad News, Really Bad News* – these investigated the ways in which news was presented, with close attention paid to the handling of strikes by unionists. Their findings revealed a bias in favour of the managers and a bias against the unionists. Most often it was simply the language used to describe the 'negotiations'; the unionists 'demanded' and 'insisted' whereas the managers 'pleaded'. There was also a pre-occupation with the amount of money that the strike was costing the firm and so all of this helped to show the workers in a negative light. The Glasgow Media Group do not hide their socialist tendencies, but through impartial analysis, show that the cultural influences of the dominant class strongly and deliberately effect news selection and presentation.

The notion of hegemony is a strong one with regard to the selection and presentation of news. The average journalist is a white, middle-class male and as such, while they try to retain impartiality, it is really inevitable that some of their dominant ideology should pervade the news. It is not as the Marxists would suggest, a consciously manipulative reproduction of dominant ideology. The news selected would be more likely to concern the middle class, have a more racist slant and even be opposed to the working class, but the hegemonic theorists press the notion that this is a subconscious result.

Marxist theorists would agree that the likes of stories about the royal family are consciously included by the media as an ideological means of getting the working class to accept the hierarchy and to even respect it. Also by running stories or news bulletins on the royals, the dominant class avoids more serious political issues. It is the idea of bread and circuses that the Marxists follow.

The three main perspectives on the media put differing stock in the notion of 'practical issues' and 'cultural theory'. The pluralist perspective would argue that the practical issues probably are more dependant in the selection of news, but it is the cultural influence of value consensus that deems these issues practical. The hegemonic theorists argue that 'seemingly' practical issues are culturally influenced in a subconscious manner by the journalists themselves, and the Marxists with their conflict theory see the negative effect of the dominant class as deeming issues 'practical' that maintains the exploitation of the working class.

The student scored the following marks for the essay:

Knowledge and understanding: 6/9
Interpretation and application: 5/9
Evaluation: 5/9
Total: 16

7 Representation

By the end of this chapter you should:

- understand the nature of representations and stereotypes;
- be able to apply these concepts to the relationship between representations and ideology as they apply to gender, ethnicity, sexuality and age;
- structure and evaluate essays on representation.

Introduction

In order to make sense of our world we need to be able to communicate with others. Communication is achieved through shared signs and symbols, the most common of which is language. The media communicate with their audiences through the process of representation. By using familiar signs and symbols, they create a representation of reality. This process of representation has several different aspects:

1. It is the way the media re-present events to us *as if* they are natural.
2. It involves focusing on some groups rather than others.
3. It is inevitably ideological. 'The media give us images, ways of imagining particular groups which can have material effects on how those groups experience the world, and how they get understood or even legislated for by others' (Branston and Stafford, 1996, p. 78).

Let's take an example. A woman in a kitchen advertising a floor cleaning product is a representation of a woman involved in a domestic task, but it may also stand for stereotypical assumptions about women as domestic labourers. The image of the woman in the kitchen embodies gendered domestic labour. We have become used to seeing images of women 'naturally' working in the kitchen; more recent adverts that have placed men in the kitchen either serve to show how 'unnatural' a setting it is for them, or that men use domestic labour as a means of obtaining rewards from women.

|i| 1. From your current viewing, identify which adverts place men in the kitchen.

|i| 2. What activities they are involved in?

|a| 3. What assumptions about gender roles are being made by these adverts?

In this chapter we are particularly concerned with the representation of different social characteristics in the media. We have chosen to focus on the following:

- Gender
- Ethnicity
- Sexuality
- Age

Stereotypes

It is not possible to examine media representations of social groups without first discussing the nature of stereotypes, as these are regularly used in the process of representation. The term 'stereotype' has become so much part of everyday speech that we assume its meaning without really unpacking it. From a common-sense position it has taken on the meaning of a negative label attached to a specific group or entity, but we need to examine it sociologically. There are several different ways in which media analysts have used the term. O'Sullivan *et al.* (1995, p. 126) define it as:

> a label which involves a process of categorisation and evaluation. Although it may refer to situations or places, it is most often used in conjunction with representations of social groups. In its simplest terms, an easily grasped characteristic, usually negative, is presumed to belong to a whole group, e.g. estate agents are insincere, devious and smooth-talking . . . in ideological terms, stereotyping is a means by which support is provided for one group's differential (often discriminatory) treatment of another.

Others see the concept in more psychological terms as a kind of 'blinkered mental attitude' (Barratt, 1986). The psychological study of stereotypes usually involves a more general concern with the origins of attitudes and it is traditionally linked with prejudice. Perkins (1979) refers to the stereotype as a compressed or shorthand way of referring to complex social relationships. The example she uses of the 'dumb blonde' illustrates this. Not only do we instantly recognise the type of person alluded to, but we are also aware that the term involves the socially subordinate position of women.

The stereotype is never neutral, but inevitably ideological, so that the representation of the individual, group or nation appears to be 'natural'. Although we must be wary of the media's use of stereotyping, we need to understand how it is an effective vehicle of representation. Walter Lippmann, as early as 1956, showed that the process could operate on different levels. It could be one or more of the following:

- An ordering process.
- A short cut.
- A means of referring to the world.
- A means of expressing our values and beliefs.

As an **ordering process** it helps us to make sense of the huge amount of data we have to process each day on the world around us. We have to use some kind of categorisation to bring order to potential chaos. However there is a problem with this as we may begin to believe that the stereotype is real.

As a **short cut**, it is a striking, simple and easily grasped form of representation, condensing a great deal of detail into a small space.

With **reference to the world**, it is the way we see particular social groups as having a set of immediately recognisable characteristics.

As an **expression of values**, the stereotype is inevitably linked to ideology because it effectively creates divisions between groups in society. This is necessarily linked to hegemony because it creates an imagined consensus; That is, 'this is what *we* think of *them*'. This may become clearer in the next exercise.

Exercise 7.2

 On the left-hand side of the following chart there is a list of groups that are often the target of media stereotyping. What you need to do is to write in the words that come to mind for each group. Place these in the right-hand column.

Type of group	Stereotypical descriptions
1. Single parents	
2. The Irish	
3. Career women	
4. The elderly	
5. Feminists	
6. The 'New Man'	
7. Australians	
8. Young black men	

We shall now examine the representation of specific groups by the media.

Representations of gender

Sociologists have highlighted the important difference between 'sex' as a fixed biological difference between males and females, and 'gender' as socially constructed differences between masculinity and femininity. They place much more importance on the social construction of gender difference than on biological explanations. We examined feminist theories of the media in Chapter 5, and it may be useful for you to refer back to them whilst reading this chapter. Feminism has had a very significant influence on research into gender representation by the media with regard to women. Feminists have generally been highly critical of many of the representations of women by the media, but they also acknowledge that the media are not solely responsible for gender role stereotyping.

Exercise 7.3

1. Which social institutions apart from the media contribute to gender socialisation?
2. Select one of these institutions and explain how it contributes to the gender socialisation process.

There is little clear evidence that media representation actually directly affects social behaviour. The main theories that examine this area are cultivation analysis, reinforcement theory and feminist theories of the media (see Chapters 5 and 9 for more detail on these theories).

Ros Gill (1988) charted the progress of research on images of women in the media from the mid 1950s through the awakening of feminism in the 1960s and onward to the work undertaken by the Centre for Contemporary Cultural Studies in the 1980s. The major methodological tool common to this work is quantitative content analysis, and Gill is very critical of this method.

Before we examine the representation of women in more detail, let's look at the typical method of content analysis. Content analysis is a means of testing the specific content of media products, and it can be both quantitative and qualitative in its approach. When quantitative, the researcher, having decided upon the particular group or event to be monitored, produces a content schedule, which is very similar to a structured questionnaire. This schedule will have a range of questions that the researcher directs to the text.

The advantages and disadvantages of content analysis

Advantages

- It is relatively cheap.
- As it does not necessitate any involvement of the researcher with respondents, it is seen as objective and 'scientific'.
- Sources are usually easy to come by as it analyses newspapers, magazines, radio and television.
- In its *quantitative* form, it produces data that is measurable, so it can document trends over time, be used in comparative research and give immediate patterns of representation. It is a highly verifiable method because it can be easily replicated.

Disadvantages

- It is far from objective. Researchers generate their own categories from which to code and these become second-order constructs.
- The researcher, usually working alone, has to place individuals in categories – this is a subjective technique.
- Quantitative research falls to examine the ideological messages about the groups being studied; while qualitative research is open to accusations of biased interpretations.
- Most content analysis is empirical research and not based upon a body of theory.

If we wished to examine the portrayal of elderly women on television, we might ask factual questions about social characteristics, including age, region, nationality, location, employment, social class, domestic/familial roles and so on. We could then do a head count of the number and types of elderly women appearing on our screens. This would provide us with some interesting statistical material, however it would tell us nothing about the messages or ideological representation of this social group.

In order to do this we would need to undertake a qualitative content analysis. This is at once richer but more subjective, based as it is on one individual's reading of media messages about elderly women. Many sociologists use a form of semiology to undertake this kind of research. Semiology – the study of signs and sign systems – has been very influential in reading media texts. We shall discuss the use of semiology in more depth in Chapter 9.

Gender and television

From children's shows to commercials prime time adventures and situation comedies television proclaims that women don't count for much. They are underrepresented in television's fictional life – they are symbolically annihilated (Tuchman *et al.*, 1978).

What does symbolic annihilation mean?

Tuchman's concept of symbolic annihilation refers to the fact that women appear far less often than men on the small screen, and when they do their roles are very limited and/or negative. She claims that the media frequently condemn or trivialise women's activities and experiences.

Female character types in contemporary television serials

Many feminists argue that women tend to be portrayed in a limited and generally negative manner on television. In her study *Ladies of the Evening: Women Characters of Prime Time TV* (1983), Meehan conducted a content analysis of American soap operas. She suggested that there were in fact only ten character types in these shows.

Exercise 7.4

1. See if you can identify Meehan's ten character types in contemporary television programmes. Concentrate on main female characters only.

Working in pairs or small groups, complete the following chart by writing the names of characters and the television programmes in the boxes.

Category	Soap opera	Situation Comedy	Hospital drama	Police drama
The imp: a rebellious tomboy.				
The good wife: a happy housewife				
The harpy: aggressive and powerful single woman				
The bitch: manipulative deceitful cheat				
The victim: passive woman who suffers disease, accident etc.				
The decoy: heroine disguised as victim. Seems helpless but is in fact resourceful				

The siren: sexually dangerous. Lures men.				
The courtesan: prostitute				
The witch: Extraordinary power, either from wealth or supernatural force. Usually gives in to a man.				
The matriarch: powerful, high-status older woman				

(Source: Adapted from Trowler, 1996.)

2. Which if any of Meehan's types have disappeared from television in the 1990s?

3. Are there any differences between genres (types of programme)?

4. What does this exercise tell you about stereotyping of women on prime-time television?

Research using content analysis has demonstrated that women are underrepresented on the screen. Television generally overemphasises certain roles for women; in particular the sexual and the domestic. Traditionally, in TV advertisements women have either been portrayed as the good wife/mother who serves, more often than not, the white nuclear family, gets excited about the latest brand of washing powder, air freshener, gravy browning and so on, and is informed about the virtues of this product by a male expert. Alternatively women's bodies have adorned a wide array of products aimed at men, ranging from aftershave to sports cars. This decorative sexual role is essentially a highly passive one for women, who are presented as objects of the 'male gaze' Mulvey, 1975; Berger, 1972 rather than social actors with independent roles.

In *Unequal Opportunities* (1980), Margaret Gallagher reviewed the portrayal of women by the media in different continents and found a remarkable similarity. The treatment of women was narrow, and they were portrayed as essentially romantic and dependent, rarely rational, active or decisive. They were numerically underrepresented and infrequently newsworthy. Whether in the cinema, in the press or on the broadcast media, women's activities focused upon the domestic sphere. Advertising directed at women was seen as condescending and manipulative, and women's bodies were often used exploitatively to sell products. 'Underlying practically all media images of women, though characterised somewhat differently from one country to another, is a dichotomous motif which defines women as either good or wholly evil, mother or whore, virgin or call-girl, even traditional or modern' (ibid., p. 71).

Feminist critiques of the media have concentrated on the relative absence of women from significant areas of the media, such as news and current affairs, political debates and sports reporting; the demeaning portrayal of women in the media, particularly in the tabloid press; and the reinforcement of gender stereotyping in advertising. They have also expressed concern about the possible effects on the attitude formation of children. For feminists, the media act as key agents in reinforcing and perpetuating a patriarchal society (see Chapter 5 for more detail on feminist theory).

The earliest systematic study of gender stereotyping on American television was undertaken in 1972 by Dominick and Rauch, who conducted a content analysis of 1000 television advertisements on New York City network stations. They found a very significant pattern of gender stereotyping in television advertising:

- Seventy-five per cent of advertisements using women were for kitchen and bathroom products.
- Being a housewife was the single most common occupation for women, with over 56 per cent of women portrayed in this role.
- Men, in contrast, were portrayed in authoritative roles. They were significantly more likely than women to be shown in outdoor and business settings.
- Eighty-seven per cent of voice-overs used a male voice, only 6 per cent used a female voice.

Bretl and Cantor (1988) noted that some subtle changes had taken place during the intervening years. Women were now seen in a wider variety of occupations, and more frequently outside the domestic setting than they had been in the early 1970s. Men and women occurred approximately in equal numbers as primary characters. European research demonstrates similar patterns. Thoveron's (1986) study of TV advertising in eight European countries found that although most of the actors in advertisements were women, there was still significant gender stereotyping. Most work settings involved men, while domestic settings mainly involved women. Women were portrayed in the home in more than 43 per cent of cases, mostly as housewives or mothers. In only 18 per cent of cases were women shown in paid employment.

The most recent large-scale British content analysis of television advertisements was conducted by Cumberbatch *et al.* (1990) for the Broadcasting Standards Authority. This study showed that no significant change in the representation of women in advertising had taken place. In general, men still outnumbered women on screen by a ratio of nearly 2:1. With respect to voice-overs, over 89 per cent used a male voice. In terms of occupational roles, men were twice as likely as women to be portrayed in some kind of paid employment (30 per cent of men, 16 per cent of women). This underrepresentation of women in work is clearly at odds with the reality of women in the employment market in the 1990s. Although housework was no longer portrayed as the dominant activity for women in the majority of advertisements (they were shown as housewives in only 7 per cent of adverts), women were still twice as likely as men to be engaged in domestic labour. In terms of physical appearance, women were still portrayed far more commonly in a decorative role than men, and far more as attractive and slim. In conclusion Cumberbatch *at al.* argued that 'women exist in what is essentially a man's world'.

Lazier and Gagnard Kendrick (1993) argue that adverts have ignored the increasing numbers of women who have become doctors, lawyers, elected politicians and entrepreneurs. Women are starting businesses at three times the rate of men.

Music videos

Since the 1980s, music videos have become an important cultural form in popular culture. Not only are there several terrestrial chart shows, but the entire airtime of MTV is devoted to music videos. Research on gender representation in this field shows that women are significantly underrepresented in music videos (Brown and Campbell, 1986). Typically women are portrayed in music videos as submissive, physically attractive and sensual, and in narrative-style concept videos there are significant gender differences both in the number of appearances of women and men and the roles they play (Sherman and Dominick, 1986).

Vincent *et al.* (1987) researched gender portrayal in music videos on MTV, based on 30 hours of programming and 300 videos. They developed a scale of sexism upon which the various portrayals of women were plotted, and concluded that sexism was a very prominent feature. Fifty-seven per cent of videos were classified as 'condescending', that is, women were shown merely as sex objects or victims. In general women were portrayed in a decorative role, and in 10 per cent of the videos women were depicted as victims of male violence. In a follow-up study in 1989, Vincent found a decrease in the condescending portrayal of women and a significant increase in the portrayal of women as people in their own right. However sexism was still a marked feature of music videos.

Exercise 7.5

 1. If you have access to MTV, it would be interesting to examine current representations of women on music videos. Choose ten music videos featuring women and fill in an extended version the following content analysis grid (10 sets of boxes).

Category	Video 1	Video 2	Video 3
Decorative: woman simply as decorative, e.g. as dancers			
Patronising: women as sex objects, e.g. dumb blonde			
Victims: women are humiliated or abused by men			
Independent: women as performers in their own right			

 2. When conducting the content analysis, did you experience any difficulty with placing women into the various categories? If so, what does this tell you about the problems associated with categorising media material?

 3. In 1996/97 Britain witnessed a so-called revolution in 'girl power', as demonstrated by the Spice Girls. To what extent do you think that this female group challenged or simply reinforced the dominant ideas of femininity?

The effects of gender representation: women and body image

Feminists have expressed concern about the limited and generally negative representation of women in the media because they believe that it has a negative effect on attitudes towards and the status of women. Recently concern has been expressed about a possible link between the representation of women's bodies on the one hand and eating disorders and the distorted body images held by young women on the other.

Since the 1980s there has been increased awareness of eating disorders among young people, especially girls, and statistics indicate that the frequency of eating disorders is increasing. Some recent reports have shown that girls as young as 11 and 12 are worried about their weight and body size and are striving to achieve unrealistic body sizes at very young ages (Bellos, 1996). This has led some researchers to question whether the media might be in part responsible for imparting unhealthy messages about body size to young women. Magazines aimed at teenage girls have come under considerable attack from some feminists for their preoccupation with romance and reinforcing a dominant ideology of femininity. Women's magazines have been attacked for their limited and traditional content, providing step-by-step guides on how to be a 'real woman' (see Chapter 5).

More recently public concern has been voiced about the 'superwaifs' of the 1990s – abnormally thin fashion supermodels. Their size has led to much speculation that many models are suffering from eating disorders and much criticism has been directed at the fashion and beauty industry for the message that 'thin is in'. Research into women's magazines (Silverstein *et al.* 1986) seems to indicate that since the 1950s models have become steadily thinner. The message conveyed in women's magazines seems to be that thinness equates with good health and attractiveness. However this is not new. One of the early American researchers into anorexia, Bruch (1978), said that she related the illness to 'the enormous emphasis that fashion places on slimness . . . magazines and movies carry the same message, but the most persistent is television, drumming it in, day in day out, that one can be loved and respected only when slender'.

The continuing emphasis on slimness and indeed 'thinness' may have consequences for adolescent girls' perception of the ideal body size and the increase in eating disorders among young women. However we must be aware that anorexia tends to be an illness of white middle-class girls and women. As Probyn (1992) argues, 'we need to ask why the historical gendered experiences of women of color [sic] generally have not led them to use anorexia as a means of voicing their discontent against the differing ways in which they are positioned in patriarchal society. If we must use the body as a heuristic [a measuring device against reality] then we must insist upon the differences [of race, sexuality, age and so on] of these bodies.'

Exercise 7.6

Research on eating disorders and the media

1. Concentrating on magazines aimed at young women, to what extent is there a dominant body image?

2. Using CD Roms or the Internet, collect a range of articles on dieting, body image and eating disorders.

    (a) How often are the media cited as a possible cause?

    (b) What other factors are cited as possible causes?

3. Discussion (you might like to discuss this with a classmate): to what extent do you think that the media might be responsible for the increase in eating disorders among young girls?

Rosalind Coward (1984) argues that advertising encourages women to view their bodies as a 'project', and one, rather like DIY, that can always be improved upon. Root (1986) maintains that this barrage of images produces in women a feeling that there is much work to be done before the their bodies can match the image of perfection in advertising. Research by Silverstein *et al.* (1986) indicates that women receive far more messages than men about staying in 'good shape' and staying slim. They examined 1200 advertisements in 48 women's and 48 men's magazines, and some of their findings are shown in Item A.

Appearance in women's magazines of food and fashion-related features

	Diet foods	Body ads and articles	Food articles	Total food Ads
Women's magazines	63	96	228	1179
Men's magazines	1	12	10	15

(Source: Silverstein, Perdue, Peterson and Kelly, 1986.)

Silverstein *et al.* argue that the sheer number of advertisements and articles involving body shape or dieting aimed at women readers in the 1980s was staggering in comparison with those aimed at male readers. However in the 1990s we have witnessed a new range of men's magazines that emphasise body size and the importance of staying in good shape. Therefore concern with body image may no longer be the sole preserve of women's magazines.

It would be wrong to argue that over the past twenty years there has been no change in the representation of women in the media. It is now commonplace to see women newscasters, women involved in current affairs and an increasing number of non-stereotypical adverts. However the question remains of whether this is evidence of a media move towards equality or simply an example of tokenism.

Looking at men

Conventional sociology has frequently been accused of being malestream in ignoring women or making them invisible: 'The realization of this failure of sociology to speak to the experiences of women, and its consequent failure to theorize comprehensively, led feminists to examine more closely why this was the case – why sociology, despite its claims to neutrality, has a malestream bias' (Abbott and Wallace, 1997, p. 4).

However, somewhat paradoxically in discussions on gender representations, until recently very little analysis of the representation of men and their bodies has been undertaken by media sociologists. We might assume that this is an example of malestream dominance because men have not been seen as either marginalised or symbolically annihilated by the media, and therefore have not been seen as needing to be investigated. 'Studies which are routinely about men, in that men constitute the acknowledged or unacknowledged subjects, are not necessarily about men in a more complex, more problematized, sociological sense' (Hearn and Morgan, 1990).

Where there has been a media focus on men as subjects, it has been around what we might term 'safe' areas: 'Conventional approaches to looking at male subjects within the media tend to be limited to acceptable contexts in which traditional masculinity is not threatened' (O'Sullivan *et al.*, 1994). These acceptable contexts tend to be televised sports coverage, where close-ups of male bodies are not connected with sexuality; unless the sportsmen are black, in which case their sexuality has occasionally been given prominence by the press. As we shall see later with representations of sexuality, the objectification of men's bodies was previously associated with gay culture. More recently in women's magazines, especially in magazines aimed at younger women such as *More!* and *Sugar*, men have been portrayed as objects of desire. It is interesting to note that relatively little has been written within media sociology or cultural studies about representations of masculinity – apart from gay representation. As Rutherford (1988) argues: 'For men to put their bodies on display contradicts the code of who looks and who is looked at. It pacifies us. Men have held the power of the look, the symbolic owning of women's bodies. Reversing the gaze offers the symbol of men's bodies on offer to women.'

In an ethnographic study Andy Jones (1993, p. 80) investigated 'how the masculine body is constructed, subjected, perceived and deployed in the experience of vulnerability'. He held several discussions with a group of young men to explore these issues, starting with an examination of popular representations of the male body in magazines and on film. They placed images of men in opposition to those of women, seeing male images as portraying power, apart from Mr Muscle (a very thin man who advertises a cleaning product), who is portrayed as 'weak and foolish'. Their discussion of celluloid heroes ranged from fairly conventional masculine heroes such as Arnold Schwarzenegger and Clint Eastwood, to David Niven and Quentin Crisp. The last two were selected for their intellect and style. It was clear from the discussion that each member of the group held different views of masculinity. As Jones says, 'Far from imposing dominant forms of masculinity upon the audience, film heroes allow the subject space to identify with an ideal self of either gender who embodies some desired power' (ibid., p. 87).

Men under threat: masculinity in crisis?

Feminists have increased our awareness of the fact that gender roles are socially constructed, and Oakley (1982) has shown us that gender roles are both culturally and historically specific. Therefore both femininity and masculinity are not fixed or static. They are always 'work in progress', always being achieved. Thus masculinity is a task to be achieved. This has always been the case, although sociological discussions around the nature of masculinity have been rare. The traditional malestream viewed masculine characteristics as those of power, strength, rationality, independence and instrumentalism. When masculinity was questioned, it frequently reflected middle-class, male subcultural theorists' concern about the delinquency of working-class youth.

Exercise 7.7

If you have studied the sociology of crime and deviance, this will be a useful revision exercise. If not, then use a sociology textbook to answer the following:

1. What did Albert Cohen mean by 'status frustration'?

2. What were the 'focal concerns' of working-class youth according to Walter Miller?

3. To what extent do you think that these focal concerns are relevant today?

Society has undergone significant social and economic changes since the 1970s, and heavy industries such as mining, shipbuilding, iron and steel have declined or disappeared. For commentators such as Jonathan Rutherford (1988), these changes have threatened traditional conceptions of masculinity. For him, what it means to be a man has become ambiguous, uncertain and varied. Along with the decline in the traditional manufacturing industries, he identifies other significant changes that have triggered this current 'crisis in masculinity'. For instance feminism as a social movement has raised the consciousness of women specifically and of society more generally. This has had widespread repercussions. As a society we have become more aware of family and sexual politics, so that male violence within the family is far less likely to be tolerated. The relaxation of the divorce laws, making divorce more easy for all, was predicted to be a 'Casanova's charter', but the new divorce legislation has been predominantly used by women.

Rutherford (ibid.) also maintains that the emergence of 'radical gay politics and black politics have produced new definitions of the world that are not attributed to the grand-narrative of White Man'. Taking this last point, it seems that the hegemonic view of masculinity has been challenged to the extent that it is now commonplace to see images of male bodies as objects for sexual appreciation.

Exercise 7.8

Men and Body Image

Choose two magazines from the following: *FHM, GQ, Men's Health, Maxim, Esquire, Arena, Loaded*. Now conduct a quantitative content analysis using the following criteria:

[i] 1. Number of articles that address the body size, dieting, fitness and attractiveness of men.

[i] 2. Advertisements featuring toiletries, food, alcohol, dietary products and exercise gear.

[e] 3. To what extent has 'looking good' become an important feature of these men's magazines?

Gendered audiences

Much of the early feminist research saw the mass media as a repressive social institution that reproduced the dominant ideology of domesticity and femininity. However this approach failed to recognise that women were active media consumers. Reception analysis, with its focus on the active and media-literate audience, has shifted the interest away from representations *per se* to the readings people make of what they watch and the enjoyment received.

> The idea of the audience member as 'a reader' is a powerful one, as it suggests a greater degree of audience activity and a degree of negotiation between the audience and the text. . . . Instead of passively 'receiving' media messages, the audience is seen to actively 'read' media texts by employing reading strategies (Jones, A. 1997, p. 3).

Studies by Ang (1985, 1991) and Gray (1992), amongst others, have particularly focused on women viewers. The relationship between women and soap operas has been of particular interest in the area of media pleasures. Soaps have been identified as a particularly feminine television genre (Geraghty, 1991). This may be due to the fact that both the characters and the audience of soaps are predominantly female. Traditionally, soap operas were associated with popular culture and few media researchers saw them as texts worthy of analysis. However research in the 1970s challenged this earlier 'masculinist' view of soaps, and researchers argued that following the narrative of soaps required considerable analytical skills. Furthermore female characters in soaps tended to be stronger and their characterisation far more complex than in any other television genre. Brunsdon (1982) maintains that watching soaps calls for three 'competences' on the part of the viewer:

- An appreciation of the devices of the soaps – cliff-hangers, lack of narrative closure, multiple narratives.
- Serial-specific knowledge of characters' past lives and key events from earlier episodes. (Buckingham, 1987, refers to these as knowledge of intra-and extra-diegetic texts. An example of an intra-diegetic text is when a character refers to a past event shown in the serial; an extra-diegetic text is when the event referred to has not been shown at all.)
- Cultural knowledge based on 'feminine competencies' associated with child care and domestic responsibilities. Geraghty (1983, p. 140) agrees with this. She considers that women viewers connect with the narratives in soaps in a way that makes real 'the conflict between work and personal relationships, the possibility of friendship with other women, a wry humour sometimes about their relationships with men'.

Modleski (1988) argues that the reader of soaps becomes an ideal mother to the characters and sees in the programmes aspects of her own family.

Women and technology

We referred earlier to recent research on media use by boys and girls. Most computer games software is purchased by preadolescent and adolescent boys. Turkle (1988) suggests that computers are popular with boys because they offer a safe and protective retreat from the pressure of dealing with personal relationships. Video games software emphasises masculine images of action and adventure, with heroes overcoming a multitude of foes. The 'quest' in many of these games is completed with the aid of technological intervention.

Exercise 7.9

 The next time you are in a computer store, check the titles of the games software. How many of them appear to be gender specific?

There is an assumption that the reason why girls and women tend to reject computers is not that they are too complex, but because they view them as male-dominated. Sherry Turkle (1988) sees computers as having a latent masculinity, so it is not that girls and women are computer-phobic, but computer-reticent, because computer technology occupies a culturally male symbolic place in society.

Gray (1992) investigated this female reticence in relation to domestic media technology. As she says, 'Men and women have unequal access to technological knowledge within our society; this is generated through familial socialisation, education and the workplace' (ibid., p. 25). She undertook a study of women's use of video cassette recorders

(VCRs) in the context of gendered power relationships within the home. Her study was based on in-depth interviews with thirty white women living with male partners. Most of them were married and in full-time employment, but they had different socioeconomic backgrounds, ages, employment and numbers of children. She found that media use varied with viewing context, that is, whether the women watched alone, with their children, with partners or with all the family together. Women of all classes gave over control of the remote control device to the men.

This study was supported by Morley (1986), who found that women felt constrained by guilt and obligation, either because they felt they should be busy with domestic work, or because they felt that their own pleasures were trifling. It was the most powerful member of the household who defined the hierarchy of what was serious or frivolous, important or trivial. This effectively downgraded women's pleasure and they had to watch the films and programmes they liked almost in secret.

Coursework suggestion: 'new lads' or 'old men'

As a topic for investigation, you might like to examine the representation and/or the reality of the 'new lad'. In response to the 'crisis in masculinity' new forms of masculinity have emerged. The emergence of 'new man' was discussed by the media and some sociologists largely as a result of advertising campaigns that emphasised men as sensitive and caring. However there has been little tangible evidence of this 'new man'. It is possible that he was simply a figment of the imagination of advertising executives wishing to extend markets (Nixon, 1996). On the other hand, the 1990s seem to have witnessed the emergence of the 'new lad' and 'lad culture'. M. Jones (1997) argues that the new lad

> epitomised the backlash against feminism and an increasingly politically correct culture. A dedicated follower of fashion, Brit-pop and football, calling women 'babes' and downing pints of lager, he took delight in behaving badly. He saw himself reflected in the pages of 'Loaded' magazine where he was encouraged to be as sexist and ethnocentric as he liked. A young man with money to spend, he was more likely to be middle-class than working-class. A laddish television culture also emerged with programmes such as 'Men Behaving Badly', 'Game On' and 'They Think It's All Over' and the comedians Newman and Baddiel.

A possible hypothesis might be: 'There is nothing new about the New Lad'.

Representation of ethnicity

We've got to get to a point where they [the media] meet our sense of right. I'm fed up of watching the telly and seeing all the time white people, white people, and never anything about blacks (an Afro-Caribbean boy from Leicester, quoted in Jones and Dungey, 1983).

We will be showing things which people haven't seen before. They will be presented by black faces rather than white faces. Wherever possible the production teams will include black people, and in many cases the director or producer will be black (Sue Woodford, Channel 4, Commissioning Editor for Multi-cultural Programmes, 1982).

It is interesting to see that these two statements were made in the same year. The first came from a fifteen year old Afro-Caribbean student in a study conducted in Leicester that examined the views and preferences of minority ethnic television audiences. One of the significant findings to emerge from this research was that members of the minority audience looked for validation. They sought people like themselves in television programmes, even when the representation was negative or humorous. The second statement came from an interview with Sue Woodford by Tony Freeth for the Campaign against Racism in the Media (CARM) about her plans for the new 'minority channel'.

Exercise 7.10

Fourteen years on, let's see whether Woodford's view of Channel 4 is reflected in its current schedules. Look through the schedules for one week.

1. How many programmes focus on the minority ethnic audience?
2. At what times are these programmes screened?
3. How many of them feature on prime time television (6.30–8.00 p. m.)?

If we are to examine minority ethnic representation we need to be clear of our terms, as there is often confusion between 'race' and 'ethnicity' and whether 'black' can be taken to include other groups, for example 'Asians'. We take ethnicity or ethnic group to refer to:

A number of people who perceive themselves to be in some way united because of their sharing either a common background, present position or future – or a combination of these . . . There is frequently a coincidence between what others feel to be a racial group and what the members think of themselves. For example, whites may think of Asians as a racial group (because of skin colour); Asians may think of themselves as united and therefore, an ethnic group (Cashmore and Troyna, 1990, p. 2).

'You've got to understand, this business is about selling, and blonde and blue-eyed girls are what sells.' This was the view of Naomi Campbell (black British 'supermodel') of the advertising industry in 1997. How far can her view be supported by the research evidence? The largest British study of ITV and Channel 4 advertising, conducted in 1996 by the Glasgow University Media Group (GUMG), found that more than 90 per cent of adverts had white actors in the leading role and only 5.3 per cent starred ethnic minority characters. Was this an underrepresentation? Greg Philo of the GUMG maintains that 'The ethnic population as a whole is only 5.5 per cent. So it's fairly representative. We couldn't find any evidence of the under-representation claimed by critics.' However, according to the *Observer* (24 August 1977) 'White actors get more lines than their black, Asian or Chinese colleagues. Whites are much more likely to be cast as middle class professionals, non-whites as sportspersons or to appear in exotic dress or as musicians.'

Alvarado *et al.* (1987, p. 201), in their analysis of race and ethnic representation in the media, used the term 'required construction' to refer to the concepts of racial difference and racism:

> These constructions and social justifications, are possibly seen at their most contorted in the situation where one culture tries to dominate another ... Racism does not necessarily require a difference of skin colour; all that skin differentiation offers is a shorthand form of visual recognition in order to define who to delimit and distinguish from oneself.

They used the following fourfold typology to examine the portrayal of black people by the media, and it will be interesting for us to see whether they are still relevant:

1. The exotic
2. The dangerous
3. The humorous
4. The pitied

The exotic

This is the sense in which minority ethnic groups are seen as 'other'. 'Black people have been represented as wondrous and strange by white Europeans, Americans and Australians. Rituals, dress, language, artefacts and food are not understood as parts of complex cultural and social formations, but are extracted, exoticised and revered by naive Western eyes' (Alvarado *et al.*, 1987, p. 204).

Hall (1990), in his examination of the cultural history of racism, from slavery, colonial conquest and imperialism to society today, argues that there are three major ways in which relationships have been discussed:

- Imagery and themes that revolve around relationships of subordination and domination.
- Stereotypes grouped around inferiority and superiority.
- Members of minority ethnic groups are described in relation to naturalistic assumptions, that is, on the basis of their supposed inherent qualities.

Hall also refers to the assumption that the viewer sees these images from a white perspective, what he calls the 'white eye'. This is similar to the 'male gaze', which is assumed to be the way images of women were viewed. The white eye assumes that the audiences are predominantly white, and that the dominant or preferred reading will be from the point of view of a white individual.

The types of programme on television that emphasises minority ethnic groups as 'other' are generally travel programmes, music and sport.

Exercise 7.11

Watch some holiday programmes that describe travel to Africa, the Indian subcontinent or the West Indies.

 To what extent are Alvarado *et al.* correct in their view of the indigenous populations as 'exotic'?

Stuart Hall (1990) has argued that ethnic representations form part of a discourse of 'racist common sense' underpinned by racist ideology. If the problem lay with the media professionals themselves, the solution would be simple – they could be replaced. The situation is much more complex, however, for although media personnel may not themselves hold racist opinions, the inferential structures – that is, the actual structures of media production – communicate a taken-for-granted or institutional racism. 'The policies of institutions that work to perpetuate racial inequality without acknowledging that fact . . . [are] not open, and visible, but . . . concealed in the routine practices and procedures of organisations such as industries, political parties and schools' (Cashmore and Troyna, 1990). This can also be applied to the media, which will become clear when we examine specific examples.

Techno-Primitives

British television science fiction and the 'grammar of race'

'Science fiction as a genre . . . offers the possibility of moving beyond the dominant narrative constraints of realism and naturalism in exploring political ideas, visions of an alternative reality and domains of fantasy' (Leman, 1991). This article examines an aspect of popular culture which does not have a mainstream place on A-level sociology syllabuses, but as it is possible to apply sociological analysis and interpretation to any aspect of popular culture, this then must include television science fiction. This makes it a really interesting subject for students of sociology because if science fiction can offer the possibility of moving beyond the taken-for-granted assumptions and stereotypes, then it could portray futuristic societies unencumbered by the social inequalities of class, gender, sexuality and race. We are interested in the extent to which Stuart Hall's 'grammar of race' (1991), can be used to understand the representations of black and minority ethnic groups in science fiction.

Television science fiction and the 'grammar of race'

Stuart Hall has argued that ethnic representations form part of a discourse of 'racist common sense' which is underpinned by racist ideology. . . .

If the problem of racism in television was simply that television companies were employing personnel whose minds were filled with bigotry, the solution would be simple. The companies could sack them. However Hall (1981) has suggested that the problem of racism is more insidious than this: 'What defines how the media function is the result of a set of complex, often contradictory, social relations; not the personal inclinations of its members.'

The media provide an important site for production, reproduction and transformation of ideologies. This is not to argue that the media are overtly or intentionally racist, but they may communicate an inferential racism, a set of unquestioned assumptions about race which appear natural. This inferential racism underlies the representation of black people on television. It is embedded in television production processes in such a way that even programme makers may be unaware of it.

So what are these assumptions? In 'The Whites of their Eyes', Hall (1981) has examined the cultural history of racism from slavery, colonial conquest and imperialism through to contemporary society. He defined three major characteristics:

- imagery and themes revolving around relationships of subordination and domination;
- stereotypes are grouped around 'superior' and 'inferior' peoples;
- members of minority ethnic groups described in relation to naturalistic assumptions.

These assumptions appear on our screens in the form of stereotypes which Hall classifies as the Slave, the Native and the Entertainer. He refers to these as 'base images' which express the assumptions of inferential racism as the 'grammar of race'. The audience for these representations is 'the white eye':

One noticeable fact about these images is their deep ambivalence – the double vision of the white eye through which they are seen. The primitive nobility of the ageing tribeman . . . the native's rhythmic grace always contain both a nostalgia for an innocence lost forever to the civilised, and the threat of civilisation being over-run or undermined by the recurrence of savagery . . . or by an untutored sexuality, threatening to 'break out' (ibid., p. 16).

Although more recent programming has been more sensitive in the portrayal of race and ethnicity, it is clear that these stereotypical images remain. Our concern was to see how far Hall's classification was relevant to popular British television science fiction. *Doctor Who* and *Blake's Seven* have been chosen as our media texts as they were both successful British television series.

Doctor Who still remains popular and has a coterie of fans and fanzines and even a series of *New Adventure* novels. The series *Blake's Seven* was televised over four years, between 1978 and 1981, on BBC1. It was written by Terry Nation (creator of Doctor Who's Daleks).

Race and ethnicity are significant factors in the representation of what is seen as 'alien' in these productions; of course, not all aliens are presented as members of ethnic minorities. Stapleford (1987) argues that, 'It would be a mistake . . . to construe the alien in science fiction simply as an exaggerated version of a man [*sic*] of another race. In many instances, the alien represents not merely someone who is different, but something *unknown and unfathomable*' (our emphasis).

In examining televised science fiction in Britain, we have found that it is not simply that the creature from another world is used to represent the 'ethnic other'; usually the opposite is the case, and ethnic minority characters are used to portray aliens. In referring to he small screen representation of ethnic minority groups. Alvarado *et al.* (1987) emphasised their 'exoticisation', and their

depiction as 'wondrous and strange'.

As this is an exploratory article, the examples chosen are necessarily selective and refer only to two British series. However, we feel that they are not atypical of the treatment of racial and/or ethnic minority groups by the genre.

The Slave

The slave figure is a recurring character in many forms of adventure stories and the black slave is no stranger to television science fiction. One of the earliest appearances of a black actor in *Doctor Who* was in 1967 in 'The Tomb of the Cybermen'. The story tells of an archaeological expedition searching for the lost tombs of the Cybermen, a race of robots. One of the sponsors of the expedition, Kaftan, has brought along her servant, the huge, muscular and silent Toberman. He does not have a speaking role and his function in the scene is simply to use his considerable muscular strength to open the doors of the tomb. . . . [H]e is defined in terms of his physicality and inferiority to whites. . . .

Toberman's inferior social position is explained not as the result of economic exploitation or colonial conquest, but as the given qualities of an inferior race.

The Entertainer

Perhaps because of the conventions of the genre, there were few examples of this category to be found. However, in a series of *Doctor Who* broadcast in 1988, three of the four black characters

were entertainers – two were musicians and the other, a singer. They were all defined in terms of their musical skills, their expressivity and their emotional natures.

The Native

Hall suggests that there are two sides to the image of Native. The good side is portrayed as a lost, simple innocence; the other side is portrayed as savage and cunning. Importantly, both sides are aspects of primitivism. The Native character is understood to be closer to nature and the natural world than the 'civilised' white characters around them. In British science fiction, the black characters who inhabit these future worlds are still recognisable either as pre-industrial 'primitives', or else they hide a close affinity with nature beneath a veneer of sophistication.

An interesting example of this is Dayna from *Blake's Seven*. . . . Dayna appears as the 'noble savage'. She has the power to sense dangers not apparent to other (white) characters such as Avon whom she has to continue to rescue. Later in the episode she is referred to as having a 'hunter's instinct'. However, her native characteristics are not simply expressed in her hunting skills; after rescuing Avon, she hides him in her cave where she soothes his brow and plants a lingering kiss on his lips out of 'curiosity' and because he was 'very beautiful'. This is surely an example of a native or 'untutored' sensuality threatening to erupt at any time.

In another episode of *Blake's Seven*, we see Avon at a conference of the 'nonaligned planers'. In this group we encounter a black character, called Hun, who is very muscular and bare-chested, but for an elaborate, jewelled chest-piece. Of the delegates, he is the only one to be in a state of undress. He rarely contributes to the discussion, although he seems to have equal leadership status with the others in the dialogue. Despite their access to advanced technology, characters such as Dayna and Hun are still defined by their closeness to nature; their innate 'natural' abilities rather than acquired skills, and the absence of civilising traits (their semi-nakedness and unchecked sexuality). Although they inhabit the future and are competent with the technology of the time, they remain fundamentally defined by their close proximity and affinity with the natural world. We suggest that they can be understood as the Techno-Primitives. . . .

The white eye in British television science fiction

How can we bring the 'white eye' into focus? One way would be to illuminate the boundaries it creates between what is considered familiar (like us), and what is considered foreign (not like us). In order to show as people from other planets, television science fiction has used non-western images. . . .

In 'Destiny of the Daleks' (1979), the Daleks enslave people from across the galaxy and force them to help search for Davros, the Daleks' lost creator. The television magazine *Invision* refers to David Yip, who plays Veldan, one of the slaves. For this story, his oriental features were intended to suggest that not all of the slaves necessarily came from Earth.' Therefore, being Chinese and coming from Earth are mutually exclusive.

Extra-terrestrial aliens are frequently made 'unfathomable and unknowable' (Stableford, 1987) by making them foreign to a Western audience. Once we understand this, the 'white eye' which is usually invisible is made visible. British science fiction views the universe not from Planet Earth, but from Planet Britain, or specifically, Planet England. The view which initially appears to be neutral, is revealed on closer inspection to emerge from a distinct cultural and political location. This is most clearly visible in the ways in which the programmes define what is and what is not from Planet England.

Conclusion

The analysis of all television images necessarily involves us in a subjective, sense-making process. To understand the representations, we have to make sense of the codes and conventions of other cultural forms in which they are located. How we interpret the images depends on our own cultural background and experience; nevertheless, we are all restricted by the viewing and reading codes which are available to us at any given time. We are, therefore, helped to make sense of representations by reference to other similar images with which we have become familiarised. Representation of particular groups in the media is always limited by power relationships because representation is underpinned by ideology. If the majority of female, working class, black and ethnic images have historically been stereotypical, it is because the media are dominated by a hegemonic (dominant) culture which is white, male and middle class.

(Source: Marsha Jones and Matthew Jones, Sociology Review, February 1996.)

Exercise 7.12

Read Item B. In this article Hall's classification of racist imagery was applied to televised science fiction in a way that had not been done previously.

 1. What theoretical framework do you think was used to analyse the programmes? Explain your answer.

 2. What evidence can you find in the text that illustrates this framework?

 3. What do you see as the main limitations of a study such as this?

 4. What strengths does the study have?

Racism in advertising: Benetton, a case study

In their analysis of Benetton advertising since 1984, Back and Quaade (1993) also refer to the 'grammar of race'. Many of you will be familiar with the now controversial advertisements produced by Oliviero Toscani for the 'United Colors of Benetton'. Toscani asserts that the advertisements are polysemic, that is, they have several possible meanings. He also maintains that these various meanings are decoded in competing ways by the audience. No single interpretation is more valid than any other. However many sociologists would refute Toscani's claim. Taking a hegemonic perspective, Benetton's advertising campaigns have reinforced the 'grammar of race'. Back and Quaade's work allows us to examine the possible racist discourses of the advertisements. They argue that there have been three distinctive campaign periods:

- Objectification and fragmentation – 1984–89.
- Racialisation and ambiguity – 1989–91.
- Catastrophe fetish: pseudo-documentary – 1992 to the present.

Objectification and fragmentation

Until 1984 the adverts had focused upon the clothes themselves, but then the emphasis changed to 'All the colors of the world'. We saw images of young people from different cultures laughing together and wearing Benetton clothes. The slogan 'United Colors' alluded to past and present conflicts such as Greece and Turkey, Israel and Palestine, while the adverts themselves featured 'stylised individuals' objectified into images of cultural difference. This phase, according to Back and Quaade (1993, p. 68), showed that: 'Firstly, images of human difference are fixed within Benetton's discourse. Race and ethnicity are presented as essentially unchanging and eternal social categories. Secondly, Toscani uses the image of boundaries between the commodified cultures/races to espouse a commitment to international harmony.'

Racialisation and ambiguity

This period was a radical shift from the first as here the images were in stark black and white (apart from a green rectangle). They included images of a black sheep nuzzling a white wolf; a black child clutching a white doll; a black stallion mounting a white mare; an albino tribeswoman against a background of black tribespeople; two hands, one black and one white, handcuffed together; and a picture of a black woman breastfeeding a white infant. 'During this period Toscani created racial archetypes to espouse a saccharin message of multi-racial transcendence' (ibid.)

Such criticisms have not just been made by researchers. In the USA many adverts were withdrawn following public complaint. The image of the black 'mamma' and the child conjured up images of slavery and exploitation. The image of the handcuffed men evoked associations of black criminality and was associated with the daily reality of young black men being arrested by white law enforcement officers. London Regional Transport refused to display Benetton's posters in the underground. Although Toscani has defended his work against allegations of racism by arguing that the meanings are polysemic, as sociologists we would argue that through the process of socialisation within the family, education and media, white audiences recognise and accept dominant readings of race.

The catastrophe fetish: pseudo-documentary 1992

These images only infrequently referred to ethnicity. This phase represented another radical shift, fusing photojournalism and advertising codes. We were presented with images of David Kirby, a dying AIDS sufferer in his final moments; a Mafia killing; and a black soldier holding what appeared to be a human femur behind his back. The following is Back and Quaade's decoding of this latter image:

> In this case, the 'white' object is the bone of a human corpse held in black hands. An iconic image, deprived of history and context, it nonetheless intersects with deep cultural codes which represent Africans as barbaric flesh-eaters incapable of embracing civilisation. The image represents a moment of barbarism, having no reference to the chain of events which lead to it (ibid., p. 76).

We are again invited by these images to take the viewpoint of the 'white eye' as 'documentary photography and the photojournalism of glossy magazines ... serve to reassure us of our own social position and provide an outlet for our fears'. 'They are putting a face on the fear and transforming threat into fantasy, into imagery, into a photograph, an object which we can look at and deal with by leaving it behind, because it is "them" not "us" who suffer' (Edwards, 1991, p. 164).

Exercise 7.13

If you have access to the Internet, find the home page for Benetton as this shows some of its advertisements.

1. To what extent is their recent campaign different from the earlier ones.

2. Read the section on postmodernism in Chapter 5 and try to apply a postmodernist reading of these adverts.

The dangerous

Here the media, in particular the British press, encouraged the notion that minority groups posed a 'threat' to the stability of British (white) society. In the 1970s the 'problem' for Britain was represented in the popular press as chiefly that of immigration, but,

> immigration is an ideological 'problem' in that the cultural residue of antagonism to the ex-colonised has been re-formulated to be appropriate for post-war Britain. Immigrants were soon assumed to be black, a term no longer connoting 'primitive', 'uneducated' and servile, but which has come to serve as a metonym for scrounger, mugger and rioter (Alvarado *et al.*, 1987, p. 210).

Exercise 7.14

Look up the term 'metonym' in a dictionary. What other words might you use in its place?

A considerable body of evidence has been collected that illustrates this element of problem and threat (van Dijk, 1991; Troyna, 1981; Hartmann and Husband, 1974). Newspaper reports have demonstrated overt racism or the more subtle, inferential racism; dramas have portrayed black people as criminals; and race issues have been covered without the necessary contextualisation of the causes of social problems.

In 1974 Paul Hartmann and Charles Husband argued that it was 'clear that the press (and the newsmedia in general) have not merely reflected public consciousness on matters of race and colour, but have played a significant part in shaping this consciousness' (Hartmann and Husband, 1974, p. 146). They considered that the media served to reinforce attitudes on race and this reinforcement was closely linked to individuals' own personal experiences. Those people who lived in predominantly white regions were more likely to rely on mediated information about race issues, and that these were 'more conducive to the development of hostility . . . than acceptance' (ibid., p. 363).

Their study was replicated by Troyna (1981), who looked at the coverage of news items about minority ethnic groups by the Manchester and Leicester local press. He found that little had changed in terms of negative reportage – stories focused upon Asian refugees, racial attacks, minority families accommodated in expensive hotels and so on. The qualitative difference was that minorities had become 'the outsider within' rather than an 'external threat' (van Djik, 1991).

Van Djik's own research examined news discourse on ethnic affairs in the British Press between August 1985 and the end of January 1986. His sample of popular and quality newspapers included *The Times*, the *Guardian*, the *Daily Telegraph*, the *Daily Mail* and the *Sun*. The main assumption underlying the research was that:

ethnic prejudices or ideologies are predominantly acquired and confirmed through various types of discourse or communication. Since many of these types of text and talk are formulated by members of various elite groups, and since the elites control the public means of symbolic reproduction . . . the reproduction of ethnic ideologies is, at least initially, largely due to their 'preformulation' by these elites . . . a country is as racist as its dominant elites are (ibid., p. 6).

The methodology of the study involved a quantitative content analysis, a more qualitative informal discourse analysis and in-depth interviews with 150 (white) newspaper readers living in Holland. The majority of these readers were middle-class, higher-educated people.

Exercise 7.15

 1. What is the term for research studies that use several different methods in the one study?

 2. What are the advantages to the researcher of using this type of research approach?

 3. Name any other study of the mass media that has used this approach.

Van Djik (ibid.) studied the headlines of the sampled British press (2755 in all) and found that as there had been urban disturbances during September and October 1985, many of the words appearing in the headlines were unsurprising. The following are a selection from the findings or the frequency of particular words: police (the most frequently used word) – 388 times; riot – 320; black – 244; race – 200; racist – 67; violence – 41; racism/racial – 31/29. Peace only appeared 20 times. As van Djik explains:

> The style register of violence [that is, the words used to describe] is amply represented in the headlines. Death, murder, terror, attack, violence, shot, shooting and similar words can be found in hundreds of headlines. . . . Together with the notions of 'riot' and 'police', they essentially define the negative ethnic situation as much of the British Press sees it. Here are a few examples from different newspapers:

HUNDREDS OF POLICE CLASH WITH MOB IN BIRMINGHAM RIOT (Times, 10.9.85)

CARNIVAL NO-GO AREA ANGERS DRUG POLICE (Mail, 26.8.85)

WEST INDIAN GANG INVADED PUB IN REVENGE RIOT (Telegraph, 23.8.85) (ibid., pp. 55–6).

The in-depth interviews with newspaper readers showed that:

- People were able to recall events that had happened two years previously.

- Other events involving to refugees and immigration, which had been given wide coverage in the press, were also recalled clearly.
- Although a diversity of opinions were expressed about immigration and refugees, they were all contextualised, 'within the boundaries of a very clearly organised ideological framework' (ibid., p. 243).

No one defined the issues within alternative frameworks such as neocolonialism, racism, and the 'First World' – 'Third World' political relationship.

Exercise 7.16

1. How do you think (a) a pluralist and (b) a hegemonic theorist would explain the findings of van Djik's research?

2. Which of the two explanations do you find more satisfactory?

3. Why?

The humorous

We are expected as members of the audience to view televised comedy as 'non-serious', it is even disconnected from the serious. If we were to challenge it, we might be accused of being 'too uptight' or lacking 'a sense of fun'. Yet in the situation comedies of the early 1970s race was a major vehicle for comedy. Programmes such as 'Mind Your Language', 'Love Thy Neighbour', 'Rising Damp' and 'Till Death do us Part' traded on racist humour. As Stuart Hall (1981) has explained, these programmes did not simply have black characters in them, they were 'about race'.

These programmes neutralised black people as a threat to the country by making them the butt of racist jokes. Sue Woodford was Channel 4's commissioning editor for multicultural programmes, and in an interview in 1982 with Tony Freeth of the Campaign against Racism in the Media (CARM) she said that television at that time was being racist by not reflecting the black community. Despite the fact that the media professionals were not themselves racist, black people had little access to the media – their voices were not being heard. As far as comedy was concerned, she said, 'I think in many ways that it is worse because more people watch it . . . it reinforces their prejudices and it makes them more comfortable about being racist. It makes it more respectable' (p. 95).

However in America there has been some evidence of some change: 'African Americans are more visible in American media . . . , more often portrayed in high-status roles in American TV fiction . . . , and are projected as less threatening in the US media by comparison to the past' (Curran, 1996).

The pitied

When we are not seeing representations of minority ethnic groups as dangerous or funny, we often see them as victims, usually of 'natural' disasters such as famine, drought or flood. Images of children are often used to elicit our sympathy and charity. The early footage of the Ethiopian famine victims, which gave rise to the first Band Aid charity concert, focused on the plight of the children. However this 'championing of "charity" (a highly patronising concept) helps to perpetuate a dependency created by the original domination of those lands . . . it diverts attention away from the international policies of governments, so that charity becomes a new justification for the nature of the relationship between First and Third Worlds' (Alvarado *et al.*, 1987, p. 220).

Effects on audiences

A possible result of these appeals is to make us feel better, having contributed to alleviating the situation, but they also launder out the stains of the earlier oppression and exploitation.

These media images leave their impression on children too. A group of 12–13 year old children in a London secondary school were asked about their knowledge of the Third World. Among their responses were poverty, dying babies, monsoons, starvation, disease, drought, refugees, flies, Oxfam, beggars, mud huts and injections. When they were asked where their information came from, they cited television programmes such as 'Blue Peter' and 'Newsround', as well as the news and 'special films' (Simpson, 1985).

Exercise 7.17

Something we didn't prepare earlier?

Simpson (1985) was interviewing children over ten years ago and since then media professionals have become more aware of criticisms of Third World coverage. In order to see how far this is reflected in children's television, it might be an interesting exercise to watch some editions of 'Blue Peter' over the next few weeks.

Whenever an issue about the Third World is raised, examine how it is dealt with. Are traditional stereotypes still in existence or is there more reference to world aid, industrialisation and urbanisation, and international politics?

Coursework suggestion

You might wish to compare the portrayal of black (and/or other minority ethnic) characters in British and American television programmes over a period of weeks. You could compare situation comedies or soap operas. It is a good idea to video the programmes as you should watch them several times to ensure that your content analysis is accurate.

Your analysis might focus upon the social characteristics of the characters – their socioeconomic status, age and gender; their importance as major/minor characters; the types of storyline that involve them, and whether their portrayal is positive or negative. It may be interesting to locate the characters in their different cultural backgrounds. (Several research studies are referred to in this chapter that would help you to focus your enquiry.)

Representations of sexuality

> A major fact about being gay is that it doesn't show. There is nothing about gay people's physiognomy that declares them gay, no equivalents to the biological markers of sex and race. There are signs of gayness, a repertoire of gestures, stances, clothing and even environments that bespeak gayness but these are cultural forms designed to show what the person's person alone does not show: that he or she is gay (Dyer, 1993, p. 19).

Dyer's comment that 'being gay doesn't show' is crucial to any debate about the representation of sexuality on the screen. Examining the representation of sexuality by the media is more complex than, for example, counting the number of times that women appear on the screen because we cannot immediately identify a person's sexual orientation in the way that we can identify markers of sex and race.

Dyer argues that there are signs of gayness, for example gestures, accents, posture and so on, but these markers of sexuality are socially constructed and are both historically and culturally specific. Dyer maintains that media texts often rely on stereotypical narratives to indicate that characters in a storyline are gay. These may include 'childlessness, loneliness, a man's interest in arts or domestic crafts, a woman's in mechanics or sports . . . each implying a scenario of gay life. As secondary characters, gays have familiar narrative functions: a woman's gay male best friend, the threatening lesbian' (ibid., p. 23).

It is fair to say that until very recently both lesbians and gay men were, to appropriate Tuchman's term, 'symbolically annihilated' by the media in general. The representation of these two groups has been particularly limited on television, whereas historically there has tended to be a greater representation of gay people in cinema. Sanderson (1995) argues that until the mid 1960s mentioning homosexuality in British broadcasting would have been unthinkable. However since the 1980s, and in particular with the launch of Channel 4, there has been a significant change in the representation of both gays and lesbians in film and television. The first programme to be specifically targeted at a lesbian and gay audience was 'Out on Tuesday', launched in 1989 by Channel 4. Unsurprisingly its reception by some parts of the mainstream press was very hostile ('What next – a show for one-eyed Mexican dwarfs?' asked *Today* newspaper) and the series later received considerable criticism from gay viewers for its content. However it lasted for three seasons and broke broadcasting ground.

Programmes that followed 'Out on Tuesday' include 'Out This week', a gay news programme on Radio Five Live; 'Gaytime TV', BBC's all gay weekly programme; and 'Dyke TV' on Channel 4. In addition Quentin Crisp provided an alternative Queen's speech on Channel 4 in 1996.

Dyer identifies four predominant gay types that have been represented in the media:

- In-betweenism
- Macho
- The sad young man
- Lesbian feminism

In-betweenism

In-betweenism is characterised for Dyer by the gay 'queen' and 'dyke'. This type of representation implies a strong correlation between sexuality and gender. Gays and lesbians are depicted as caught between the male and female genders. Therefore the 'queen' is portrayed as effeminate, 'not a real man', while the dyke is masculine, 'butch', 'not a real woman'. These typifications are clearly underpinned by an ideology of gender that assumes true masculinities and femininities. Dyer maintains that these types are frequently portrayed in a negative light by the media because in terms of the dominant culture they have failed to achieve the status of 'real men and women'. Therefore they are often seen as 'tragic, pathetic, wretched, despicable comical ridiculous figures'. Dykes challenge dominant ideas of gender and are therefore frequently portrayed as dangerous and threatening.

Macho

This is only applied to gay men and is an exaggerated form of masculinity. Dyer argues, 'in marking off the macho man from the simply straight man, this gay type retains the idea of male homosexuality implying something different in relation to gender, but here is no notion of a biological betweenism but an excess of masculinity'. Thus the macho type is clearly nearer to the real man, but he is defined as 'other' and in opposition to this type due to his excess of masculinity, for example the body builder.

The sad young man

This gay type emerged in American cinema in the 1960s. Here was an image of troubled adolescence, of soft young men, heads hung low, troubled expressions, an air of yearning. These adolescents had not yet achieved adult masculinity and were therefore not real men. The characters played by James Dean in films such as 'Rebel without a Cause' and 'East of Eden' epitomise the sad young man. The lowering of the head in these films echoed the Christian traditions of martyrdom and suffering. Dyer argues that these types have become icons of beauty, and famous 'sad young men' in film have included James Dean, Montgomery Clift and Dirk Bogarde. This image of the sad young man has recently been used by advertisers to sell men's fashion and cosmetics.

Lesbian feminism

Dyer agues that this gay type has portrayed lesbian culture as closer to nature and naturalness. This type of lesbianism reflects a strand of radical feminist thinking that women are closer to nature than men and their bodies have a natural affinity with aspects of nature. Thus lesbians have been portrayed as hippies who are close to nature and healing, and involved with craft making.

Exercise 7.18

It is interesting to see how far gay and lesbian representation has recently become part of mainstream television, rather than simply being marginalised in minority programming. In programmes such as soaps there is some representation, but is it stereotypical?

Think about the narratives around gay and lesbian characters in popular soaps:

 1. How many characters can you think of?

 2. How useful is Dyer's typology in interpreting the representation of these characters?

Representation of age in the media

Much of the representation of age in the media is linked to expressions of ageism. This is usually manifest as negative feelings towards and/or discriminatory behaviour against a person or group because of their age, and usually refers to older rather than younger people. It is worth noting that, despite ageism, some groups of people – for example politicians and judges – continue to wield power and command respect to a much greater age than the majority of citizens (Lawson and Garrod, 1996). Although it does not simply refer to the elderly, ageism is mainly used against those who are over retirement age, but as the retirement age is relatively fluid rather than fixed, ageism does not start at a specific point in time. Ageism, if we take a hegemonic perspective, serves to legitimate the way society deals with ageing. 'Ageist representations represent our historical and political definitions of age as the intrinsic and natural essence of the ageing process' (Alvarado *et al.*, 1987) p. 226.

Exercise 7.19

 Let's look at the words that we generally associate with different ages. Fill in the following grid with descriptive words that come to mind about each age group:

Age	Positive descriptions	Negative descriptions
Childhood Youth Old age		

 1. Which group has the most negatives and which the most positives?

 2. What reasons can you give for these differences?

What is problematic about the underlying assumptions about age is that they rely upon natural, biological characteristics to categorise different life stages and ignore the social construction of age:

- Children are presented mainly as innocents.
- Adolescents are presented as rebellious.
- The elderly are presented as sexless and helpless.

In a very important sense these assumptions actually serve to hide the ways in which age is affected by social characteristics such as class, gender and ethnicity. One of the ways in which we can monitor how age is represented is through content analysis. As we have said elsewhere, this is by no means a perfect method and leaves many questions unanswered, but it is useful in allowing us to see how age is portrayed even at a quantitative level. One such study compared the portrayal of elderly men and women on primetime US television. It covered two weeks of programming – one week during autumn 1987 and the second during summer 1988. Overall it was found that elderly women were underrepresented compared with men, and traditional sex-role stereotyping was evident (Vernon *et al.*, 1990).

Men were more likely to be portrayed as having desirable attributes, such as 'active', 'creative', 'healthy', 'wealthy', 'socially involved' and 'highly intelligent', while women were more likely to be given negative traits, such as being 'rigid' and 'unpleasant'. However the differences between the genders were not overly significant. Another dimension to ageism was that the 'girlfriends' of older and middle-aged men were typically 10–15 years younger than them. Vernon *et al.* concluded that one implication was that women should remain 'youthful' in appearance in order to be socially acceptable, whereas this did not apply to men.

Exercise 7.20

Take a copy of any daily newspaper and look at the advertisements in it.

1. How many advertisaments do you think are addressed to people over 55?

2. What types of product are advertised in these particular advertisements?

3. What does this tell us about older people as consumers?

(You could also do a similar exercise by looking at television advertising.)

Television and the elderly

All societies tend to treat their elderly differently from the rest of society. In our society, with its emphasis on beauty and youth, we tend to see old age as something we should try to avoid at all costs. Youth is the desirable age, old age is not. In general, unless they are members of the elite, elderly people are, to borrow Tuchman's phrase, 'symbolically annihilated' by the media. In 1987, for example, people over 65 accounted for approximately 11 per cent of the British population and only 2.3 per cent of the televised fictional population (Alvarado *et al.*, 1987, p. 243).

As Alvarado *et al.* assert, the older woman gets an even worse deal. She has always been a problematic figure in fiction – portrayed as a witch, hag or crone. Not only are older women underrepresented by the media, but they make up a socioeconomic subgroup in society too, being more dependent on the state for their pensions and living longer than their menfolk.

Women of all classes are affected by ageist assumptions, because after a certain age women no longer have a fulfilling domestic role to perform and they are seen as being less physically desirable.

On television, elderly characters are often portrayed as vulnerable and/or comic. We can illustrate this with some recent situation comedies portraying elderly characters.

Exercise 7.21

The following programmes portray elderly characters.

1. 'One Foot in the Grave'
2. 'Waiting for God'
3. 'Last of the Summer Wine'
4. 'Harry Enfield and Chums' – sketch of the 'old gits'

You may not be familiar with all of these programmes, but you may have watched some of them. They are all humorous programmes and the nature of the humour is often located around the age of the characters and their appropriate or inappropriate behaviour.

  1. Do you notice any differences in the portrayal of the elderly in these shows?

 2. What messages, if any, about old age are conveyed in these comedies?

3. As students of sociology you may have studied the social construction of age. If so, you will be familiar with the way in which old age tends to convey negative assumptions. To what extent do the images of the elderly in these comedies reinforce these negative labels?

In relation to situation comedies, humour about the elderly often centres on sexuality, which is either viewed as impossible or undesirable. Sexuality among the elderly may threaten our belief that sexual activity is a youthful thing and that in the elderly it verges on the obscene. We could call this ideology of youth, 'youthism'. 'Ageist humour serves the same function as the myth of childhood innocence in sustaining our dominant regime of sexuality by making alternative definitions of what constitutes the sexual, seem natural' (Alvarado *et al.*, 1987, p. 248).

Exercise 7.22

Now let's turn to the genre of soap opera. Draw up an extended version of the following grid and list the characters over 65 years old in two soaps with which you are familiar.

Soap	Name of characters	Positive aspects	Negative aspects

 1. List the characteristics that you consider to be either negative or positive that are shown by these characters.

 2. Are most of these representations negative or positive?

 3. How might you use each of the following theories of the media to interpret your findings: (a) Marxist, (b) hegemonic, (c) pluralist?

Examination focus

As examiners, we are acutely aware that providing up-to-date examples of essays is a prerequisite for gaining good marks for the skill domains of interpretation and application. This is nowhere more clearly demonstrated than in questions that ask for media representations and stereotyping. You must remember that media representations are not fixed and static, but fluid and changing. They will inevitably reflect both dominant ideologies and changes in public attitudes. This is most apparent in the recent representation of sexuality by the media. That we now have gay characters as a matter of course in our daily soap operas, whatever their portrayal, indicates a sea change in attitudes.

In the light of this, we would recommend that you keep up to date with examples of representation in the contemporary media, which will enable you to apply current examples to existing sociological theories.

Examination questions

Essays on gender

1. 'Studies of how females are represented in the mass media demonstrate that the media reinforce the production of stereotyped images of gender differences.' Critically discuss this statement with reference to relevant sociological evidence (AEB, Winter 1995).
2. 'The mass media reflect rather than create stereotypical images of women.' Evaluate the sociological arguments and evidence for and against this view (AEB, June 1997)

The following are the opening paragraphs from two students' answers to question 2. Read both extracts carefully and then in pairs decide which is the most effective introduction to the question.

Extract 1

It is debatable whether the mass media reflect or create stereotypical images of women. This could be through television, news or radio. The media are defined as communication from the few to the many, thus giving power to the few (the owners and controllers of media companies). The few largely consist of white men. Radical feminists see men as the enemy, therefore media create gender stereotypes and inequalities as the ownership and control lie in the hands of men.

Extract 2

There have been various studies of how females are represented in the mass media. All of these suggest that this institution is a major source of stereotypes. Female sociologists have become more aware of the lack of attention paid to women in the media; as Griffin showed, the media promote unequal images of men and women, a situation she refers to as 'male as norm'.

Essays on ethnicity

1. With reference to sociological studies, assess the claim that the media are biased against ethnic minorities (AEB, June 1993).
2. Assess the view that that the mass media are the major source of stereotypes of ethnic minorities. Illustrate your answer with reference to sociological evidence (AEB, June 1996).

In order successfully to answer question 2 above, you will need to provide definitions of both stereotypes and ethnic minorities (do not assume that you can discuss ethnic minorities as if they are an homogenous group). You will also need to consider other sources of stereotyping, for example social institutions such as education and law enforcement and their role in the reinforcement of ethnic stereotypes.

The following introduction comes from a student's answer to question 2 written under timed conditions. Remember that the introduction to an essay sets the parameters of the debate. A good introduction should make it clear how the essay will progress.

Student's answer

> There are many ways in which media create and amplify the creation of stereotypes of ethnic minorities. This began with the 1970s 'Crisis of Capitalism' (crime reported to be increasing, subcultures becoming more widely spread, rises in unemployment and an economic crisis). During this time the term 'mugging' was introduced from the USA. Mugging was not actually a new crime but gained a real name. Media began to over-exaggerate and amplify the term 'mugging', which in turn created a moral panic within society. Because the ethnic minorities were a surplus population of workers, the blacks were more likely to be unemployed and, therefore, more likely to commit crimes, and the term mugging was applied to them. This was due to media amplification. The ethnic minorities gained labels which in turn produced a self-fulfilling prophecy.

You can clearly see that the student actually answered a different question – perhaps one he had prepared for in the hope that it would appear in the exam paper. These are some of the problems with his introduction:

- No definition of stereotypes given and no explicit interpretation of the question.
- He assumes that the media 'create and amplify . . . stereotypes'.

- He treats ethnic minorities as a single group.
- He refers to the material on amplification rather than stereotyping. Although the material might be relevant later in the essay, it is not well-focused here.

akuie Now it is your turn. Try writing an introduction that avoids the problems we have noted. When you have completed this, compare it with that by a member of your class. How similar are your paragraphs?

General essays

1. Critically examine the arguments and evidence which suggest that the content of the mass media is biased (AEB, November 1992).
2. Assess the view that the output of the media is always ideological (AEB, June 1997).

(Hint: although questions 1 and 2 do not explicitly mention representation in their titles, you could legitimately apply the material in this chapter to these debates.)

Choose either question 1 or 2 and produce a spider diagram or a mind map in preparation for a possible examination answer.

8 Deviancy amplification and moral panic

By the end of this chapter you should:

- understand the term moral panic;
- understand the process of deviancy amplification;
- be able to apply examples of moral panics;
- understand competing theories of the origins of moral panics;
- structure an essay on this topic.

Introduction

This chapter examines the relationship between acts of deviance and their coverage by the media to produce a moral panic. There has been a history of such public panic in our society and it is interesting that the concept has become part of everyday language. Let's examine the origin of the concept. Used first by Jock Young (1971) with reference to the reaction to drug takers in Nottinghill, it is generally associated with his colleague, Stanley Cohen (1972), who defined it as follows:

> A condition, episode, person or group of persons emerges to become defined as a threat to societal values and interests: its nature is presented in a stylised and stereotypical fashion by the mass media: the moral barricades are manned by editors, bishops, politicians and other right-thinking people; socially accredited experts pronounce their diagnoses and solutions; ways of coping are evolved or (more often) resorted to (Cohen, 1972, p. 9).

A moral panic can be recognised in the intensity of feeling expressed by a large number of people about a specific group of people who appear to threaten the social order at a given time. These people become 'folk-devils', about whom 'something needs to be done'. This 'something' usually takes the form of increased social control, which might mean stricter laws, longer sentences, heavier fines and increased policing of specific areas. After the imposition of these new controls, the panic subsides until a new one emerges. It is interesting to analyse the contexts of moral panics because they invariably occur when powerful interests groups in society are facing troubled times (Goode and Ben-Yehuda, 1994).

For instance, in the 1970s British capitalism was facing a series of threats: strikes, disturbances in the inner cities and the activities of the IRA in Northern Ireland. In order to divert public attention away from this crisis, it is argued that the agents of social control exaggerated the threat posed by a relatively infrequent offence – street crime – gave it a new label, 'mugging', and a new moral panic was created (see Chapter 4).

Ben-Yehuda (1980) points to the same phenomenon in Renaissance Europe, when 'witches' were seized upon as the major threat to society, when it was in fact Catholicism that was being threatened by the Protestant Reformation. We shall now examine the characteristics of moral panics and the role of the media in their development.

Characteristics of a moral panic

Most societies at some time have been gripped by a moral panic and we need to know how to recognise one when it occurs. Sociologists are interested in the development of issues into moral panics. It is important to consider who actually has the power, if power is the appropriate term here, to define the event as a moral panic. We also have to decide at what point concern about a specific phenomenon becomes a moral panic. What are its major characteristics? Can we know that we have experienced one only after the event?

We can at least find some common ground on what constitutes a moral panic. Goode and Ben-Yehuda (1994) outline what they see as the five main features of a moral panic: concern, hostility, consensus, disproportionality and volatility.

Concern

There must be awareness that the behaviour of a particular group or category is likely to have negative consequences for the rest of society. This gives rise to public concern, which may be shown through public opinion polls and, significantly, through media coverage.

Hostility

There must be increased hostility directed at this group, and they may be referred to as the enemy of respectable society. They become 'folk-devils' and a clear division opens between 'them', the threateners, and 'us', the threatened.

Consensus

There must be fairly widespread acceptance that the threat posed by this group is a very real one to the rest of society. The consensus does not necessarily have to be nationwide, but it is important that the moral entrepreneurs are vocal and that the voices of the opposition are weak and disorganised.

Disproportionality

It is implicit in the term 'disproportionality' that the societal reaction to the event is out of proportion. In a moral panic the public is given evidence in the form of statistics, which are often wildly exaggerated. Furthermore the statistics for drug addiction, attacks, victims, injuries, illnesses and so on are disproportionate to the actual threat exercised by the group or category.

Volatility

Moral panics, as the term implies, are volatile. Any moral panic has a limited 'shelf life', although it might lie dormant for a long period of time and might also reappear during different historical periods. (The panic over satanic ritual abuse in the 1980s had Medieval antecedents in witchcraft accusations and trials.) In general they erupt suddenly and just as quickly subside. However, irrespective of whether or not there is a long-term impact, the public hostility generated during a moral panic is relatively short-lived: it is difficult to sustain antagonism at fever pitch for any length of time, public interest may wane or the news agenda setters may change the focus of attention.

Exercise 8.1

Let's examine 'volatility'. Think back to a recent moral panic:

 1. Who or what was it focused on?

 2. What was the eventual outcome? (For example was there a legal change as a result of it?)

Moral panics occur most frequently in societies that are modern or undergoing modernisation; when this is the case, they may serve as a means of both strengthening and redrawing the moral boundaries in those societies. 'When a society's moral boundaries are sharp, clear and secure, and the central norms and values are strongly held by nearly everyone, moral panics rarely grip its members – nor do they need to' (Ben-Yehuda, 1985).

The progress of a moral panic

> A small group or category commits a deviant act

↓

> The media report the story as 'interesting': a problem group is identified

↓

> The media search for similar stories, then sensationalise and exaggerate their significance. The causes are not analysed in any depth. Easy targets for blame are located

↓

> The original group or category becomes the folk-devil(s) and fear of them is encouraged

↓

> More deviance occurs as this group is further marginalised. Media interest is heightened

↓

> A moral panic occurs as people become aware of the group as a result of media coverage. Public concern is expressed in calls for ways of dealing with the group. The media and the public press for increased control by the authorities

↓

> Greater social control is exerted. Politicians, police and magistrates respond by introducing harsher measures to stamp down on the deviants. New laws may be introduced

ITEM A *Exercise 8.2*

Study the progression in Item A and see the extent to which you can apply one of the following examples to it. (You will probably need to visit your library or resource centre for this. See how much you can find out in a newspaper on CD Rom.)

1. Dangerous dogs.
2. CJD (Creutzfeld Jacob's Disease) and its connection to BSE (bovine spongiform encephalopathy).
3. Drug taking by young people (especially Ecstasy).

Muncie (1987) argues that the moral panic thesis not only allows us to identify instances of media exaggeration and distortion, but also demonstrates that selective reporting by the media can be instrumental in generating crime waves and social problems. In this way the agencies of social control actually create more deviance as a result of the process of moral panic. This is often referred to as *deviancy amplification*, because people 'pre-disposed to the initial illegal activity may gravitate to the places where reporting is taking place, thus actually increasing the incidence of the phenomenon' (Lawson and Garrod,

1996). Despite the fact that the reported phenomenon has existed for a long time, the increasing media attention invokes public concern. People start to ask, 'what is to be done about x?' and we enter a social process whose eventual outcome is likely to be legislative change.

Exercise 8.3

Using the index in your main sociology textbook, look up the following terms: interactionism, labelling, deviancy amplification. Write a paragraph explaining each one.

Cohen's concept of the 'moral panic' lies within the perspectives of interactionism, labelling and even anomie theory, so it can be encompassed by deviancy theory. However Hall *et al.* (1978) place it within a different tradition. Critical of the interactionist approach for its failure to examine of power relations, they instead place the concept within a clear hegemonic framework of relations between the state, the law and social class.

For Hall *et al.* a moral panic is a means of distracting attention from a crisis within the capitalist state. Moral panic forms part of a legitimising process of identifying 'enemies within' while at the same time strengthening the power of the state. This ensures that the law and order debate will be promoted without public understanding of the social divisions and conflicts that help to produce the deviance and political conflict (Muncie, 1987). In Britain the mugging panic resulted in the imposition of more military-style policing in inner city areas.

Mass hysteria and collective delusion

Moral panics can also be related to mass hysteria and collective delusions. According to Miller (1985), three features are associated with mass hysteria:

- A mistaken belief that a threat is being posed by an 'agent'.
- Heightened emotion, especially fear.
- Mobilisation on the part of a substantial part of the population.

There is probably very little incidence of true mass hysteria, and even in the classic example of the reaction of some people to the radio broadcast of 'The War of the Worlds' in 1938 there was actually little mass mobilisation. (This event is examined in more detail in Chapter 9.)

While it may be true that a considerable number of people have felt threatened by an outside 'agent', they have rarely resorted to flight. However there have been many examples of collective delusion. If we accept the idea that moral panic is generated by fear of a threat and, often, an inability or unwillingness to check the facts, then we can say that moral panic must be based on an aspect of mass hysteria, that is, exaggerated fear.

We shall now look at some contemporary examples that might be seen as moral panics.

Child sexual abuse

Allegations of child sexual abuse have been reported by the press throughout the 1990s. Specific cases of organised abuse were reported to be occurring in the Orkneys, Manchester and Nottingham, all of which were given wide coverage.

Kitzinger and Skidmore (1994) examined the media coverage of child sexual abuse during 1991, the year when the Orkney case was dominant. They were interested in the process of news production and the extent to which concern about child sexual abuse (CSA) could be seen as a moral panic. They found that social workers attracted the most negative coverage, and the difficulties and successes of their child protection work were rarely discussed. Instead the 'reporting of CSA in 1991 was about cases and intervention and rarely about the underlying causes of abuse, how to prevent it or the help that is, or should be available to survivors' (Skidmore, 1995). Child abuse is linked to domestic violence in general, and according to Clarke (1997):

> The New Right has tended to argue that abuses against women and children are symptomatic of the current crisis in the family caused by a decline in morality and family values this century. . . . Others, however, believe that rather than any absolute increase in family violence, we are witnessing a classic 'moral panic', an upsurge of public and expert attention towards a phenomenon which for many years had been neglected.

This debate has been brought up to date recently with the call for the names and addresses of convicted paedophiles to be made public after their release from prison.

Exercise 8.4

 Give three reasons why the names and addresses of convicted paedophiles should be made known to the community and three reasons why they should be allowed privacy.

Satanic child abuse

Linked to fears of organised child sexual abuse was concern about the ritual 'Satanic' abuse of children. Satanic abuse implies that the ritualistic sexual abuse of children forms part of devil worship. In the early 1980s the belief began to take hold that many hundreds or even thousands of children were at risk of being sexually assaulted or even murdered by satanic worshippers. This was the subject of much heart-searching in Britain by media professionals, social workers and sociologists. 'Survivor' stories were printed in the press and chat show hosts interviewed several people who claimed that they had been victims of satanic cults.

What is particularly interesting to sociologists is why such stories should have been believed in the first place, given that the stories were so unlike 'real life', involving as they did the devil and his followers. An enquiry into alleged cases was undertaken by Professor Jean La Fontaine (1994). The study employed a range of methods, including postal surveys of the police, social services and NSPCC; secondary analysis of files; and case studies of reported cases. Despite interviews with self-professed Satanists and victims alike, no concrete evidence was produced that ritual satanic abuse had ever taken place. When the moral panic subsided it was discovered that the whole episode had started as a result of a training programme for social workers by some American Christian fundamentalists.

The victims of the moral panic remain the many children who were snatched from so-called 'dangerous' homes and placed in care, and the parents who were accused of ritual abuse. The moral panic over satanic abuse qualifies as persecution (Goode and Ben-Yehuda, 1994, p. 112). Persecution can be defined as severe repressive actions that result from an almost obsessive public fear of the perceived danger posed by a particular group of people.

It is easy to see why satanic abuse was taken up as an explanation of child abuse. People are often reluctant to believe that parents could do such things to their own children, hence some involvement with external or 'evil' forces can help to explain it. 'The notion that unknown, powerful leaders control the cult revives an old myth of dangerous strangers. Demonising the marginal poor and linking them to unknown Satanists turns intractable cases of abuse into manifestations of evil' (La Fontaine, 1994, p. 31).

'Back to basics': the single-parent family

'Our greatest fear and most urgent need is to guard against the possibility of the viewing family becoming a reflection of the families it views' (Kershaw, 1980). Kershaw, speaking at the UK Association Conference for the International Year of the Child 1980, was voicing the fears of many moral entrepreneurs of the time. Indeed his statement might be taken as the rallying call of what was soon to become familiar as the 'New Right' movement of the Thatcher era.

The concern about inadequate families focused upon the lower working class, especially upon single parent households. Contemporary societal ills were blamed on the fecklessness of the one-parent family, which became part of the demonology of the new right, supported in part by some sociologists (Dennis, 1992) who, although professing 'ethical socialism', actually adopted the agenda of the Tory politicians and began to research the phenomenon of the dysfunctional single parent family.

The family, usually taken to mean the nuclear or 'cereal packet' family, is never out of our collective consciousness. Families are part and parcel of our daily media diet, whether reported in salacious detail by the tabloids if they happen to be hapless royals or other 'media celebrities', or as familiar friends and neighbours in soaps and situation comedies on our television screens. But what do we really know about families in Britain today? Nowadays families are characterised by change: there are fewer first marriages, an increasing number of remarriages as divorce has become commonplace, and we have experienced a new form of family structure, the reconstituted family.

However our focus here is upon the single or lone parent family. It is this particular family form that has given rise to both political and media concern in the recent past and formed a significant factor in the 'Back to Basics' morality drive of the Conservatives in 1993–4. Although the previous Thatcher government had expressed some concern about the need to return to 'Victorian values', it was the government under John Major that purposefully took up the issue. In 1993 various government ministers issued statements to the effect that traditional family values were under attack, and at the annual party conference Major used the term 'Back to Basics'. This viewpoint was most clearly expressed in the verse read by Peter Lilley (Social Security Minister) at the Tory Party Conference in 1992 (Item B).

ITEM B

'I've got a little list, of benefit offenders, who I'll soon be rooting out

And who never will be missed, they never would be missed.

There's young ladies who get pregnant, just to jump the housing queue

And Dads who won't support the kids of the ladies they have . . . kissed.'

ITEM B *Exercise 8.5*

With reference to Item B:

1. What stereotype of the lone parent is Peter Lilley invoking here?

2. What does he mean by 'benefit offenders'?

Lilley's voice was not a lone one and several other Tory MPs gave their support, as the following quotes demonstrate (quoted in the *Guardian*, 9 November 1993; Wagg, 1994).

> Teenage pregnancy often leads to a whole life of state dependence (Michael Portillo, Chief Secretary to the Treasury, 15 September 1993).

> We must emphasis our belief that the traditional two-parent family is best for society and above all for children (Michael Howard, Home Secretary, 5 October 1993).

> How do we explain to the young couple who want to wait for a home before they start a family that they cannot be housed ahead of the unmarried teenager expecting her first, probably unplanned child? (Sir George Young, Minister for Housing, 7 October 1993).

The response by the media to this political critique was not a homogeneous one and many different voices were heard. The quality broadsheets were concerned with factual evidence surrounding lone parents, especially the accusation that the children – the sons in particular – of lone mothers were more likely to become delinquent. The popular tabloids paid lip service to the debate, but soon became more concerned to challenge the government for hypocrisy.

Morgan (1994) refers to the way in which private troubles, such as those experienced by lone parents, have become matters of public consumption through a process of amplification:

> A politician may make references to single parents at a party conference, perhaps drawing upon some statistical surveys. The press will not simply report this speech, but will provide its own experts . . . but also supplying more individualised human interest stories of its own. Other leaders or experts may themselves comment on these press accounts and so a kind of spiral of amplification will take place.

Morgan argues that three main factors affect the likelihood of an ostensibly private issue becoming a focus for public concern:

- The size of the problem (by this he means the possibility of a considerable financial burden being carried by the state).
- Whether causal relationships are involved (it is clear here that the lone parent family is attributed with the responsibility for generating delinquency and other forms of moral degeneracy).
- When linked with the second reason, lone parent families are seen as symptoms of a general social malaise, indicating a breakdown in community or wider societal values.

Morgan maintains that the processes by which single mothers became constructed as a social problem involved the relationship between political speeches and media accounts that included political references in their reportage. The lone parent family has been constructed as a potential threat to wider family values and as an indication of a decline in moral standards, especially among the working class.

So the single parent, usually young and working class, preferably housed in council accommodation, became another folk-devil. The ensuing legislation introduced the now much-criticised Child Support Agency, whose function was to chase up errant fathers who were failing to provide adequate maintenance for their abandoned families, who were seen as a burden on the state. The moral panic, if it can be categorised as such, was volatile. It did not actually disappear from the media, but even the Conservatives became less overtly critical as several senior MPs and ministers were discovered to have flouted basic family values and engaged in extra-marital relationships – some had even fathered illegitimate children, hence producing more single parent families (Linné and Jones, forthcoming).

Exercise 8.6

If your school/college library has CD ROM facilities, take either the *Guardian* or *The Times* CD ROM for 1993 and find as many references to single or lone parent families as you can. Read through the articles.

 To what extent is the reporting supportive or critical of these families?

In October 1997 those attending the Conservative Party Conference in Blackpool witnessed a volte-face in the Tory attitude towards single parents. Michael Portillo, former Conservative defence secretary, reassured single parents, together with other minority groups such as homosexuals, that the Conservatives had become a party of compassion. Whilst voicing support for the traditional nuclear family, Portillo said:

> we admire those many people who are doing an excellent job raising children on their own. The important thing is that people recognise the responsibility they have when they conceive children and do all they can to provide a warm, caring and balanced home for them. Our society has changed. For good or ill, many people nowadays do not marry and yet head stable families with children. For a younger generation, in particular, old taboos have given way to less judgmental attitudes to the span of human relationships.

Exercise 8.7

The policies of political parties change as the political climate changes. In the Conservative case, the party suffered a tremendous electoral defeat in May 1997 and it seems that a change to their policies was inevitable. It may be interesting for you to follow up the single parent issue and to document the two main parties' attitudes to wards the issue to see whether their standpoints have become more similar or more remote.

Undertake a content analysis of newspapers over a particular period of time and examine the coverage of lone parents. Take particular note of instances when politicians are quoted. Look for any differences in emphasis in the news coverage and see if you can tell the political sympathies of the newspapers.

Coursework suggestion

Exercise 8.7 could form the basis of a coursework enquiry. Here are some questions for you to consider:

1. How many newspapers will you need to carry out the content analysis?
2. What period of time will be necessary to get a fair coverage?
3. What will your hypothesis be?
4. Will your analysis be quantitative, qualitative or both?

The US drug panic of the late 1980s

What is interesting about this panic was its unexpectedness, coming as it did after the relatively liberal attitude to wards illegal soft drugs that prevailed throughout the 1970s. Drug abuse did not appear on opinion polls between 1979 and 1984, but in 1986 it was called the nation's 'number one problem'. In September 1989 it was cited by 64 per cent of the respondents in a New York Times/CBS News poll, although by November the figure had dropped to 38 per cent. Why did the escalation occur? There were several contributory factors:

- The introduction and urban use of crack cocaine in late 1985.
- The death of two popular athletes from cocaine overdoses in June 1986.
- Coverage of these deaths by the national media.
- The essentially conservative political climate during the 1980s under Ronald Reagan.
- The 1986 congressional election – the bandwagon effect of talk about drugs by senators.
- Nancy Reagan, the US 'first lady', began to make speeches stressing the dangers of drugs – it was she who coined the 'Just say no' slogan.

- The appearance of stories about crack-addicted babies, which gave rise to a public outcry against drug-abusing women passing on the addiction to their babies.

Was the drug crisis a moral panic? Goode and Ben-Yehuda (1994, p. 222) give this a 'qualified yes', but there is no evidence of an increase in measurable chronic use accompanying the increase in public concern. Nonetheless drug use became 'the major problem' of US cities until it moved away from centre-stage in the early 1990s.

Theories of moral panics

Why are there moral panics? What causes the public to mobilise against a specific 'folk-devil' at a particular time? Goode and Ben-Yehuda (1994) propose three models that can be used to address these questions: the grassroots model, the elite-engineered model and the interest-group model.

The grassroots model

This model argues that a panic starts when the general public becomes anxious about a specific problem or issue. When this concern is also voiced by the media and politicians they are simply expressing the more widespread concern. This model rejects the idea that politicians and the media generate the panic, because they can not create a concern where none has existed before. One example of grassroots concern relates to the increased distribution of heroin and crack cocaine in the USA in the late 1980s. A response to this concern was the passing of antidrug legislation in 1986 and 1988. Stolz (1990) argues that the policy making may have been, 'a response to concerns of the general public, not just those of interest groups (or elites)' (quoted in Goode and Ben-Yehuda, 1994, p. 129).

The elite-engineered model

This is the idea that elites deliberately and consciously undertake a campaign to create public fear and panic in order to divert attention away from the 'real problems' in society. The mugging panic of the 1970s can be fitted into this model as Hall *et al.* (1978) argue, that the reaction to the crimes was out of all proportion to the actual threat posed by the crimes. Mugging was a 'perceived or symbolic threat' rather than an actual one. The moral panic was arguably a diversionary tactic as capitalism was facing several crises. Although the situation is cited as an example of hegemony at work rather than a conspiracy of the ruling elites to subjugate the masses, it is unclear why the issue of mugging, rather than any other, should have been taken up in this way. The public had to be convinced that the real enemy was not the crisis of capitalism, but black youth on the streets. So the moral panic about mugging was 'engineered or orchestrated' by the elite, or capitalist class, together with the media, the legislature, the police and the courts (ibid., p. 138).

Interest-group theory

This is the most popular approach. It opposes the elite-engineered approach because it challenges the idea that elites are involved at all. This approach considers that the power exercised to produce the moral panic comes from middle-level groups such as professional associations, police departments, media professionals, and religious and educational groups. So for any moral panic we need to ask 'who benefits?'

> Interest-group activists may sincerely believe that their efforts will advance a noble cause – one in which they sincerely believe. . . . Advancing a moral and ideological cause almost inevitably entails advancing the status and often the material interests of the group who believes in it, and advancing the status and material interests of a group may simultaneously advance its morality and ideology (Goode and BenYehuda, 1994, p. 139).

It was argued that in 1986 in the USA, politicians helped to stir up the panic about drug abuse in order to be reelected. This was not part of a conspiracy, but rather a situation where the politicians actually believed there was a drugs crisis.

The interest-group model can also be applied to the issue of satanic ritual child abuse in Britain in the 1980s. As Jenkins (1992) argues, the situation 'offered ideological confirmation of the limitations of liberal theology'. Religious fundamentalists and evangelicals believed in the reality of the devil and that Satanism was a real issue.

In line with this model, it could be argued that social workers stood to gain from the panic in two ways: (1) by an enhancement of their status and (2) by increased funding in the wake of public demand for additional state funds to fight the Satanic rituals that were apparently being carried out on children and young people. However as Skidmore (1995) has pointed out, social workers attracted the worst of the negative coverage, so it is difficult to argue that their status was enhanced. In the 1996 case of the death of Ricky Neave – a six year old whose mother was tried and acquitted of his murder, but jailed for abusing him – social workers received more attention from the media for their apparent negligence than his mother received for the actual abuse of the child.

Exercise 8.8

1. Try to apply the moral panic models (the grassroots model, the elite-engineered model and the interest-group model) to the following public concerns: joy riding, public naming of convicted paedophiles, video nasties, school security, hand guns. In each case, say briefly why they fit the model (or models as some may overlap), as shown in the table below.

Issue	Grass-roots model	Elite-engineered model	Interest-group model
1. Joy riding	Complaints from working-class communities		
2. Naming of convicted paedophiles			Advancing the interests of social workers and the police
3. Video nasties			
4. School security			Advancing the interests of school staff and pupils
5. Hand guns			

2. Below are a number of evaluation statements of the concept of moral panic. Identify which are the strengths and which are the weaknesses. Record your answers in a two-column table. When you record your answers, indicate which strengths and which weaknesses you find most compelling. Justify your reasons to another student.

1. In *Policing the Crisis*, Hall *et al.* (1978) show that the media emphasis given to the crime of mugging was simply a diversionary tactic to benefit the capitalist class.
2. The concept of moral panic enables us to see the process of social control at work.
3. The idea of deviancy amplification as a result of a moral panic assumes passivity in the audience.
4. Not all moral panics produce public calls for changes to the law.
5. Studies of moral panics assume rather than empirically test the fact that public reaction follows that of the moral entrepreneurs.
6. There is little evidence to indicate a copycat effect as a result of media coverage.
7. It is important to note that there are different types of moral panic with different causes and beneficiaries.
8. The concept allows us to monitor how some people react to reports of specific events.

3. Using the above points and any others you can think of, in no more than 250 words describe how useful you think the concept of the moral panic is.

Examination focus

Although there may not be an examination question specifically on deviancy amplification in the mass media section of your exam paper, you may find a similar question in the crime and deviance section. For example the following question, although primarily connected with the nature and extent of deviance, will benefit from your knowledge, understanding, interpretation, application and evaluation skills from studying the media aspects of the topic.

Essay

'Assess the extent to which the mass media cause the amplification of deviance' (AEB, winter 1992).

In order to produce a good response to this question you need to examine the relationship of the media and other agencies to the process of deviancy amplification. Appropriate ideas and studies could be taken from this chapter and applied to the question.

You might also introduce the debate about the effects of screen violence (see Chapter 9).

Evaluation skills

1. You might challenge the idea that deviancy amplification actually exists outside the sociological literature. It was apparent that during and after the 'dangerous dogs' moral panic, many people came to view dogs such as Pit Bull terriers, Rotweillers and Alsatians as potentially harmful. However this is a very different case from the others discussed in this chapter. For instance it is very unlikely that more parents chose to take on lone-parent status and that the claims for welfare benefit by existing lone parents were amplified as a result of the coverage of the 'Back to Basics' campaign.
2. It is important to consider whether the role of the media in amplifying deviance is exaggerated or not. Other agencies are also responsible, such as the police, courts, prisons and so on. It is necessary for you to examine their role alongside that of the media.

9 Audiences and the effects of the media

> By the end of this chapter you should be able to:
>
> - understand the development of the effects research tradition;
> - critically assess the adequacy of different approaches to effects research;
> - differentiate between mediacentric approaches and active audience approaches;
> - understand the debate about screen violence and its possible effects on the audience;
> - structure an essay on this topic.

Introduction

> Some kinds of communication on some kinds of issues, brought to the attention of some kinds of people under some kinds of conditions, have some kinds of effects (Berelson, 1948).

There are many different ways in which researchers have analysed the effect that various media have on their audiences. This chapter will focus on social science research.

The potential for negative effects on audiences has been a matter for general concern since the earliest days of the mass media, and this public concern preceded the research into effects. Many hundreds of studies have been undertaken to examine the effect(s) of media on different audiences. Researchers have examined the contribution of cinema, the press and, especially, television to aggressive behaviour, antisocial behaviour, prosocial behaviour, attitudes, prejudice, sexual habits, morality and so on. It is still commonplace today for people to believe strongly that television exerts a powerful influence on the behaviour and general social attitudes of children and young people. However, why should the idea that media violence causes real violence be part of our 'collective consciousness'? How has the idea emerged? This chapter will attempt to answer these questions.

It is possible to map the media research chronologically, although this would tend to oversimplify the complex ways in which researchers have addressed the issue. Even from the early research evidence it is clear that the media did not have a uniform effect on their audiences. However if we take a more general view we can see that research has moved along a continuum from a position in which the media are seen as all powerful (a mediacentric approach) to a position where the audience is perceived as individuals, each actively engaged in a sense-making process of reading and interpreting media messages.

Many different research methods have been used to investigate possible media effects. It is important to remember that a piece of research is only as good as its methodology.

Exercise 9.1

1. Linking methods to research studies, which methods do you see as most appropriate for the following studies?
   (a) The representation of childhood in advertising.
   (b) Audience preferences for television genres.
   (c) A sociohistorical study of legislation associated with broadcasting.
   (d) An understanding of the place of television in family power relations.
2. In each case justify your choice of method.

This chapter will examine the research tradition from the direct-effect 'hypodermic syringe' model, where the media are seen as powerful and the audience passive and easily manipulated, to the most recent 'reception analysis' approach, which sees the audience as active interpreters of media text. We will examine the issue of media, violence and young audiences as a special case.

Media strong, audience weak: the hypodermic syringe model

The first systematic research into the effects of media on audiences started in the 1920s with the Payne Fund studies. These studies into the effects of cinema films on their audiences were pioneering studies that established the field of mass media research in general. One of the conclusions of this early research was that 'The films were an influence on attitudes; they provided models for behaviour; they shaped interpretations of life. They probably had as many prosocial influences (or at least harmless influences) as those that disturbed adults of the time' (Lowery and De Fleur, 1988, p. 52).

Even though this research found no direct detrimental effects on cinema audiences, the research approaches to media effects assumed that the new mass media were powerful enough to exert a direct influence on their audiences. This 'hypodermic syringe' model was based upon earlier studies of persuasion and propaganda, which took for granted the idea that mass audiences, like crowds, were easily manipulated. Belief that the new mass media had the potential for enormous influence characterised much of the period up to the 1940s.

The importance of this model is that the basic premise that the media are powerful is still held, especially as a commonsensical view of the media. For instance whenever some incident takes place that offends the public's sense of morality, there are people looking to scapegoat the media for encouraging the underlying behaviour. This was apparent with the murder of Jamie Bulger in 1993 (see p. 175 for details of this case).

Violence on the media was seen as a contributory factor in the murder by a student of headmaster Philip Lawrence in 1995 when he went to the aid of a boy who was being attacked. Lawrence was fatally stabbed when he tried to intervene. A call to ban violence on television was part of his widow Frances Lawrence's manifesto against violence in 1996.

Exercise 9.2

[i] 1. Collect a copy of one tabloid newspaper every day for a month. Find all items that report acts of violence resulting in tragedy and read them carefully.

[i] 2. Are the mass media referred to as being in any way to blame for the violence? If so, which specific media are referred to, and in what way are they held responsible?

[i] 3. To what extent do you think the blame is justifiable?

An incident that became the classic example of the powerful influence of the media was the radio broadcast in 1938 of H. G. Wells' book *The War of the Worlds*. The dramatised adaptation was so convincing that it generated mass hysteria in many American states. What is significant, though, is that not all of the six million listeners responded in the same way. The broadcast was a dramatisation of an invasion of Martians into a rural area of New Jersey, USA. 'Long before the broadcast had ended, people all over the United States were praying, crying, fleeing frantically to escape death from the Martians' (Cantril 1940 p. 7). Research on the audience response was undertaken by Cantril (1940), who found that several factors were significant determinants of who believed the broadcast to be true. For example listeners who had not heard the beginning of the programme were more likely to be taken in by it, and those who were not able to check out the story with neighbours, to 'reality test' it, were convinced by the broadcast and reacted accordingly. So even in these early days we can see that the audience was differentiated (Lowery and De Fleur, 1988).

Much of the direct-effects research was conducted in the 1960s by behaviourist psychologists working under laboratory conditions. Notable amongst these were Bandura and his associates, who examined the relationship between imitation and aggression. Their experiments involved a film of an adult hitting a 'Bobo' doll (a large inflatable doll with a rounded base that rolled back when hit) will a mallet. After seeing the film, groups of children were left alone with an identical doll and a mallet and their behaviour was observed. Some were even provoked into feeling of frustration before being left alone (Bandura *et al.* 1963; Bandura, 1965). It is unsurprising that most of the children used the mallet to hit the doll – it is somewhat difficult to think what else they might have done with these objects, which were the only objects left in the room. One child was allegedly overheard saying to her mother before the experiment, 'Look Mummy, there's the doll we have to hit' (Noble, 1975).

Limitations of the laboratory method

Exercise 9.3

List the reasons why sociologists would not trust laboratory data that assumes a link between media influence and social behaviour. The first two are done for you:

1. The laboratory is an artificial environment that cannot replicate the way that families watch television.
2. Demand characteristics: the subjects may wish to please the researcher by exhibiting the behaviour they think is desired, which may not be a valid response.

Strengths and weakness of the hypodermic syringe model

Strengths

1. It was the first approach to try to analyse media effects systematically, within a positivistic tradition.
2. It did attempt, however clumsily, to isolate the effects of the media from other influences.

Weaknesses

1. In general the major problems associated with direct-effects research lie with the methodology used and the mediacentric assumptions.
2. The research tended to rely on laboratory situations, the results of which cannot be said to hold for situations in the real world.
3. The researchers assumed that the media were the most significant influence on individuals and failed to acknowledge the way that social relations, especially within the family, have an effect on media consumption.

The failure of this approach to produce convincing evidence of a direct effect on individuals led researchers towards new strategies in their research.

The two-step flow hypothesis

Now we move into the 1950s and a new approach. Through their book, *Personal Influence* (1955), Elihu Katz and Paul Lazarsfeld changed the perspective of media research for a decade. They were able to show that rather than the audience being made up of isolated individuals with no power to defend themselves against the media, within the audience there were active individuals who influenced others. These were 'opinion leaders' whose personal characteristics enabled them to draw other people towards their viewpoint. Katz and Lazarsfeld maintained that opinion leaders' greater exposure to the media informed their decision making, although the link between exposure and decision making was a complex one The research focused on specific areas where opinion leaders influenced other people: shopping, fashion, going to the cinema and ideas about current affairs and politics.

Two assumptions were particularly significant to this approach. First, the authors assumed that personal influence was set within the context of interpersonal relationships. These relationships helped to anchor opinions, attitudes and behaviour, which in turn might be affected by the media.

Second, networks of relationships were affected by the communications process, so that the degree of individuals' exposure to media messages differed according to their position in a set of interpersonal relationships.

Strengths and weaknesses of the two-step flow hypothesis

Strengths

1. It moves away from the mediacentric approach by placing the media within a social context.
2. It examines the way personal relationships, for example friendship, may help to mediate messages from the media.
3. It demonstrates that the relationship between leaders and follower is a variable are depending on the topic concerned.

Weaknesses

Exercise 9.4

Below we have listed three weaknesses of the two-step flow model, what others can you think of?

1. It doesn't explain how we can pick out the opinion leaders from the rest.
2. It doesn't explain why only opinion leaders should be active, rather than anyone else.
3. It doesn't justify why it is a 'two-step' process – it is possible to have a multistep process.

Audience needs and satisfactions: the uses and gratifications approach

The 'uses and gratifications' approach is mainly concerned with the choice, reception and response of audience members, hence they are assumed to be involved in the reading of media messages. However the approach essentially focuses upon the psychology of needs. Audience members are perceived as active, motivated in their media use and aware of their own social and psychological needs. These 'needs' have been grouped under the following headings:

- Diversion and escape (from the routine of domesticity).
- Personal relationships (as topics of conversation and 'company' for the isolated person).
- Personal identity (as a means of comparison with oneself).
- Surveillance (gaining information about the world).

Although we are attempting to follow the research tradition chronologically, to step back in time a little, questionnaire research was done as early as 1944 by Herzog among women listeners to radio serials. These women were shown to have gained satisfactions such as emotional release, vicarious pleasure and identification with characters from their regular listening.

As McQuail (1994) points out, this approach has been updated more recently. The emphasis on the 'needs' of the audience has been reduced as the concept of needs is a very difficult one to research. Also, the expectation of researchers that differentiating the audience by their perceived uses and gratifications would help in understanding the effects of the media has been much reduced. More recent research has indicated the importance of the 'pleasures' of audience members. This is dealt with in detail later in this chapter in the section on reception analysis.

Strengths of the uses and gratifications approach

1. The audience is seen as more actively involved with the media.
2. The audience is seen as differentiated (by gender for example), rather than homogeneous.
3. It allows us to see that some media are used differently by different audience groups.

Exercise 9.5

To test out your own 'uses and gratifications', choose a television programme that you try not to miss.

 1. List the reasons why this programme is important to you.

 2. Now try to see how far you can fit these reasons into the gratifications listed above.

 3. What weaknesses can you find in this approach?

Reinforcement theory

Moving on from uses and gratifications takes us to the position where the central focus of the media is critically challenged. Rather than researchers asking what the media do to their audiences, this approach asks what *we do* with the media. The focus ceases to be on the media, but on the social factors that operate to influence the individual. Viewed from this perspective, it is clear that the media operate within a set of other social factors. Children who sit alone in front of television from an early age and watch without a parent figure will have a different relationship with the media from children whose parent sit with them and interpret what is happing on the screen.

The reinforcement theory approach was developed as a response to the fear that violence on screen generated aggressive behaviour in viewers. Halloran (1995, 1970, p. 29) directed attention away from the mediacentric approach to one where the media were seen in a social context:

> It is not so much a question of the influence of television per se, but of its influence through interpersonal relationships and social settings. For example, what is learned from television models and from watching television generally may be tested and applied in everyday relationships and social settings. If it seems to work, if it goes down well, or provides some form of social satisfaction, then reinforcement will occur and a pattern of influence may be established.

Strengths and weaknesses of the reinforcement approach

Strengths

These are very similar to the strengths listed for the uses and gratifications approach (see above). We would also add the following:

1. The approach acknowledges that television has an important reinforcing influence, but one that affects individuals in different ways depending upon their social circumstances.
2. The role of television as a socialisation agent is emphasised, but within the context of other important agencies, such as the family and peer groups.

Weaknesses

1. The approach does not allow us to predict which media texts will be used as reinforcers by specific individuals.
2. We can only analyse the reinforcement effect after it has taken place.

Structuring reality: towards the active audience – cultivation analysis

Most of the earlier work summarised above has looked for short-term effects, but there is a substantial body of research that maintains that the effects of the media are more significant over the long term. Among these is the 'cultivation' hypothesis of Gerbner (1973). This approach sees the crucial importance of television in daily life, so much so that it dominates our 'symbolic environment'. What Gerbner means by this is that some people in the audience come to believe in the reality, or 'mediated reality', shown on television rather than their own personal experiences of reality. Of course this does not affect all viewers and he maintains that the important difference lies between heavy and light viewers. The former are those who, because they watch more television, come to believe in this mediated reality. In essence the world presented to them is *mean*. It is full of violence, bad language and fear.

Cultivation analysis is part of a research tradition referred to as 'cultural indicators'. It investigates:

- the institutional processes underlying the production of media content;
- the images represented to the audience within media content;

- the relationships between exposure to television's message and audience beliefs and behaviours (Signorelli and Morgan, 1990).

The central assumption of this theory is that the media represent the world in a highly selective, stereotyped and distorted way. The effect of this is cumulative, so that heavy viewers come to assume that the images they see are a reflection of the world outside their windows. Gerbner and his associates have undertaken many content analyses, examining in particular the amount of crime and violence on American television.

Strengths and weaknesses of cultivation analysis

Strengths

1. It attempts to differentiate audience responses and emphasises an active audience.
2. It considers the differences in media influence on light and heavy viewers.

Weaknesses

1. There are many methodological problems with this approach, not least the assumption that all heavy viewers respond in the same way to media output.
2. To date there has been little corroborative evidence of the thesis from European countries.
3. Reinterpretation of Gerbner et al.'s work demonstrates other methodological problems. Measuring the long-term attitudinal effects of the media on individuals is very difficult because so many of our attitudes are a result of early socialisation.
4. It is impossible for researchers to quantify the possible effects of the media in isolation from other social influences.

If we apply the 'left realist' work of Lea and Young (1993) to an understanding of the relationship between the media and crime, then factors such as social class, ethnicity and neighbourhood may have a more significant influence on the audience's perception of crime than their television viewing. Lea and Young assert that anxiety about crime is realistic because people who live in areas of high recorded crime do see and experience a great deal of crime in their lives. This lived experience – that is, 'situational reality' – and knowledge of crime is the root cause of their anxiety. However we could combine Gerbner's approach with Lea and Young's work by acknowledging that although situational reality may generate a fear of crime and violence, heavy viewing of television violence may reinforce this fear among people living in high-crime areas.

The portrayal of crime on television – mediated vs situational violence

ITEM A

Male offenders found guilty of or cautioned for indictable offences: by age and type of offence in England and Wales, 1995

| Offence | Ages (per cent) | | | | Total |
	10–13	14–17	18–20	21–34	All aged 10 and over (000s)
Theft and handling stolen goods	8	24	16	37	160.9
Violence against the person	4	21	14	43	41.8
Burglary	8	30	20	37	43.9
Drug offences	–	13	24	53	71.9
Criminal damage	10	24	15	39	12.2
Sexual offences	4	14	8	30	6.8
Robbery	7	36	19	32	5.3
Other indictable offences	1	8	17	58	52.4
All indictable offences	5	20	18	43	395.2

(Source: Social Trends, vol. 27.
© Crown Copyright 1997)

ITEM B

Women offenders found guilty of or cautioned for indictable offences: by age and type of offence in England and Wales, 1995

| Offence | Ages (per cent) | | | | Total |
	10–13	14–17	18–20	21 and over	All aged 10 and over (000s)
Theft and handling stolen goods	12	28	12	32	60.1
Violence against the person	8	36	11	34	7.7
Burglary	12	43	15	24	1.9
Drug offences	–	10	19	56	7.9
Criminal damage	8	27	13	35	1.2
Sexual offences	6	13	6	50	0.1
Robbery	7	55	16	20	0.5
Other indictable offences	–	9	15	59	5.0
All indictable offences	10	26	13	36	84.4

(Source: Social Trends, vol. 27.
© Crown Copyright 1997)

ITEMS A AND B *Exercise 9.6*

Conduct a content analysis on two screenings of 'Crimewatch UK'.

i 1. Make a list of the crimes that are most frequently investigated on the programme.

i 2. For each crime state (a) the typical victim, (b) the typical offender.

*i**a* 3. Imagine that you had to rely solely on 'Crimewatch UK' for your information on crime, what picture of crime in Britain would you gain?

4. Using Items A and B, compare the official statistics on crime in England and Wales with your data from the content analysis of 'Crimewatch UK'. Does your investigation support or refute Gerbner's view that the representation of violence on television distorts the official picture of crime?

Coursework suggestion: crime on television

This is an opportunity for you to undertake your own content analysis study. It might be a useful starting point for your own A Level coursework too.

Look through the television schedules for one week (you might exclude screened films at this stage). Count the number of crime-related programmes for that week. Work out the percentage of programming given over to these programmes. You could also separate them into types of programme (genres):

- Drama: police series (for example 'The Bill', 'NYPD Blue,' 'Thief Takers').
- Documentary: fly-on-the-wall (for example 'The Nick').
- Detective drama, (for example 'Cracker', 'Prime Suspect', 'Inspector Morse').
- Studio presentations (for example 'Crimewatch UK').

Types of crimes dealt with. From the data you could conduct several different analyses:

1. You could compare the output from different countries.
2. You could look at the representation of perpetrators and victims – this might highlight gender, class, age and ethnic differences.
3. You could analyse the picture of crime that we obtain from television series.

Don't forget that by itself, content analysis does not help us to understand or interpret an individual programme, nor does it explain how we as viewers might respond to different texts. Quantitative content analysis is like all other forms of quantitative analysis – essentially superficial and lacking the richness and depth of more qualitative methods.

Reception analysis: media weak, audience active

We have finally arrived at our 'active audience', but there are still no straightforward answers to the relationship between media and audience. Reception analysis does not look for an effects relationship as such, it is more concerned with the way audiences read media texts and is popular among cultural studies theorists and researchers. It attempts to demonstrate how we make sense of the messages and images of popular culture through a process of interpretation. Most reception studies use an *ethnographic* approach, using qualitative methods such as in-depth interviewing, participant observation and group discussions (Hobson, 1982; Morley, 1980, 1986; Buckingham, 1993). Some, for example Ang (1985), have used viewers' letters.

These researchers have all attempted to explore audiences' interpretations of the texts. So being a member of the audience is a complicated business. We don't just sit in front of the set and watch. Television viewing is a 'cultural practice'. 'How we watch television is, therefore, part of the cultural context in which programmes, commercials and other televisual paraphernalia are placed' (Lewis, 1991, p. 49).

Morley's (1980) study on the nationwide audience used the typology designed by Hall (1980) and separated the groups of viewers into three types of textual reader: those who took a dominant reading and accepted the preferred meaning as encoded (that is, the meaning intended by the programme makers); those who took an oppositional stand – they did not simply reject the preferred reading, but actively challenged it; and those in the middle who negotiated the meaning to make sense of it for themselves. Morley's analysis takes us some of the way towards an understanding of the audience, but does not allow us to predict who will take which particular reading and why.

Morley was attempting to link the social position of the audience with their readings of media texts, and he maintained that their textual readings were partly socially determined. However, Morley's work does not take into account the cultural competencies of the audience members. His categories of class, occupation, locality, family structure, educational background and so on are too broad to explain why groups such as apprentices, bank managers and schoolboys should share a dominant reading of the text.

Morley's later research (1986), although not addressing this issue, is nevertheless important for the light it sheds on power relations between family viewers. For his book *Family Television* Morley conducted in-depth interviews with eighteen south London families about their viewing habits. He first interviewed the parents and then invited the children of the family to join them. The families were from the same local area and were, broadly, lower-middle and working class. All were white. Morley found that gender played an important part in differentiating viewing behaviours. Concentrating on the context of family viewing, he discovered from the interviews that power relationships entered into the dynamics of viewing choice. Masculine power was predominant and manifested through monopolisation of the remote control device. Few women in the family used the remote control regularly, while for the men it symbolised their power over the other family members. One of the children interviewed said that her father kept the controls for the video and the television on either arm of his chair. Many of the men were accused of 'flicking' channels to check what was showing elsewhere; this occurred while other family members were watching TV.

> Woman: 'And that's what you do [her husband], isn't it? Flick, flick, flick – when they're in the middle of a sentence on the telly. He's always flicking over.' Husband: 'The remote control, oh yes, I use it all the time' (Morley, 1986, p. 149).

Only in the cases where the men were unemployed was there evidence of more flexibility over control of the device. In these cases the men taped the programmes that they wanted to watch and let other family members watch at the scheduled times. They were able to watch the taped programmes during the day.

There were interesting differences in people's manner of viewing. The men preferred to pay close attention whilst watching and found it frustrating that their wives chatted or did household tasks while they watched. As the following quote shows, many of the women felt that there were always other jobs to be done and felt guilty if they simply sat and watched:

> There is always something else, like ironing. I can watch anything while I'm doing the ironing. I've always done the ironing and knitting and that . . . You just sit down and watch it, whereas you've got things to do, you know and you can't keep watching television. You think, Oh my God, I should have done this or that (ibid., p. 151).

This woman illustrates that men define the home as a site of leisure, separate from work, whereas for women, home is always work, whether they are employed outside it or not.

Like Gray (1992), Morley found that women infrequently programme their video recorders. Gray refers to this lack of technical expertise on the part of women as 'calculated ignorance', which they adopt in case they are called upon to take responsibility for yet another domestic task. This is one that can safely be left to the children and the men.

Most of the recent work examining media use has been ethnographic.

Strengths and weaknesses of reception analysis

Strengths

1. It sees the audience as active and media literate.
2. Like reinforcement theory, it places television within the context of other social agencies.

3. It sees the audience as differentiated by social characteristics, such as age, gender, ethnicity and social class, as well as their previous media experiences.

Weaknesses

1. Although it takes account of audiences, it loses sight of the debate about ownership and control over the content of the media.
2. By concentrating on the pleasures of audiences, it fails to examine the possible differences in cultural capital between groups, and ignores the media rich, media poor issue. (You will be able to explore other weakness in Exercise 9.7 below.)

Exercise 9.7

Read Martin Hammersley's article 'Introducing Ethnography' in *Sociology Review*, vol. 2, no. 2 (1992).

1. What is the nature of ethnographic research?

2. What are its strengths and limitations in analysing media use by families?

Semiology

We cannot leave the study of audiences without making some reference to semiological analysis. This method of analysis is increasingly being used to interpret media texts, and while it is more usually associated with cultural studies, it is finding a place in media sociology. Its origin at the beginning of this century is attributed to a Swiss linguist, Ferdinand de Saussure (1857–1913), and an American philosopher, Charles Peirce (1839–1914). They were both interested in the study of signs as conveyors of meaning, and the method of making sense of signs became known as semiology or semiotics. For de Saussure, a sign was divided into two parts – the signifier and the signified. The signifier is something that is aubible or visible, for example a sound, printed word or image, and the signified is its associated meaning. 'These signs or symbols can consist of simple pictures, letters etc., although in today's world the vast array of electronic imaging all serve to mediate our experience of reality, and in turn have become objects of semiological study' (Woodhams, 1993).

The sign itself has no intrinsic meaning, it is essentially arbitrary; for example we use the signifier 'car' to mean a person-driven road vehicle, in French the word is 'voiture', but in both countries those words call up a similar image of the signified object. However we can further contextualise the word 'car' and find different associations – what do the following names of cars mean to you: Skoda, Lada, Rolls-Royce, Porsche? Pierce divided signs into three types:

- Icon: a sign that is identical to what it represents, such as a photograph or reproduction.
- Index: a sign with a direct link to what it represents. This could be the smell of the perfume always worn by a particular person, or the sound of thunder indicating a storm.
- Symbol: a sign that has a symbolic link with what it represents, for example a no-entry road sign, the Union Flag.

Therefore we can only make sense of a sign when it is set in a meaningful context. There are two processes that help with this sense-making process:

- Denotation: describing what the signifier is; a description of what we can see.
- Connotation: 'the associations produced by the denotative order in the mind of the person or persons who interact with the sign' (Price, 1993, p. 64).

As an example of this we could take the signifier 'rose' or an image of a rose:

Signifier	Denotation	Connotation
Rose – the word or an image	A beautiful flower with a strong perfume	Here there could be several: romance, love, England's rugby team, the English counties Yorkshire or Lancashire, and, more topically, New Labour

Exercise 9.8

Produce a chart like the one above for the following:

1. Blue
2. Cigars
3. A red flag
4. A mobile phone

Some sociologists have used semiology to interpret the 'styles' of different groups. In *Subculture: The Meaning of Style*, Hebdige (1979) analysed various youth groups not according to their position in the class structure, but their appropriation of different cultural forms such as music, clothes, hairstyles and so on. This brings us to another concept: 'bricolage'. This is a 'structured improvisation, where something, the trilby [hat] for example, is taken from one signifying code, the dress of the city gent, and placed in another (the skinhead)' (Woodhams, 1993, p. 25).

Strengths and weaknesses of semiology

Strengths

1. It shows how we learn to read signs in different combinations or codes without being consciously aware of the process.

2. Used alongside other sociological methods, it can be a useful addition to textual analysis.
3. It demonstrates the polysemic nature of media texts.

Weaknesses

1. By removing a text from its context, the analysis is in danger of being ahistorical.
2. As it ignores the production of texts, it does not make any reference to the structure of media industries as producers of texts.
3. It does not provide a set of methodological guidelines for 'doing semiology'.

Coursework suggestion

You might incorporate semiology into a coursework project on the representation of specific groups in the media. For example, if you were to look into the way men are represented in magazine advertisements, you could examine the items they are shown with – hats, briefcases, watches, cars, planes and so on. What do these things signify about the men?

Media, violence and children: a special case?

As we have seen, no analysis of the relationship between media output and audience can ignore the debate about effects. It is important to recognise that the effects debate tends to depict the mass audience as consisting of the 'weaker and more vulnerable' members of society. In reality, these vulnerable groups consist of young people in general and working-class women in particular (Branston and Stafford, 1996).

This section is concerned with screened violence, especially violence on television, and its supposed effect on the young audience. This issue continues to provoke public concern. Anxiety over the portrayal of violence on television is inextricably linked to a view of children as vulnerable to and victims of powerful media influences. This case study on media violence and its effects will review some of the major studies in the field and evaluate their strengths and weaknesses. Before we examine the evidence, several points need to be made about the definition of violence:

- Defining violence is highly complex, for example cartoon/fantasy violence does not equate with news footage of real-life violence.

- Operationalising a concept of violence in media research will inevitably involve the use of second-order constructs by researchers. These constructs may not be shared or understood by respondents, particularly if we are dealing with children. Therefore research that imposes definitions of violence on a young audience is likely to be problematic.
- The broader one's concept of violence (for example verbal abuse, swearing, threats of violence, comic strip violence, physical and sexual violence), the greater the number of violent acts that will be encountered.
- Violence on TV needs to be contextualised in order fully to understand its meaning and significance. For example many violent acts by TV 'criminals' are not condoned and the 'Baddies get caught'. Therefore these acts are often encoded with the message that crime and violence is not acceptable.

Children and the effects of television

Exercise 9.8

This exercise asks you to question your own assumptions about TV and its possible effects. We can begin with the premise that television is a powerful influence on the socialisation of children.

1. List 10 different ways in which children might be affected by what they watch on TV (we have listed two below).
2. Now divide the list into two columns: those which you consider to be *prosocial* (promoting good behaviour) and those which are *antisocial* (encouraging bad behaviour). We have placed our two examples in the appropriate columns to get you started.

Prosocial effects	Antisocial effects
1. Help with learning to read	1. Provokes fear
2.	2.
3.	3.

3. Now compare your answers with those of other students. Do you agree or are there major differences in your concepts of pro- and antisocial effects?
4. Why might it be difficult to measure the effects of TV on children?

A brief history of the concern about media effects

Public concern about the potentially harmful effects of the media is nothing new. In the nineteenth century, newspapers called 'Penny Dreadfuls' were thought to corrupt their readers because of their salacious reporting of violent crimes (Barker, 1983). Fear was even expressed by moral entrepreneurs of the time about the suitability of the novel for young women.

We would take the term 'moral entrepreneurs' to mean church leaders, politicians and some campaigners who take the moral high ground on social issues, for example Mary Whitehouse, who as president of the National Viewers and Listeners Association vociferously campaigned to eradicate sex, violence and bad language from television. Generally, moral entrepreneurs mobilise and call for action after a significant violent incident has taken place, for example calls for the banning of firearms after a serious shootings incident.

In 1888, Edward Salmon wrote:

> Let us go into the houses of the poor, and try to discover what is the effect on the maiden mind of the trash the maiden buys ... the higher flown conceits and pretensions of the young girls of the period, their dislike of manual work and love of freedom, spring largely from notions imbibed in the course of a perusal of their penny fictions (Branston and Stafford, 1996, p. 312).

In the early twentieth century the popularity of the cinema brought with it the 'dangers of darkness' (Barker, 1983). Television in the home was accused of destroying family life; video brought with it concern about the easy accessibility of 'video nasties' for young people; and recently public concern has been voiced about pornography on the Internet. As each new form of media technology emerges, so a new wave of public anxiety follows close behind. Many commentators argue that the media have been conveniently scapegoated for the social ills of society (Skeggs and Mundy, 1992, p. 78; Buckingham, 1993).

ITEM C

Extract A

'One powerful agent for the depraving of the boyish classes of our towns and cities is to be found in the cheap shows and theatres, which are so specially chosen and arranged for the attraction and ensnaring of the young. When for three pence a boy can procure some hours of vivid enjoyment from exciting scenery, music and acting ... it is not to be wondered at that the boy is led on to haunt them, becomes rapidly corrupted and demoralised, and seeks to be the doer of the infamies which have interested him as spectator' (*Edinburgh Review*, 1851, quoted in Murdock and McCron, 1979).

Extract B

'The V-chip backed by President Clinton and Congress, may soon alter the way everyone watches television and give parents an easy tool to control what their children view' (CNN Los Angeles, 29 February 1996).

Extract C

'The only people who need more research on this matter are those who produce television programmes. The argument is quite simple: violent television is a pollutant, like nicotine or drugs, and if you give people an addictive habit, they'll be influenced by it. From the age of five or six children are put in front of a machine which glorifies violence' (Shulman, 1973).

Extract D

'There are lots of other factors which make people violent . . . Britain was a far more violent place before television and film. It's as if all these angelic people suddenly became violent when TV arrived' (film director Michael Winner, *Daily Telegraph*, 8 April 1994).

ITEM C **Exercise 9.9**

Refer to Item C and other sources and answer the following questions:

1. What evidence is there to suggest that concern about media effects is not new?

2. In what ways do you think the V chip might alter viewing patterns?

3. What does extract B assume about the way 'everyone watches television'.

4. Read Item C again carefully. Which of the arguments do you find most convincing and why? Now compare your answers with those of someone of your parents' generation. What differences do you find?

It is interesting to note that concern about the potentially harmful effect of violence in the media has united the political left and right. Gauntlett (1995, p. 2) maintains that both sides of the political spectrum agree that 'TV is a powerful force which can seduce children away from their better nature and which constitutes an attack on more authentic or essentially human behaviour'.

This view of the power of the media is inextricably linked to the late-twentieth-century Western ideology of childhood, which sees children as essentially innocent, vulnerable and in need of protection from the potentially harmful influences exerted by the media (Wagg, 1992). Theorists from both the left and the right have tended to see children as a passive, homogeneous audience that is unable to differentiate between mediated (on screen) and situational (lived) reality. *Situational reality* is the social reality lived and experienced by individuals, whereas *mediated reality* is the picture of the world that the media produce. Although this image of the world may seem natural and 'seamless', it is actually constructed by media producers.

The effects debate was clearly articulated in the well-publicised case of the murder of the toddler James Bulger in 1993 by two young boys.

Supposedly having watched the horror film 'Child's Play 3' on video (although there is no incontrovertible evidence that they actually did), they reenacted some of the atrocities portrayed in the film. Many commentators cited as clear evidence of a moral panic the judge's summing up of the Bulger case – he said that he suspected that exposure to violent video films might provide a partial explanation – and the subsequent parliamentary call for action (see Chapter 8 for more detail on moral panics). However, what is of more sociological interest is the fact that other children who had watched the film did not go on to commit a copycat murder. Estimates at the time suggested that at least 181 000 children had watched the film on satellite television, 42 000 of whom were aged nine and under, but there was no subsequent upsurge in the child murder rate after the screening of the film.

This debate raises another key issue that students often find confusing: the distinction between a social and a sociological problem. A social problem is a phenomenon that society identifies as needing positive action, because of its negative effects on individuals or on society as a whole. Although social problems such as violence, hooliganism, crime and poverty are often the focus of sociological interest and study, sociologists do not limit themselves to the more problematic aspects of social life (Lawson and Garrod, 1996). Hence sociologists were just as interested in why the many children who were alleged to have watched 'Child's Play 3' did not imitate the film's violent acts as they were in the James Bulger murder case.

Exercise 9.10

 Discuss the following question with another sociology student:
Why do you think that so much research on television and its effects has focused on antisocial rather than prosocial behavioural effects?

Public fears versus social research evidence

When reviewing the existing literature on violence and the media, it is very important to differentiate between what might be termed 'public fears' and the actual evidence produced by media researchers in this field. For the purposes of this case study, we will first outline the public concern about the possible effects of media violence on children and young people and then evaluate the findings of some of the major research studies. We have categorised these general 'fears' into three types:

1. Television zombies
2. Desensitisation
3. Copycat violence

Fear 1: 'TV zombies'

This first fear presupposes that TV is an all-powerful medium and that its young audience is highly impressionable and vulnerable to its influence. The medium is seen as responsible for exploiting un-critical children who mindlessly lap up everything they see on the screen. Television has also been referred to as the 'plug-in drug'(Winn, 1985).

This view clearly differentiates between what are considered to be desirable and undesirable activities for children. TV is portrayed as an 'evil' that dulls the minds of otherwise inquisitive and lively young children, and brings them into contact with issues such as sex, with which they are considered too young to cope (Postman, 1985). This fear has also been frequently expressed by moral entrepreneurs in Britain, for example: 'More and more children are growing up in a moral vacuum, which for so many is being filled with fetid junk from the lower depths of our popular culture – video nasties, crude comics and violent television' (*Daily Express*, 26 November 1993).

Fear 2: desensitisation

This fear is based on the assumption that regular viewing of mediated (screen) violence will desensitise the young audience to situational (real life) violence because they become accustomed to seeing it on their television screens; that is, as a result of frequently viewing violent acts on TV they lose their sensitivity to the shock and horror of such violence. The fear that children become desensitised is really only based on a common-sense assumption of the power of the media.

Fear 3: imitation – 'copycat violence'

Children clearly do imitate what they see on television and film. You will have undoubtedly seen young children pretending to be Power Rangers, Turtles, Super-heroes and so on. They imitate the language, skills and narratives of what they have seen on screen. Children are often given dressing-up copies of the clothes worm by these fictional characters in order to pretend-play. This imitation is encouraged by some adults as a form of imaginative play and it is viewed as a positive stage in child development.

However fear has been expressed that media violence creates 'copycat' violence among children and young people. Those con-cerned about imitation stress that children who watch violence will be excited or seduced by these on-screen acts and will subsequently reenact them in real life. It is assumed that children are particularly at risk from the effects of violence on screen because of their lack of sophistication and ability to differentiate between mediated reality and real life. This view of effects sees an all-powerful mass media exerting a tremendous influence over a vulnerable and essentially passive young audience. The prospect of copycat violence has raised a great deal of public concern, which is voiced by moral entrepreneurs each time a particularly shocking violent crime is reported.

We have already mentioned the case of James Bulger and the accusation that the boys who murdered him had imitated the violent acts portrayed in the film 'Child's Play 3'. The following year (1993) three young people were found guilty of the torture and murder of a sixteen year old girl. According to the presiding judge, the crime was 'As appalling a murder as it was possible to imagine'. It was alleged that one of the culprits had imagined herself to be the character Chucky in the film 'Child's Play'. She was alleged to have chanted 'I'm Chucky, wanna play?' before sadistically torturing her victim.

In the USA, the young defendants in several well-publicised murder cases blamed a specific film or television violence in general for their crimes. For example the defence lawyers of sixteen year old Nathan Martinez, who murdered his step-mother and half-sister, attributed the murder to his viewing the film 'Natural Born Killers' in 1994. Fifteen year old Ronnie Zamorra, who shot and killed a neighbour, was said by his lawyer to be unable to distinguish between real life and television programmes.

The difficulty in these cases is proving causation; that is, proving that a particular film or television programme was directly responsible for provoking the violent behaviour. Later, we will examine evidence from research on children and imitation.

Media research on violence

Now that we have outlined the public fear about the power of screened violence, we will examine the results of major research studies in this field. It is interesting to note that much of this research was conducted as a response to these early fears.

Our review of media research outlines and evaluates earlier American research in comparison with more recent European work on media violence. There will be some overlap with the earlier sections in this chapter, but this section focuses on violence and young audiences. We will not repeat the strengths and weaknesses of the various approaches presented earlier in the chapter. The following effects models will be examined:

- Catharsis effect (USA).
- Stimulation effect (USA).
- Observational learning effect (USA).
- Reinforcement effect (UK and USA).

- Cultivation analysis (USA).
- Reception analysis (UK).

Catharsis effect

This is a psychological approach, grounded in Freudian psycho-analytic theory. It asserts that the stresses of daily life build up such a high degree of frustration in the individual that it may lead to aggression. Feshbach (1961), one of several American supporters of this approach, argues that viewing violence may in fact act as a deterrent to real life violence because watching violence on our screens relieves our feelings of frustration. Therefore the viewing of screened violence may actually defuse potentially aggressive behaviour in individuals. Feshbach and Singer (1971) maintain that this cathartic effect may be more pronounced in working-class viewers because their socialisation has resulted in their being less self-disciplined than the middle classes.

Exercise 9.11

1. What assumptions does this approach make about social class socialisation and self-discipline?

2. Think about your own viewing of violent films; to what extent do you think that catharsis theory is valid?

Stimulation effect

In contrast to catharsis theory, the stimulating effects theory assumes that viewing violence is likely to create aggression in the viewer. Berkowitz (1962) maintains that watching violence stimulates emotional and physiological responses so that the likelihood of aggressive behaviour is increased. However this stimulus–response model is far from simple. Berkowitz argues that it depends on the individual having feelings of frustration before the viewing begins. This is particularly relevant when the situations shown on screen are similar to the anger-provoking circumstances experienced by the viewer.

Observational learning effect

This is based on the assumption that people learn to be aggressive. Bandura and Walters (1963) maintain that people may model their aggressive behaviour on screened violence. Therefore television increases the likelihood of aggression and violence by showing situations that the viewer can imitate. They argue that audiences are more likely to imitate violent screen behaviour if they perceive that the behaviour is rewarded by others. However Cumberbatch (1989, p. 36) questions the idea of children imitating criminal or violent acts simply because they have watched them on TV. Imitation hypotheses ignore the individual motivation to act and also conveniently forget that most police action on TV glorifies crime fighting rather than deviant or criminal acts, therefore any simulation, if the hypothesis is correct, should involve prosocial rather than antisocial effects.

Reinforcement effect

As its name implies, this perspective argues that violence on television will reinforce any propensity for violence that already exists within the viewer. Media violence neither increases nor decreases the possibility of audience aggression. For Klapper (1960), violence is not created by the media, rather it results from a complex interaction of norms values, peer situations, family life and social roles. These factors determine how violence is understood and reacted to by the audience. Halloran (1964) has developed a more critical approach. He rejects the mediacentric position and argues that the media are only one of many factors that influence the audience.

The reinforcement effect approach is sociological rather than psychological, as it locates the media within the social situation of the child. It is impossible to separate the possible effects of violence on television from other areas of social life. Children do not watch television in a social vacuum as they are influenced by their experiences of family life, schooling, religion, policing and so on. The causes of violence are therefore much more complex than simply the result of viewing screened violence. As Halloran (1964, p. 20) has argued, 'We must get away from thinking in terms of what TV does to people and substitute for it the idea of what people do with TV.'

Cultivation analysis

Gerbner and his associates (1980) have conducted social surveys on and content analysis of prime-time television for over twenty years in the USA. One of the main premises behind their work is that television portrays a distorted view of social reality. Violence is significantly overrepresented on screen, and social groups such as blacks, women, gays and lesbians (as we have already seen in Chapter 7) are noticeably underrepresented. As a result of this distorted media representation, Gerbner *et al.* argue that heavy viewers of television (those who watch the most TV) develop very distorted views of the outside world and as a result express more prejudiced attitudes towards some minority groups. They also become more fearful of crime and violence than lighter viewers of TV.

Cultivation theorists assert that over a prolonged period of time, heavy viewing of TV violence leads to a greater fear of crime. However critics argue that the correlation does not appear to be strong. Wober (1978; Wober and Gunter, 1982) has challenged the cultivation effects model by arguing that heavy viewers of television may have been particularly anxious about the outside world in the first place, hence television reinforces rather than causes their fears.

ITEM D

Case study of the problems of researching the effects of screened violence

Belson's (1978) study of the effects of TV violence attempted to measure the effects on adolescent boys of long-term exposure to television. His research was based on interviews in London with 1565 boys aged 12–17. The boys were asked to recall 100 television programmes broadcast between 1959 and 1971. These programmes had been allocated an 'objective' violence score by a panel of adults, and these scores were translated into a ten-point violence scale. The boys were also invited to discuss any violent behaviour they had been involved in during the previous six months.

Belson then measured the boys' viewing habits against their violent behaviour. His findings indicated that, on average, boys who watched more violence on screen tended to commit a greater number of violent acts, particularly those of a more serious nature. He concluded that extensive exposure to TV violence does influence real-life aggression.

Belson's work has gained a great deal of attention from sociologists in the field.

However, despite the large sample size, the work has been strongly challenged by some researchers. Murdock and McCron (1979) argued that Belson's conclusion that TV violence had a direct effect on the boys' behaviour ignored other significant factors, including social class and home background: 'Whereas only 13% of boys from higher non-manual families admitted committing four or more 'serious' acts, the figure for those from lower working class homes was almost three times as high, 38%.'

Somewhat paradoxically, Belson found that the boys who scored the highest on real-life aggression were only moderate viewers of violence. Cumberbatch (1989) notes that 'very high viewers of violence were 50% less aggressive than the moderate to high exposure group'. We could therefore argue that aggression could be as easily reduced in society by increasing the amount of violence on screen as by decreasing it. We might wonder, then, if watching a great deal of on-screen violence actually serves to deter real life violence!

ITEM D *Exercise 9.12*

Evaluation is an essential skill to employ when investigating methods and methodology. We want you to evaluate Belson's study by answering the following questions:

 1. What problems may emerge because of the sole reliance on interviews with boys?

 2. The questions relied on retrospective memory. How reliable is this data?

 3. Can we generalise from Belson's findings?

4. Why do you think Belson excluded girls from his study?

5. What assumptions are being made in this study about masculinity?

New conceptions of children and television – reception analysis

> In recent years . . . new wave TV cartoons and video games have served as a focus for a whole range of concerns about consumerism, violence and sexism. . . . Yet there has been very little attempt to investigate the ways in which young people use the media and the meanings and pleasures they derive from them: here again, they are defined largely as passive victims of powerful and exclusive negative effects (Buckingham, 1993, p. 5).

Earlier effects research was based on the assumption that the majority of children respond in similar ways to the same media and are vulnerable to psychological damage from the media. However it has recently been argued by European researchers that the concept that the media exert direct effects is too deterministic and ignores the extent to which children are a sophisticated and active audience. This shift in focus has been particularly associated with researchers involved in reception analysis. Today most media sociologists would totally reject the notion of the media as all powerful: it is extremely simplistic to argue that any given media text will affect all members of an audience in the same way. Indeed most analysts accept the proposition that media texts are read differently by different members of the audience according to their subjective experience, cultural knowledge and social characteristics. The old debate that focused on television as a 'problem' has been replaced with one that is concerned with the motivations for watching and the pleasures received. Buckingham (1993) criticises effects research on children for the following reasons:

- Despite decades of research, all correlations between violence and antisocial behaviour in children are so weak or qualified that they are untenable.
- Many studies ignore the meaning of violence for those who watch it and those who perpetrate it.
- Children are not a homogenous group: issues of gender, class and ethnicity must be addressed.
- A child does not have a fixed identity – identity is socially constructed and in constant negotiation.
- Children are far more sophisticated and media-literate than researchers previously assumed.

This new method of researching children as active audiences of television incorporates a much more ethnographic approach to understanding the meanings children attach to their viewing.

An example of reception analysis is Julian Wood's (1993) small-scale study of young people's use of video. This ethnographic study of working-class teenage boys aimed to discover what the boys watched on video and in which circumstances. As part of his study, he attended an 'after-school horror viewing session' of Steven King's 'It' at one of the boy's homes whilst his family was away. Wood describes how one of the boys, Colin, became the spokesperson and explained what sort of film it was: '"It's a really bad horror," he tells us enthusiastically.' (p. 189) Wood quotes the lads' comments after watching the film:

'I thought you said it was bad', says Steve. Colin defends his choice, but Steve has the advantage of taking a more macho stance. 'It was [a] fucking tea party!' he says. 'And they was like poofs.' Steve is referring here to the fact that the male characters do a lot of American-style 'bonding', getting into big huddles at various stages – although it had struck me earlier how these on-screen cuddles mirrored so closely the way the three friends were sitting almost on top of each other on the sofa (quoted in Buckingham, 1993, p. 191).

Later, Julian Wood interviewed Colin on his own:

JW: Did you see lots of strong stuff when you were younger then?

Colin: I saw them all – Texas Chainsaw Massacre, Evil Dead, Driller Killer, all them. They were pirates mostly.

JW: Did you enjoy them?

Colin: Yeah. Except one. I think it was The Burning. That bit with the shears got me.

JW: Where he cuts fingers off kids in the summer camp?

Colin: Yeah. It was weird, that. I suppose it gave me a few nightmares.... Different things get different people, I suppose (ibid., p. 193).

Wood argues that for these boys and perhaps other young people, watching horror films takes on the status of a 'rite of passage'. Fears are to be overcome and videos 'dared to be' watched. Certification is to be flaunted. A higher certificate is simply indicative of stronger and more valued material. This approach is a far cry from the direct effects research by Belson and others.

ITEM E **Exercise 9.13**

Using Item E and the relevant sources, answer the following questions:

1. What do you think are the strengths of Wood's approach?

2. What are its limitations?

3. What pleasures do you think the boys derived from watching these films?

4. How do you think Wood's presence affected the validity and reliability of the data he collected?

In response to public fear about supposed 'copycat' violence in the 1990s in Britain and concern that the level of violence had increased on screen from 1993–94 (NVLA, 1994), Hagell and Newburn of the Policy Studies Institute (PSI) were commissioned in 1994 by the British Board of Film Classification to investigate the viewing habits of young offenders. They aimed to establish whether there were significant differences in what young offenders enjoyed watching compared with non-delinquent youngsters. The study was based on interviews with 78 juvenile offenders (nine girls and 69 boys, aged between 12 and 18) and questionnaires with a representative sample of 538 school children.

The overall findings of the study indicated that there were no significant differences in the viewing of violence by the two groups. For both groups, soap operas were the most popular choice, with male young offenders listing 'The Bill' as their favourite programme and school children choosing 'Home and Away'. The overall favourite film for both offenders and schoolchildren was 'Terminator 2'. Hagell and Newburn (1994) found no evidence to suggest that juvenile delinquents were exposed to or chose to watch more screened violence than their 'conformist' counterparts. They concluded that 'considerable doubt can be cast upon claims of some direct causal connection or correlation between television and anti social behaviour'. They could find no evidence of television viewing being the cause of their persistent offending and argued instead that 'The overriding impression gained from interviewing was of lives that were full of change, chaos and deprivation, in which the media were of less significance than was the case for the non-offending peers' (ibid.).

A move to the right?

In the same month as the above research was published, Elizabeth Newson's discussion paper (1994), a review document of largely American research on the effects of television violence, was released to the press. Her conclusions lent support to a campaign launched in 1993 to protect children from the supposedly harmful effects of video nasties. She claimed that 'professionals in child health and psychology under-estimated the degree of brutality and sustained sadism that film makers were capable of inventing'. She maintained that studies had proved there was a significant correlation between violence on screen and real life aggression in children. She argued that children both identified with and mimicked the violence they witnessed on screen.

However Newson's conclusions have not gone unchallenged. Von Feilitzen's (1994) work contradicts Newson's findings by suggesting that 'Mass communication research has not been able to discern any corresponding causal relation between entertainment violence and violent crimes.' She argues instead that 'different persons experience excitement, violence, horror and power – as well as other media and cultural contexts very differently, need it differently and attach different meanings to it'(von Feilitzen, 1994, p. 159).

Barker (1997) also criticises Newson, describing her report as 'wildly misleading' and 'common sense writ large'. In relation to the Bulger case, although Newson does not assert that the two boys convicted of the murder actually saw the film 'Child's Play 3', she depicts the boys as 'exemplars of a new cruelty in children'. According to Barker, Newson's assumption was that we were witnessing a new kind of film that had disturbing messages. Barker challenges what he sees as the commonsensical views expressed by Newson and her readings of the various films she offers as evidence. His main point is that the concept of 'media violence' is subject to a multitude of definitions by numerous observers:

> It is supposed to encompass everything from cartoons (as in Tom & Jerry and Wily Coyote), children's action adventure films (the dinosaurs in the film, Jurassic Park, alongside playground scuffles in Grange Hill and last-reel shoot-outs in Westerns); news footage from Rwanda and Bosnia; horror films from Hammer to cult gore movies; the range from Clint Eastwood, as the voiceless hard man of Dirty Harry, to Arnie as the violent humorist of almost any of his films, etc. etc. (Barker, 1997, p. 27).

He argues that the single factor linking all these media products is simply that certain critics don't like them. It would therefore appear that social researchers have competing interpretations of the significance of these findings on television and violence.

However the conclusion reached by Buckingham (1993) and Hodge and Tripp (1986) is that children are highly sophisticated audiences who are able to understand and criticise what they watch. Furthermore Buckingham, *et al.* (1990), in their work on children and television, found that they had considerably underestimated children's ability to be critical of TV. More recently there has even been a move away from seeing children as an active audience to seeing them as an 'interactive' audience with the introduction of the Internet, CD ROM and multimedia products.

In short we have witnessed nothing short of a revolution in media research into the relationship between violence on screen and the young audience. From a sociological perspective we have identified a clear shift in paradigms concerning this debate. However this is not to say that we have reached any concrete conclusions about the potential effects of televised violence on young people. Perhaps the only safe conclusion to draw from the evidence is that most sociologists rarely point to television as the main cause of violence in society. As Linné (1995) has argued, 'All the research findings, when mentioning violence on television, treat television as a possible contributory factor in real life violence, but never as the sole cause.'

However it does not follow that we should be unconcerned about what is portrayed on screen and the circumstances in which these portrayals of violence are viewed. In fact it seems that there has been a move towards a revisionist position among some contemporary researchers. Miller and Philo (1996), two members of the Glasgow University Media Group and hence long-time observers of the media, present a radical challenge to what they call the 'critical theorists'. They maintain that as the media influence audiences through news reporting and advertising, we should take seriously the claim that screen violence may also have an effect. They call for yet more research:

> Certain essential questions for further research seem to remain. How does violence become part of the human vocabulary of potential behaviour, and do the media in contemporary society have an influence in this? If violence can be seen as efficient in achieving goals, or as pleasurable in its own right, do media images encourage or develop such perceptions in the viewer? . . . What we need is a sociology of the development of motivation, belief and interpersonal response. It is no longer enough to stick to vague negative assertions that 'There is no evidence' (Miller and Plillo, 1996).

Returning to the conclusions by Hagell and Newburn (1994), we find that the 'debate has to progress beyond the simplistic argument that screen violence is to blame for juvenile crime. Perhaps the only thing that is not in dispute is that this is a debate that is set to run and run.'

Examination focus

Although in the past there have been no specific essay questions on the effects of screen violence on audiences, the material in this chapter can easily be applied to more general essays on audiences and media influence. We have selected number of questions for which the material in this chapter would be useful.

Essays

1. Assess the sociological evidence for and against the view that the effects of the mass media vary according to the social characteristics of the audience (AEB, June 1992).
2. 'Any sociological explanation of the influence of the mass media needs to take into account the social situation of the audience.'

Explain and evaluate the view expressed in this statement (AEB, November 1993).

3. '"The hypodermic syringe" model sees the individual as a member of a passive audience, who is easily influenced and manipulated by the mass media.' Assess this model with reference to sociological evidence and arguments (AEB, June 1995).

As examiners for AEB A level sociology we are aware of the difficulties that many students have with interpretation and application skills. The following exercise might prove useful and you could use it as a model for all your essay work.

Take each one of the essay questions above and, concentrating on interpretation and application, list the appropriate evidence that you would use for each one. The following grid, which relates to question 2 above, should help you.

Appropriate studies	How do they relate to the question?
1. Buckingham and Wood's studies	They allow us to see that even children and young people are not a homogeneous audience, but are differentiated by age, gender, class, ethnicity and so on
2. Morley's work	Again we are shown that audiences do not read texts in the same way. Morley uses the typology of Stuart Hall: preferred/dominant, negotiated and oppositional readings. Texts are polysemic

Now continue the exercise yourselves.

10 Politics and the media

By the end of this chapter you should:

- have a critical understanding of the role of the media in a democratic society;
- be able to analyse the effect of media coverage of elections on the voting intention and behaviour of the electorate;
- recognise political bias in the press and on television, and audience perception of this bias;
- be familiar with the 'packaging of politics';
- have an understanding of the relationship between the state and the media;
- structure an examination essay.

Introduction

In this chapter we will examine aspects of the relationship between politics and the media. This could be a very broad task indeed as it is clear that there are many areas that could be included under the blanket concept of 'politics'. Politics and what constitutes 'the political domain' affect many aspects of media institutions, from their ownership, organisation, selection processes and the nature of media content itself. Hence many issues are 'political' in the broadest sense. For instance:

- The way that dominant groups act as both gatekeepers and agenda setters of media content is political.
- The systematic marginalisation of minority groups is also a political issue.
- So is the representation of women and ethnic minorities by the media.
- The debate on ownership and control is also highly political.

However in this chapter we are mainly concerned with the politics of government and how this relates to the media. Some important issues will be addressed in this chapter:

1. The role of the media in a democratic society.
2. The effect of the media coverage of general elections on the voting intentions and behaviour of the electorate.

3. Political bias in the press and on television, and how audiences perceive it.
4. New media, new politics: the 'packaging of politics'.
5. State regulation and the media

The role of the media in a democracy

Democracy is a system of government that involves some form of election by the people. It has an ideological aspect too, as it is seen as a valued feature of modern societies (Lawson and Garrod, 1996).

Browne (1994) lists the competing views on the role of the media in a modern democracy. The following factors are those that he considers promote democracy:

1. The media are not controlled by the state, so government censorship is limited and free speech is upheld. Journalists are therefore free to publish and comment, within the legal limits.
2. A wide range of media mean a wide range of opinions. Because the media are able to comment on government policies and actions, the media play an important 'watchdog' role.
3. The media provide impartial accounts of news and current affairs.
4. The media accurately reflect public opinions that already exist in society rather than creating new ones. People make conscious choices about what media they use.
5. Anyone can put across their views by setting up a newspaper, distributing leaflets and using other media.

A democratic society can only work properly if there is a well-informed electorate. In modern societies, political information is mainly provided by the mass media and they have been seen to take on the position of 'watchdog of the constitution' or 'fourth estate' (Newton, 1990). However any bias or misinformation presented by the media may have an adverse influence on the voting public.

'The media have failed democracy. We live in a political society in blinkers. The information society is a myth. What we have is the misinformation society' (Golding, 1993). In this statement Golding presents a very pessimistic view of modern societies and the role of the media within them, but it is possible to argue that there has never really been a 'golden age of democracy'.

At the beginning of this century the British media, especially the press, were 'segmented according to style, political complexion and perceived readership' (Wagg, 1994). Quality broadsheets such as *The Times* and the *Daily Telegraph*, which were read by the middle and upper classes, were mainly Conservative in outlook, whereas the *Manchester Guardian* (now the *Guardian*) was allied to the Liberal

Party. The only daily newspaper allied to the Labour Party was the *Daily Herald*, which later became the *Sun*.

Different proprietors held different opinions about the relationship between politics and the press, with Lord Beaverbrook of the *Daily Express* taking a radical position by saying that the main purpose of his paper was to print propaganda.

In the late nineteenth century and early days of the twentieth century, press owners were closely linked to political interests and factions. This connection continued into the early decades of the twentieth century. Between 1911 and 1915, for example, funds from the (Tory) Unionist Central Office were secretly paid to four national newspapers, in 1901 the *Daily News* was bought by a leading Liberal family, the Cadburys, and in 1924 the *Morning Post* was bought by a Conservative syndicate.

In 1949 Lord Beaverbrooke made his position very clear when he said 'I run the *Daily Express* for the purpose of making propaganda and with no other motive'. Similarly Lord Rothermere expressed his overt support of the British Union of Fascists during the 1930s with headlines such as 'Give the Blackshirts a helping hand' and 'Hurrah for the Blackshirts!' The conservatism expressed by the popular press arose from a deep attachment to Britain and Empire and was overtly patriotic and ethnocentric, and openly anti-Semitic in the case of Rothermere's papers.

Until recently, political bias reflected the essentially Conservative leanings of the British press. As a result of increasing concentration of ownership of all kinds of mass media, a relatively small group of multimedia/multinational corporations control a considerable amount of what we see, hear and read (see Chapter 3):

> Instead of showing the competitive features of a free market demanded by the liberal theory of democracy, the privately owned media seem to be in the hands of an oligopoly. Moreover, three-quarters of the national dailies . . . give strong support to the Conservative Party, about one-fifth to the Labour Party and none at all to the Liberal Party . . . This suggests rather little of the political pluralism which the free market is supposed to produce (Newton, 1990).

However this Conservative bias changed in the early months of 1997 when Rupert Murdoch pledged support for Tony Blair and New Labour.

Exercise 10.1

 The following terms may prove useful when you are writing an essay (if you don't know their meanings, look them up in a textbook or a dictionary of sociology):

1. Oligopoly
2. Propaganda
3. Marginalisation
4. Impartial
5. Syndicate

Exercise 10.2

Using material from this chapter, write a paragraph on the following: to what extent do you agree that the press promote democracy in Britain?

Elections, voting behaviour and the media

If you have studied politics you will be familiar with the changes that have taken place in electoral behaviour in this country. Here we will provide a brief outline of the main changes. From the end of the Second World War until the 1970s it was relatively easy to explain voting patterns. There were three simple deciding factors:

1. **Partisan alignment** (or party loyalty): people were socialised into voting for a particular party, mainly by their families. Around 90 per cent of voters supported one of the two main parties.
2. **Class alignment**: as the social classes were relatively stable it was easy to correlate class with voting, as apart from 'deviant voters' the working class largely supported the Labour Party and the middle-class supported the Conservatives.
3. **Electoral stability**: there was stability in voting over time as party loyalties were strengthened. For example between 1950 and 1970 the Conservative share of the vote ranged between 41.9 per cent and 49.7 per cent, while the Labour vote ranged between 43.8 per cent to 48.8 per cent.

These three factors changed radically after the 1970s to become:

1. **Partisan de-alignment**: by 1987 the share of the votes won by the two main parties was only 73.1 per cent and there was a rise in support for the third party, the SDP/Liberal Alliance Party, later to become the Liberal Democrats.
2. **Class dealignment**: splits within the working-class, forming a 'traditional' and 'new' working class, together with increased division between the north and south of the country, have seriously challenged class alignment (see Marshall, 1987). Until 1997 there was a significant decline in support for the Labour Party by the working class as a whole: the percentage of working-class Labour Party voters declined from 50 per cent in 1979 to 38 per cent in 1983, but rose to 45 per cent in 1992.

Some commentators were of the opinion that Labour would never again be elected to government.

3. **Electoral volatility**: it has become much more difficult to predict people's voting behaviour as some change allegiance both between and during election periods. It has been argued that the electorate has become more concerned with issue voting than with maintaining party loyalty, and this is where the media might be playing an important role in informing and even influencing them.

The coverage of general elections brings into sharp focus the major concerns about the political influence of the mass media. There are two main concerns here and both can be seen as focusing on the role of the mass media in a democratic society. The first is whether the media do influence the electorate as a result of their coverage of general election campaigns; and second, the ways in which the media might affect wider political struggles and debates.

There has been a long-running and contentious argument as to whether the media coverage of election campaigns has any influence upon the electorate. It is clear that the media have affected the nature of political life in general, but the nature and extent of this influence is much more difficult to quantify.

Many empirical 'before and after' studies have examined the influence of media campaigns on actual voting behaviour. However, as we shall see, most of this work has produced inconclusive or, at best, tentative results. One of the earliest of these studies was *The People's Choice* by Lazarsfeld *et al.* (1948) on the American presidential election of 1940. This was a large-scale, longitudinal social survey conducted throughout the campaign and based on interviews. One of the main findings of the study was the existence of 'a considerable amount of interaction between the social characteristics of voters, what they select and use from the political propaganda presented by the media, and their ultimate voting choice' (Lowery and De Fleur, 1988, p. 93). An important finding was that exposure to the media was not uniform throughout the sample. Some people paid close attention to information on the radio and in newspapers and various magazines, but the majority of the sample paid the campaign only scant attention. Those who paid most attention to the media and showed the most interest had already made up their minds and were mainly from higher socio-economic groups. This study was the first to discover the influence of 'opinion leaders' on other people's attitudes. These well-informed members of the audience were influential and were able to advise and inform others less interested in the media coverage. This was the two-step flow hypothesis (see Chapter 8): 'Ideas often flow from radio and print to the opinion leaders and from them to the less active sections of the population' (Lazarsfeld *et al.*, 1948, p. 151).

In their study of a British general election, Blumler and McQuail (1968) hypothesised that there would be differences in political impact between those who watched political programmes out of genuine interest and those who watched simply because they were heavy viewers of television. The researchers found a very interesting change in allegiance towards the Liberals among heavy viewers, and this favouring of the Liberals increased with exposure. This finding seemed to be replicated in the 1983 campaign, when the Alliance Party was given almost equal television coverage as the two main parties, whereas its press coverage was minimal.

ITEM A

The effect of televised election campaigning on voter's choice, 1983 (per cent)

Reason for choice	All voters	Late deciders	Switchers
Conservative TV broadcast	6	14	8
Labour TV broadcast	5	12	7
Alliance broadcast	9	26	22

(Source: Adapted from BBC TV/Gallup survey, June 1983.)

ITEM A   *Exercise 10.3*

Item A shows the percentage of people who were influenced by party political broadcasts (PPBs).

1. Which voters were most influenced by the broadcasts?

2. What might this table tell you about the influence of PPBs at election time?

Studies of media influence in political campaigns are open to criticism, not least because they concentrate on the campaigns and ignore the day-to-day coverage of political news. As Negrine (1991) argues, long-term social, political and economic changes may be more relevant to predicting the outcome of an election than events in the short period running up to the election itself.

The relationship between media and politics is by no means straightforward. Attitudinal shifts within the electorate take place during and between elections as a result of many different events, the reporting of which will have different effects on different sections of the electorate. So it is very difficult to determine the actual impact of the media on the electorate, and we also have to examine the possibility of different kinds of influence being exerted by the different kinds of medium. Blumler (1977), who has produced a great deal of research evidence in this field, admits that 'the magnitude of measured communication effect has typically proved modest'.

Another factor in measuring the political effects of the media is the number of resources the audience members have access to, or how 'media-rich' they are. Voters have access to many different media sources, for example television, radio, the press, political journals and video, but it is very important to remember that they also have non-media sources such as families, friends and workmates. The assumption that the media exert the most significant influence on the voter reflects a mediacentric view and few sociological researchers would accept that this is the case today. There is also a possible danger of media 'overkill'. An example of this took place during the 1987 British election campaign, when television audiences appeared to experience 'election fatigue'. The audience for BBC1's extended 'Nine O'clock News and Election '87' fell by nearly three million during the campaign and ITV's 'News at Ten' audience fell by half a million (Negrine, 1991).

Politicians and party political broadcasts

There are also instances of political communications being misunderstood, for instance party political broadcasts, which are intended to communicate directly to the electorate, do not always hit the mark.

Item B concerns a party political broadcast on behalf of the Labour Party in the 1992 election campaign. It is interesting, firstly, as an example of a political message being misunderstood by the audience, and secondly, because of the manipulation of the message by some newspapers.

ITEM B

'The War of Jennifer's Ear': 1992 election

The Labour Party's party political broadcast on 24 March 1992 was intended as a critique of the way the Conservative government was handling the National Health Service; however it badly misfired and gave the Conservative tabloids ammunition to use against the Labour Party. The story was based on two actual children: Jennifer Bennett, whose parents had approached the Labour Party about her case; and the son of Conservative MP Michael Mates, who had allegedly paid £1300 for an operation on his son. The broadcast gave rise to heated debate and it was the Labour Party that was accused of sleaze and having gone 'too far'.

What is significant is that the debate about health funding was lost under a barrage of 'facts' about the real Jennifer and her parents, who were split in their political allegiances. The headline in the *Daily Express* on 26 March read:

'Kinnock on the run as TV "fiction" explodes in his face – THE BIG LIE'

The article on the front page went on to denounce Kinnock as 'unfit to govern'. Jennifer's mother, who had always voted Tory, said that she 'did not want one person to vote Labour as a result of my child being used as a political football'. And so the storm raged. The loser appeared to be the Labour Party, and the potential political mileage it had hoped to gain from a debate about health funding was not forthcoming.

ITEM B   *Exercise 10.4*

1. Using *The Times* and the *Guardian* newspapers on CDROM (1992), look up references to the 'war' cited in Item B.
2. From the articles, can you tell whether either newspaper is more or less sympathetic to the Labour Party? Give reasons for your answer.

Newspapers and voting behaviour

As a Mori Poll in 1992 indicated, it would be wrong to suppose that there is a simple equation between the politics of a newspaper and the voting intentions of its readership. People routinely read newspapers whose political position is at odds with their own, a point which questions the power of newspapers to alter the opinions of their readers and to act as a tool of political persuasion. The Sun, for example had been a fierce critic of the Labour Party yet nearly half of its readership indicated that they intended to vote Labour in the 1992 election (Denscombe, 1993, p. 43).

However in the 1997 general election the *Sun* came out in strong support of Tony Blair and New Labour.

ITEM C

Newspaper readership and voting intentions, British 1992 (per cent)

	Conservative	Labour	Liberal
Daily Telegraph	71	13	15
Daily Mail	66	17	15
Daily Express	61	19	13
The Times	61	18	17
Financial Times	50	35	14
Sun	39	48	10
Independent	31	40	26
Daily Mirror	19	59	10
Guardian	12	59	22

(Source: Adapted from Denscombe, 1993.)

ITEM C   *Exercise 10.5*

    1. Which of the newspaper(s) in Item C have readerships whose views are closest to their own?

    2. In what ways does the evidence in this table challenge the instrumentalist view of the media?

ITEM D

The following articles refer to the influence of tabloid coverage of the 1992 general election on the final vote.

'Perhaps it was The Sun "wot won it" for Major'

'A press blitz on Kinnock does seem to have reduced Labour's share of the vote, reveals Brian MacArthur.

There is serious evidence for the first time in election history that the Tory tabloids may indeed – as Labour leaders are already complaining – have influenced how the nation voted. According to MORI, there was a 4% swing to the Tories among Sun readers last week, 3% among Daily Express readers and 2% for the Daily Mail. If MORI is right, and its research is based on a huge sample of 22700 voters, at least 200000 Sun readers swung to the Tories last week, while another 200000 were shifted by the Daily Mail and the Daily Express, enough to turn a potential Labour victory to defeat in many of their target seats' (*The Sunday Times*, 12 April 1992).

'Tony, Tony, Tony . . . and John'

'Politicians and journalists alike are convinced that a newspaper's final endorsement will make a difference to how people vote. The truth is that what these papers say in the last week of an election campaign is largely irrelevant. What counts is what has been written in the years before, during the lengthy process of agenda-setting.

Elections are not won and lost amid the hysteria of that final three-week campaign. Despite Margaret Thatcher's alarms in 1987 and the Kinnock camp's enbarrassment over Jennifer's Ear in 1992 . . . there is no way press coverage could have influenced the eventual outcome of those battles in their final moments.' (*Guardian*, 2 December 1996).

ITEM D   *Exercise 10.6*

    Carefully read the extracts in Item D. Which argument do you find more convincing and why? Use sociological evidence in your response.

The 1997 general election

It is a common-sense, but incorrect, assumption to say that when party political broadcasts are televised, people take a coffee break. It is suggested that during 1996, party political broadcasts were watched regularly by about 10.5 million viewers. According to Grice (1996), in previous election campaigns the Tory government had spent between £30000 and £50000 on each five-minute broadcast; Labour had averaged £30000; and the Liberal Democrats had spent under £20000. Equal air time was given to the Tories and Labour (five times five minutes), whereas the Liberal Democrats were allowed only three broadcasts.

The Conservatives started their campaign in July 1996 with the unveiling of their 'New Labour. New danger' campaign against the Blair-led Labour Party. It was estimated that the Conservative Party spent £10–15 million pounds during the campaign, using the services of the advertising agency M. and C. Saatchi, compared with the Labour Party's budget of £2–4 million pounds and the Liberal-Democrats' £100000.

Complaints about the Tories' 'demon-eyes' posters were made to the Advertising Standards Authority and initially it was decided to ban them. However they were not withdrawn, which quickly brought them into the public consciousness. The Labour Party responded to these posters with the slogan 'Same old Tories, same old lies', which did not seem to have the same power.

The necessary money for a political campaign was of little relevance to one new challenger in this election. The Referendum Party, created by Sir James Goldsmith, was said to have spent £20 million on its election campaign and gained not a single seat as a result. As Grice stated:

> Naturally, the admen in all four parties believe they can make a difference. Whether advertising can win elections is another matter. Most party strategists believe it can swing floating voters, but it cannot turn a political tide. . . . The Tories' tax record may be damaged by the rises since 1992, but Labour is not complacent. 'The ability to lie and to spend is a dangerous combination', a senior Labour strategist points out. Whatever the outcome, the election will test the power of advertising (Grice, 1996).

So we can see that election campaigns have come to be treated not so much as a political contest, but as a some kind of race where the only important factor is who wins and who loses. This is quite understandable because it is far more interesting to witness a political battle between personalities, than a long, drawn-out, complicated discussion of economic affairs. Also, recent general elections have been accused of becoming increasingly 'Americanised'. As Axford (1992) has argued:

> a presidential style is seen as embodying the triumph of appearance over substance. It involves identifying and marketing the singular qualities of individuals. Essentially, it is all about leaders . . . the

personal life and habits of the candidates are considered legitimate objects for scrutiny by press and television.

Axford identifies three broadcasting styles for political coverage:

1. The reactive style, where party campaigns are reported in a mainly descriptive fashion. Photo opportunities and leader profiles are evident here.
2. The rebellious style, where broadcasters set their own agenda, not always as the parties would wish. 'These are occasions for the broadcaster media to cock a snook at the attempts by the parties to manage their output' (ibid., p. 19).
3. The reflective style, which is a more analytical or thoughtful approach taken by broadcasters when analysing the issues and policies.

Each of these three styles puts a different complexion on the political issue being broadcast, and the rebellious and reflective approaches are more likely to affect the way leaders are represented.

Exercise 10.7

1. Watch a televised interview with a political leader. Which of Grice's three broadcasting styles, referred to above, is evident in the interview?
2. To what extent does the style of the televised interview affect what is being discussed? Explain your answer.

The general election campaign of 1997 was the longest this century, lasting for six weeks (17 March to 1 May). It proved to be record-breaking in other respects too. On the morning of 18 March the newspaper allegedly 'wot won it' for the Tories in 1992, announced 'The Sun Backs Blair: Give change a chance'. In what it called an 'historic announcement from Britain's No.1 newspaper', the *Sun* maintained that as this was the election for the millennium, then the people of Britain needed 'a leader with vision, purpose and courage who can inspire them and fire their imaginations ... that man is Tony Blair. He is the best man for the job, for our ten million readers and for the country.'

Although the paper voiced reservations about some of the New Labour's policies, it was clear that it was loosening its support for the Tories. The latter were seen by the *Sun* as 'tired, divided and rudderless'. However the *Sun*'s support for New Labour was not particularly consistent as by the third week of the campaign it had printed as many pro-Tory articles as pro-New Labour. A team of researchers that included Professor Peter Golding and David Deacon of Loughborough University monitored and coded 1633 news items on the general election between 31 March and 18 April. Some of their findings are shown in Item E.

Framing the debate: number of newspaper articles that were clearly positive about one of the main parties

Newspaper	Pro-Tory	Pro-Labour	Pro-LibDem	Neutral
The Times	28	22	6	34
Guardian	20	19	5	50
Telegraph	22	21	4	48
Independent	17	25	10	41
Financial Times	21	28	1	44
Sun	35	35	0	25
Mirror	18	50	1	29
Star	30	34	2	32
Mail	35	17	1	45
Express	32	12	3	49

(Source: quoted in the Guardian, April 1997.)

The 1997 election resulted in a massive landslide victory for the Labour Party, which took 419 seats (44 per cent of the votes cast). The Conservatives took 165 seats (32 per cent of the votes) and the Liberal Democrats 46 seats (17 per cent of the votes). Other parties claimed a 7 per cent share of the votes.

The opinion polls

The opinion polls of 1992 had almost exclusively predicted a Labour victory, so their reputations were rather tarnished when the Conservative Party succeeded once again in taking the target number of parliamentary seats. However in 1997 the polls, predictions of a landslide victory for Tony Blair's New Labour were quite correct. Brian Gosschalk of Mori claimed that they had had a good campaign: 'I think the polls come out of the 1997 general election a great deal better than most of the pundits who refused to believe in the possibility of a landslide' (quoted in the *Guardian*, 3 May 1997). Each of the five major polling organisations had predicted the final result to within a margin of plus or minus 3 per cent.

Election results predicted by the polls in 1997

Poll	Lab.	Con.	L.Dem.	Other	Lead	Error
Harris	48	31	15	6	17	+4
NOP	50	28	14	8	22	+9
ICM	43	33	18	6	10	−3
Gallup	46	33	16	5	13	0
Mori	47	29	19	5	18	+5
Poll of polls	47	31	16	6	16	+3

(Source: Guardian, 3 May 1997.)

Exercise 10.8

1. What is an opinion poll?

2. What method is used to collect data for opinion polls?

3. What sampling method is used for the collection of this data?

4. Although the 1997 predictions proved to be correct, to what extent is the opinion poll a *reliable* and *valid* form of data collection?

'New' ways of seeing

We have seen that it is very difficult to argue in favour of the direct effects model of political communication. One of the 'new' methodological approaches is the 'constructionist' approach. Neuman *et al.* (1992, p. xv) see this as focusing on 'the subtle interaction between what the mass media convey and how people come to understand the world beyond their immediate life-space'. According to Negrine (1996, p. 128), the constructionist approach proposes the view that 'individuals make sense of the media's menu of issues by "framing" them in ways which draw on past personal, and other, experiences'. It differs from earlier approaches by examining the framing of issues by the media as well as by audiences.

The approach's research agenda and methodology differs from the social survey method of examining media influence. Negrine identifies four features of the approach:

1. It examines individuals such as children and teenagers, rather than groups. Attention is paid to how these individuals think and feel about political issues.
2. Like reception analysis, it concentrates on how individuals make sense of media messages.
3. The methodology involves in-depth interviews with individuals or small groups.
4. The constructionist approach suggests that individuals rely on frames, 'to convey, interpret, and evaluate information' (Neuman *et al.*, 1992, p. 61).

Exercise 10.9

1. Look up 'constructionist approach' in your textbook. To what extent do you think this approach is a 'new' one,? and why?

2. What important social characteristics are missed out if we concentrate simply on individuals?

Case study: children and politics

Earlier work on children and politics involved the idea of political socialisation, that is, children were introduced to ideas about politics at home and at school. Himmelweit *et al.* (1985) maintain that the family is the primary agent of socialisation. Children's political socialisation depends upon 'the political involvement of the parents, their agreement on matters politic as well as the relation of child to parent. Where both parents are actively involved in politics, share the same political outlook and have good relations with their children, influence should be maximal, particularly where the wider community provides supporting cues' (ibid., p. 51).

Today we have many different media influences, such as satellite television, videos and computer technology, and these have to be taken into account when examining the political socialisation of children and young people. From research into development stages it is evident that children think about political issues in different ways at different ages. This is hardly surprising as they do the same with other issues. At age five or six their political consciousness 'is a collection of scraps of information, unrelated to each other', but by age seven they are able to 'distinguish a political and governmental world' (Connell, 1971).

Neuman *et al.* (1992) use 'frames' to explain how children organise information about the political arena. Connell (1971) uses a similar approach, but refers to four significant factors:

1. Hierarchy: children hold some notion, however crude, of differential power.
2. Conflict: they have ideas of violent conflict from an early age, but 'issue conflict' requires greater sophistication. This usually occurs at around twelve.
3. Elite–mass relationships: generally, children do not understand popular sovereignty, but they can understand the concept of an elite group having power over the public.
4. Political parties: older children are more likely to make connections between parties when they are linked to elections, and that there is often conflict between the parties.

[A]ll these studies tend to suggest that children to a large extent reproduce the ideas handed on to them by adults in family contexts, in schools and from the media. However, even this process of reproduction leaves room for the children to contribute something of their own (Negrine, 1996, p. 137).

Coursework suggestion

An analysis of the political socialisation of young children

You might adopt a 'constructionist' approach to discuss political ideas with young children – the topics discussed could be personalities in politics, political parties or wider, environmental issues. The following are some of the questions that you might consider:

1. What would be an appropriate age to sample?
2. How can I make the questions meaningful to young children?
3. Would photographs of politicians be a useful stimulus for the children?
4. Would it be useful to interview them individually or set up discussion groups?
5. Which of the two methods in number 4 would produce the most valid data?

Political bias in the media

According to the three main theories of the media there is political bias in the press. Bias is 'a deviation from some assumed "truth" or objective measurement' (Lawson and Garrod, 1996, p. 18). Therefore, in relation to the press we would expect to see statements that are either supportive or critical of particular political parties or politicians. In Chapter 3 we looked at the concentration of ownership of the British media, Item G below shows the ownership of the national press.

ITEM G

Ownership of the major newspapers

Owner	Newspaper	Share of market (%)
News International plc	*The Times, The Sunday Times, Sun, News of the World*	34.2
Mirror Group	*Daily Mirror, Daily Record, People, Sunday Mirror*	27.1
United Newspapers plc	*Daily Express, Sunday Express, Daily star*	13.3
Daily Mail and General Trust plc (Associated Newspapers)	*Daily Mail, Mail on Sunday*	12.7
Hollinger Group	*Daily Telegraph, Sunday Telegraph*	5.3
Guardian and Manchester Guardian Evening News plc	*Guardian, Observer*	3.1
Newspaper Publishing plc	*Independent, Independent on Sunday*	2.4

(Source: Adapted from The Media Guide, 1994, p. 14.)

The owners of newspapers have an impact on the newspapers' political content and leaning. The table in Item H gives a rough guide to the perceived political bias of some daily newspapers prior to the 1997 general election.

Political bias of daily newspapers

Newspaper	Political sympathy
The Times	Traditionally pro-Tory, changing to Centre
Daily Telegraph	Traditionally pro-Tory, but likes 'New Labour' under Tony Blair
Guardian	Anti-Tory, pro-New Labour
Independent	Mainly pro-New Labour
Daily Mail	Pro-Tory
Daily Express	Traditionally pro-Tory, but changing under Lord Hollick
Sun	Was pro-Thatcher, less keen on Major, Supported Blair in the 1997 election
Daily Mirror	Traditionally pro-Labour, not wholeheartedly New Labour
Daily Star	Pro-Tory, but politically apathetic

ITEMS G AND H   *Exercise 10.10*

Study Items G and H.

1. What percentage share of the newspaper market was pro-Labour in 1997?
2. What percentage share was pro-Conservative?

As we saw earlier, the Marxist or manipulative theorist would argue that political bias in any newspaper demonstrates the influence of the proprietor of that newspaper. The hegemonic theorist would see it as an inevitable part of the inferential structures within which the journalists operate, and the pluralist would argue that there is an inevitable bias, but that this should not concern us because readers are able to judge for themselves and can recognise bias when they see it.

The press and BSE*

Extract A

'The Government reacted angrily last night to an EU decision to ban British beef exports indefinitely. John Major said it went well beyond any action justified by the scientific evidence and persuaded Jacques Santer, the European Commission President, to reconvene a meeting of EU officials today to hear the views of Britain's chief medical officer and a leading expert on mad cow disease' (*Daily Telegraph*, 26 March 1996).

Extract B

'The Government last night attempted to brazen out the gathering crisis over beef, rejecting plans to cull cattle herds in the hope that international confidence in the industry will be restored and the Treasury saved from huge compensation claims . . .

On the foreign exchanges the impact of the BSE crisis drove down sterling amid a meltdown in domestic consumer confidence' (*Guardian*, 26 March 1996).

---

* BSE (bovine spongiform encephalopathy) is a disease in cattle that has resulted from feeding them foodstuffs containing offal from sheep and other cattle.

ITEM I *Exercise 10.11*

This exercise asks you to examine political bias in the quality press. We have already discussed the relationship between the tabloid press and political sympathy; it is important for you to discover whether such sympathy is also evident in everyday news items in broadsheets. Read the two extracts in Item I:

 1. Which article is pro-government and which is against?

 2. Which specific words indicate the strength of their political allegiances?

Exercise 10.12

Now it is your turn to search for bias. Take two broadsheet newspapers published on the same day and look at their front pages.

 1. Look at the lead story in each paper and compare them if they are on the same news item. If they are not, choose a story covered by both papers.

 2. What specific evidence can you find of the political bias of your particular newspapers? (You will need to examine the vocabulary of each item in detail, look especially at the adjectives used to describe the people and situations involved.)

Political bias on television

Unlike newspapers, which do not have to maintain a politically neutral position, BBC television, according to the terms of its charter, has to maintain a state of balance and impartiality between the major political parties. However there is research evidence to show that television audiences also perceive political bias in programming. For example in 1979, 1985 and 1994, samples of viewers were asked whether they thought that ITV and BBC favoured any political party. Items J and K show the results of the surveys.

Response to the question 'Does ITV favour any political party' (per cent)

	1979	1985	1994
No	74	71	69
Yes	10	15	14

Of those who answered 'Yes', these were the parties they perceived as being favoured:

	1979	1985	1994
Conservative	3	6	5
Labour	6	8	7
Liberal Democrat	1	1	1

(Source: Television: The Public's View 1994, Fact File, Carel Press, 1996.)

Percentage of people who said 'yes' in response to the question 'Does BBC favour any political party?'

	1979	1985	1994
Conservative	12	22	22
Labour	5	4	6
Liberal Democrat	1	1	0.5

(Source: Television: The Public's View 1994, Fact File, Carel Press, 1996.)

ITEMS J AND K   *Exercise 10.13*

 1. Study Items J and K. What general patterns in viewers' perception of political bias can you see emerging between 1979 and 1994 with regard to both ITV and BBC?

 2. What differences can you find between the viewers' perception of ITV and BBC biases?

These audience perceptions provide interesting evidence for the debate on the influence of the media, as does the following research data (Item L).

Perceived impartiality of news and current affairs programmes on the four main TV channels towards different groups, 1994 (per cent)

	Fair towards	Biased towards	Biased against
Politicians	59	25	13
Women	77	7	12
Ethnic minorities	71	13	12
Police	68	13	16
Govt depts/ministries	63	22	11
Trade unions	62	6	27

(Source: Television: The Public's View 1994, Fact File, Carel Press, 1996.)

Exercise 10.14

1. In Item L, identify the following:

   (a) the groups who suffer most from bias in the media;

   (b) the groups who are most favourably treated.

2. Item L is based on a sample of 1000 people aged 16 and over with a working television at home.

   (a) To what extent is this a useful source for sociologists studying the perceptions of audiences?

   (b) What other methods would you recommend that would produce more *valid* data?

Television in parliament

The televising of parliament came relatively late to Britain. It was first suggested by Aneurin Bevan in 1959, when he said 'We should seriously consider re-establishing intelligent communication between the House of Commons and the electorate as a whole. That, surely, is the democratic process.'

It took thirty years for his wish to be realised. The televising of the House of Lords started in 1985, and the cameras eventually entered the Commons on 21 November 1989 as a short-term experiment. Initially there was considerable fear on the part of MPs: 'The main fear was of television itself. Excluded from the Commons the medium had developed its own alternative political debate with participants, selected by the programmers, not the parties, paid to wrestle in mud or be grilled by "impartial" interviewers, forced to face hypothetical questions, give hostages to fortune and easy answers to complex questions' (Mitchell, 1991). On 19 July 1990 the Commons voted to make the televising of parliament permanent.

Exercise 10.15

There are obvious advantages and disadvantages to televising parliament. Make a list of as many as you can think of (the first of each have been done for you).

Advantages

1. It has allowed greater opportunities for politicians, not least because of their greater visibility. Parliamentary Question Time has given the prime minister and the leaders of the opposition parties a platform upon which to demonstrate their leadership qualities to the viewing public.

Disadvantages

1. Parliamentary affairs can become trivialised.

Exercise 10.16

The media and politics in Britain have become inextricably entwined. Think for a moment about the run-up to a general election:

- Imagine there is no television coverage.
- Imagine there are no radio interviews with MPs and cabinet ministers.
- Imagine there are no daily opinion polls.

 1. How would we obtain information about the parties' policies?

 2. How could we choose between the parties?

New media, new politics?
Packaging politics

It took time for politicians to recognise the usefulness of television as an electioneering device. Prime ministers and MPs were used to giving public performances as they were essential aspects of their role, but only after 1950 did they use television to address a mass audience rather than a few hundred people in a town hall on an electioneering tour. According to Seymore-Ure (1991) 1959 was a watershed in the relationship between politicians and the media. Before that time the BBC held the monopoly, and TV news and current affairs programmes were still in their infancy; however with the introduction of ITV in 1955 the situation changed dramatically. Competition for ratings between the two companies became all-important, and one result of this was the changed attitude towards MPs:

> This was arguably the single most important moment in the history of political broadcasting ... From now on, broadcasters were to make qualitative judgements about the news value of election campaigns; the relative importance of issues, personalities, minor parties; and how they should all be treated. Broadcasters increasingly took politicians at the broadcasters' value (ibid., p. 162).

The 1960s saw considerable expansion in political programming, not least irreverent satirical programmes such as 'That Was The Week That Was', which was considered so controversial that it was taken off air during the run-up to the 1962 general election. These satirical programmes were not easy targets for politicians because if they attacked the programmes they risked making themselves into even bigger objects of ridicule.

In 1964 BBC2 went on air with a remit to produce 'serious' programming, including political programmes. In 1974 the first election phone-in took place on the radio, giving the 'ordinary person' access to airtime. It was at that time that the prime minister, Harold Wilson, saw the potential of television as a medium for putting across political ideas. After Wilson it was almost impossible for a PM not to be a 'TV personality'. The ability to perform well on TV has now become essential for most if not all prospective parliamentary candidates, and it would be unthinkable for a would-be PM to lack a positive TV 'manner'. By the 1990s 'TV was no longer an instrument to be applied *to* politics: it was part of the environment *within* which politics was carried on' (Seymour-Ure, 1991, p. 176)

Franklin (1994) calls this new media–politics relationship the 'packaging of politics'. According to some, this new dynamic caused the media to be increasingly managed by politicians and their public relations officers, now known colloquially as 'spin doctors'. As Franklin states, 'Enthusiasm became an obsession as politicians tried to influence and regulate the flow of political information and messages via the mass media to an unprecedented degree. In this process, politicians and policies have become packages for media presentation and public consumption' (ibid., p. 4). He argues that a number of developments were significant in influencing this packaging process:

- The current generation of politicians had a different experience of television – they had grown up with it and were therefore familiar with its qualities.
- There was a growing professionalisation in the presentation of politics by the media.
- There was a tremendous increase in the number of media outlets so much greater use could be made of media opportunities, for example chat shows and comedy shows as well as current affairs.
- The media gained access to areas that were previously private: in 1978 radio was used to broadcast parliamentary affairs, in 1985 television cameras were allowed into the House of Lords, and in November 1989 television started to broadcast from the House of Commons.

All of these changes brought parliament and its members into everyday communication with the electorate. As a result, politicians began to realise that in order to be successful they would have to court the media, but what was really new was the sense that politicians could no longer operate effectively without the media.

The relationship between politicians and the media has become 'increasingly choreographed – it follows a pre-arranged format, including press conferences, televised addresses, "walkabouts", "photo-opportunities" and short statements or "sound bites"' (Wagg, 1994). 'Hence, the constant hunt (by politicians and journalists alike) for "photo-opportunities", which may make for good journalism although they are pseudo-events contrived for the media . . . "tabloid television" demands little of its audience in terms of concentration and under-standing' (Newton, 1990).

It is important to note that while politicians use the media to promote their policies and images, they then have to live up to the media images that they themselves have helped to create. This has been apparent in the cases of 'sleaze' in the recent past. Item M includes some reported cases of sleaze involving MPs and ministers.

ITEM M

Sleaze

'John Major's Government may well go down in history as the sleaziest. Scandal has become so common we are almost numb to it: the new ones merge with the old; the big ones are obscured by the small. They are bewildering, but they are important' (*Independent on Sunday*, 23 July 1995).

The term sleaze has entered our vocabulary in relation to politics since the mid 1980s. The *Independent on Sunday* lists 39 cases that have occurred since 1990, 34 of which concerned Tory MPs, four involved Labour MPs and one involved Paddy Ashdown, leader of the Liberal Democrats.

The first case was that of Alan Clark, MP for Plymouth Sutton until 1992 and minis-ter for defence procurement. During a dis-cussion between Clark and some machine tool manufacturers, Clark was alleged to have advised them 'to phrase applications for licences to export machinery to Iraq in such a way as to emphasis its "peaceful purposes"' (*Independent on Sunday*, op. cit.) This was seen as an official endorse-ment to break an international arms sales embargo on Iraq.

It is likely that the number of incidents under the heading of 'sleaze' in political life has not increased that significantly, but there are factors that have served to exaggerate the extent of sleaze over the last decade:

● The inability nowadays to keep things out of the media.
● The Willingness of 'wronged' women to tell their stories.
● Public scrutiny has become more effective.

The various allegations of sleaze have included adulterous sexual liaisons; un-disclosed 'gifts'; arms to Iraq; the £234 million provided to the Pergau Dam project in Malasia in exchange for a £1 billion trade deal; possible insider dealing of shares of a television company; and cash for questions. It is interesting to note that few MPs actu-ally felt the need to treat these incidents as resigning offences.

The Nolan Committee – a response to sleaze

At the end of 1994 John Major set up the Nolan Committee to investigate standards in public life. This committee still sits. In May 1995 it produced the following recommendations:

- MPs should be barred from working for lobbying firms, and if hired for their parliamentary services they must disclose it. The register of members' interests should be updated regularly.
- There should be a new code of conduct for MPs.
- There should be a Parliamentary Commissioner for Standards to investigate complaints.
- Ex-ministers should wait three months before taking up any outside job, and appointments should be vetted.
- Ministers should be subject to a clearer code of conduct – more information should be available for public scrutiny.
- A Public Appointments Commisioner should oversee fairness in appointments to quangos.

(Source: Independent on Sunday, 23 July 1995.)

Exercise 10.17

1. If you have access to CD Rom facilities, look up references to the Nolan Committee. What further developments have taken place (for example have any of its recommendations become law)?

2. Check the recent press for examples of possible political sleaze.

   (a) How are they reported? (Do the press take sides?)

   (b) What are the outcomes of the cases?

The importance of the role of the media in political life can be seen in the dramatic increase in the amount of central government resources given over to public relations. MPs can call upon the advertising, marketing and campaigning services of 850 press and information officers. Advertising budgets have increased substantially. As Franklin (1994) shows, the public expenditure budget for political campaigns rose from £60.5 million in 1982–3 to £200 million in 1988–9. In September 1989 the advertising campaign for the privatisation of electricity alone cost £76 million.

These recent changes have had a number of consequences, some more beneficial than others. There have been both advantages and disadvantages for the electorate. Some writers argue that the increasing openness of political agendas has helped to inform the public while others point to an increase in misinformation.

The following is a list of advantages and disadvantages of the opening up of politics by the media (adapted from Franklin, 1994). Read them and in a two-column table list the advantages and the disadvantages separately. Justify your reasons to another sociology student.

1. A diminishing of the political process as media distort as well as communicate messages.
2. Audiences are better able to assess the competence of government ministers.
3. The content of political debate comes second to its presentation – images dominate political substance.
4. The electorate gains by being better informed and more aware of political issues.
5. It is simply the inevitable result of new technology and is beneficial to audiences.
6. It places the emphasis on personalities and leads to 'presidentialism'. Politicians become more concerned with their voice and appearance.
7. The media oversimplify and trivialise political issues.
8. Overall, there is increased public knowledge and citizen participation, and hence greater governmental accountability.
9. Packaging political debates serves to manipulate the public.
10. Parties are marketed like high street commodities and we become disempowered consumers responding only to the images on the boxes.
11. The political message becomes less powerful than the projected image. At worst, this could be a means of subverting democracy.
12. A widespread lack of public interest in politics associated with a cynical evaluation of politicians in general.

Media and political parties, 1997 style

The 1997 general election campaigns witnessed the closest ever relationship between the media (especially but not exclusively television) and political party headquarters. The Labour campaign headquarters at Millbank and the Conservative Central Office were staffed around the clock, and the staff stayed in close contact with the political media professionals.

It was interesting that new technology also played a significant role in this election, with party headquarters using mobile phones, fax machines and e-mail to supply their constituency workers with up-to-date information. Furthermore each of the main parties provided an Internet website.

The Labour, Liberal Democrat and Conservative Parties each gave daily press conferences, which were broadcast live on Sky TV.

The state and the media

Another issue that is relevant to the topic of politics and the media is that of the role of the state in press and broadcasting. Although it is possible to view the media as part of the multinational, global market economy, it is clear that as they operate in the public domain they are accountable to the public at some level. After the Second World War there was the assumption of a 'free press', that is, free from direct government control and shaped by market forces. (Seymour-Ure, 1991). Broadcasting was also distanced from government control, so it seems that the government had a policy of 'no policy.' This did not mean, of course, that there was no government intervention in the press and broadcasting, but it was *ad hoc* and more concerned with the structure and organisation of the media than their content. Seymour-Ure sums up the intervention of government in media affairs in Britain as 'fragmented, compartmentalised and uneven' (ibid., p. 214).

So if government policy has been characterised by *ad hoc* intervention, how can the media be seen as accountable? Journalists have considerable autonomy, but within the confines of decision making by editors and the print unions. Journalists and broadcasters see themselves first and foremost as professionals, and therefore as self-regulating. The media also have to operate within legal restrictions that can act as an important restraint on broadcasters and journalists, although accountability remains narrowly defined.

Newspapers have no more legal right than any private citizen to do or say anything they like. The main legal controls are the Official Secrets Act (set up in 1911 and renewed in 1989), the Prevention of Terrorism Act of 1976, and laws concerning libel and contempt.

The Official Secrets Act

The Official Secrets Act, which was passed in 1911 as an antispy measure, prohibited any unauthorised passing on of information by anyone holding office under the crown, so all civil servants were bound by it. The new act of 1989 limited the scope of what is deemed as classified information, but the law of secrecy on civil servants remains. In 1984 Sarah Tisdall was imprisoned for six months for leaking to the *Guardian* newspaper a confidential memo from Michael Heseltine to Prime Minister Margaret Thatcher concerning the arrival in Britain of American cruise missiles. The *Guardian* was forced to disclose its source and she was convicted. In 1985 Clive Ponting, a civil servant in Heseltine's office, leaked information about the Falklands War. He too was prosecuted but subsequently acquitted. The Spycatcher incident, which ran from 1985 to 1988, highlighted the inconsistencies in the system. Peter Wright, a former MI5 agent, disclosed classified information in his book *Spycatcher, The Candid Autobiography of a Senior Intelligence Officer*. The British government tried to quash publication of the book in the USA and Australia, but it failed and the book went on general release in 1987.

In 1989 the new Official Secrets Act was passed. This was intended to prevent the disclosure of security or intelligence matters by current and past members of the security services, crown servants and government contractors. Importantly for the media, the Act also covers the disclosure of information by journalists, and if editors are believed to be encouraging their journalists to disclos information without lawful authority, they too are in breach of the law. Although the Act seemed to make freedom of information even less likely, in 1993 The Major government published a white paper, 'Open Government', which proposed a new Whitehall code of practice that would allow greater freedom of access to public information.

In 1992 the Scott Inquiry was set up to investigate 'the role of ministers in the sale of arms to Iraq and specifically, the alleged alterations of the guidelines and misinformation given to the House of Commons' (Allan *et al.*, 1994, p. 41).

Contempt of Court Act, 1981

This prevents journalists from publishing anything that might interfere with the outcome of a trial. The media are not allowed to be seen as taking sides, although there have been instances when the tabloids seemed to step outside these limits. 'Trial by Media' can prejudice a fair trial, but the law has also been seen as a means of preventing the legitimate dissemination and discussion of items of public interest.

Libel

The law of libel means that journalists can be sued for publishing anything that is defamatory; that is, damages or diminishes the reputation of an individual. Many cases have been brought against the tabloid press in recent years, but it is a costly business and usually available only to the rich. It is an interesting consequence of the increased invasion of privacy by the tabloid press during the 1980s that many more libel cases were taken out. Koo Stark, a one-time friend of Prince Andrew, brought eight successful actions in four years, including damages of £300 000 from the *People* in 1988 for alleging an adulterous affair with Prince Andrew. Also in 1988, Elton John agreed an out-of-court settlement of £1 million with the *Sun* for allegations against him, and in 1989 Sonia Sutcliffe, wife of Peter Sutcliffe, the 'Yorkshire Ripper', was awarded £600 000 against *Private Eye* magazine (the latter amount was reduced on appeal). There have been several more recent cases involving media personalities, including William Roache (Coronation Street's Ken Barlow)

D Notices

D Notices ('D' stands for defence) were set up after the 1911 Act as a form of guidance. D Notices are formal letters of warning or requests signed by the secretary of the Defence Press and Broadcasting Committee. Although a D Notice has no legal authority, being merely a voluntary restriction, it is supposed to protect the national interest. If an editor contravenes a notice, she or he may be liable to prosecution under the Official Secrets Act.

The Broadcasting Act 1990

This act introduced what was called the 'light touch regulation' of independent television (Channel 3). This effectively released Channel 3 from its public service obligation. Another major change was the requirement that the BBC and all other terrestrial broadcasters had to commission up to 25 per cent of their programmes from 'independent producers'.

Exercise 10.20

i Watch one evening's television on BBC1 and look at the credits at the end of each programme to find out who actually made them. How many are coproductions and how many are produced by the channel broadcasting the programme?

Collective self-regulation

The media themselves have created mechanisms to control media excesses and allow public opinion to be expressed:

The press council

This was set up in 1953 to address complaints against the press from the public, but it was an organisation with no real teeth. In 1991 it became the Press Complaints Commission and was required to tighten standards or be replaced by a statutory press council.

The broadcasting complaints commission

This was set up in 1981 as a body to which the public could complain if they believed they had been misrepresented or unfairly treated. It later became the Broadcasting Standards Council (BSC), which monitors complaints from the public and funds research projects on broadcasting. It is interesting to see who actually does complain. A survey was undertaken for the BSC by David Gauntlett (1995b) of the Institute of Communications Studies at Leeds University. He examined the profiles of 2215 people who had sent in letters of complaint about broadcasting. It was found that most of the complainants came from the south of England (46 per cent) and the majority were likely to be clergymen, teachers or retired forces personnel. They were divided equally by gender, but men were more likely to complain about 'bad language' and women about sex. A quarter of complaints focused on declining standards. The programmes that attracted the greatest number of complaints between July 1993 and December 1994 were 'East Enders' (47 letters), 'Cracker' (46), 'Jeremy Hardy Speaks to the Nation' (38) and 'Billy Connolly's World Tour of Scotland' (34).

Privacy laws, 1997

On 31 August 1997 Diana, Princess of Wales was killed in a car accident in Paris. On hearing the news of her death, the British media initially blamed the foreign paparazzi for chasing her car and causing the crash. However as more details emerged of the events leading up to the crash it became clear that several other factors were involved. Nonetheless the intrusion of the paparazzi into the private lives of members of the royal family, celebrities and ordinary members of the public became a matter for public concern. The tabloids themselves gave assurance that they would no longer use photographs purchased from freelance photographers. There already existed a Press Complaints Commission code of conduct, which limited intrusive photography, but there was a call for the introduction of more effective privacy legislation. The death of Diana, Princess of Wales brought to a head the escalating concern about privacy and the individual.

We might ask to what extent can public figures really expect to be free of media intrusion? Belsey (1992, p. 90) is opposed to privacy legislation: 'The British press is already too restricted by the repressive use of laws of official secrets, confidence, libel and contempt of court, and to add privacy to this list would be to invite further misuse of the law by public figures with something to hide.'

Exercise 10.21

Using the information on the state and regulation in this section, construct a Marxist and a pluralist response to the view that regulation of the media serves to maintain the interests of the powerful. You could complete the following grid.

Marxist	Pluralist
1. It serves to prevent serious investigation of the business affairs of individuals because of the constant threat of libel writs on journalists (e.g. Robert Maxwell's case).	1. A democratic society needs freedom of information and the press provide people with information that they need. A code of conduct is needed rather than legislation
2.	2. It is the role of the press to promote a fairer society – they should be free to investigate any abuse of power.
3.	3.

Examination focus

There are few direct questions on the role of the media and politics, but you could apply the material in this chapter to the following question.

Essay

'Critically examine the arguments and evidence which suggest that the content of the mass media is biased' (AEB, Summer 1992).

Mark scheme (knowledge and understanding)

4–6 marks   Towards the bottom of the mark band candidates will have presented an adequate account of one/two studies on bias in the media and/or on how the ownership of the media plays a role in this. Towards the top of the mark band candidates will have presented a more accurate and broader range of knowledge on the problematic nature of bias (for example whose definition, its ideological nature), perhaps with reference to contemporary examples (for example the debate on TV impartiality, the role of the tabloids, gender/race issues in the media).

7–9 marks   To obtain these marks candidates will have presented a detailed, accurate and coherent account of a range of studies within an appropriate theoretical framework drawn from the mass culture debate and/or the debate between Marxists and pluralists. The problematic nature of content bias may have been fully explored in terms of its relationship to the ownership of the media, media vocabulary and the ideology of 'content balance'.

As you can see from the mark scheme, the question is a broad one that could be answered in several different ways. You could use the material in Chapters 4 and 5 to examine the debate from a theoretical perspective. Chapter 7 on the representation of various groups by the media would also be useful. However it is also possible to examine the ways in which political ideas and politicians are represented by the media. Complete the question under examination conditions.

11 Globalisation, new technologies, new futures

By the end of this chapter you should:

- understand the concept of globalisation;
- be aware of competing theories of globalisation;
- understand the relationship between globalisation and cultural imperialism;
- be able to apply concepts of globalisation to the mass culture debate;
- be able to relate the debate about new technologies to the future of the media, both locally and globally;
- be able to answer an examination question on this topic.

Introduction

> People don't want nationalism or soil; they want satellites and Sony (Ohmae, 1991, p. 72).

So far we have analysed the media mainly from a national perspective, focusing primarily on the British media system. However it is no longer feasible to study the mass media solely from within the boundaries of our own nation-state. We now live in a society within a global system, therefore we are affected by global processes in our everyday lives. What we mean by this is that the world has 'shrunk'. From the comfort of our sofas we can be spectators of events as they happen across the globe. As well as this, we have become consumers of global products. As Giddens (1994) argues:

> The day-to-day actions of an individual today are globally consequential. My decision to purchase a particular item of clothing, for example, or a specific type of food-stuff, has manifold global implications. It not only affects the livelihood of someone living on the other side of the world but may contribute to a process of ecological decay which itself has potential consequences for the whole of humanity.

Globalisation has been defined in various ways. Bilton *et al.* (1996, p. 54) see it as 'the process whereby political, social and cultural relations increasingly take on a global scale, and which has profound consequences for individuals' local experiences and everyday lives'.

This chapter will start by examining the process of globalisation and the role of the media in its development, and will end by focusing on the possible future of the media.

What is globalisation?

Exercise 11.1

This simple exercise tests the evidence for globalisation in your own life.

[i] 1. Go to your wardrobe and check the labels on your clothes. Which countries did they originate from. (You might be surprised that clothes you thought were British were actually manufactured in another country.)

[a] 2. You can do the same with food. Think of your local town or city; how many different types of restaurant can you list?

Some social analysts maintain that globalisation has been one of the most significant changes to have taken place over the last thirty years and its impact has been felt by individuals and nations world-wide. As well as being an important concept used by sociologists, economists, geographers and political scientists, it has also become a 'buzzword' among media professionals and appears regularly in the press.

Exercise 11.2

[i] 1. If your school or college has the *Guardian* and *The Times* CD-ROM disks for the current year, note down the number of articles per month in which the term 'globalisation' appears.

[i][a] 2. Produce a bar chart of the frequency of the term's appearances over a year.

[i] 3. Are there any differences between the newspapers? If so, what are they?

[e] 4. What are the limitations of quantitative data such as this to a sociologist?

There is general agreement among sociologists that globalisation is taking place. However there is considerable disagreement over its possible consequences. Some who take an optimistic approach see globalisation as having many benefits, especially in empowering local communities to produce their own media products.

However, writers who take a more Marxist standpoint link globalisation with cultural imperialism and the 'Americanisation' of culture. We will examine this debate at a later point in the chapter, but first it is important to see how the process of globalisation has come about.

The development of globalisation

As Giddens (1997, pp. 63–4) says, 'The global system is not just an environment within which particular societies – like Britain – develop and change. The social, political and economic connections which cross-cut borders between countries decisively condition the fate of those living within each of them.' Welsh (1997) suggests that the following factors are important in the development of globalisation:

- The increasingly global nature of capital and the rise of global markets.
- The increasing global movement of people.
- The increasing importance of information technology in production, consumption and leisure.
- The increasing awareness of environmental issues that affect the whole planet.
- A growing awareness that politics has stretched beyond the nation-state.

We can see then that globalisation fundamentally affects three areas of society. Firstly, in the *economic sphere* there has been a tremendous intensification of economic competition around the production, exchange, distribution and consumption of goods and services. Markets have become global and economists refer to the 'global market place'. The increasing importance of the global economy has emerged from changes in the role of the state and an increased emphasis on the free-market economy.

Until the 1970s the state played a considerable role in the British economy. However in the early 1970s there were a number of economic crises, and new right politicians and economists argued that a major cause of the crises was the overinvolvement of the state in economic affairs. In the 1980s the Conservative government, under Margaret Thatcher, aggressively promoted free-market economic policies.

> In response to the economic crisis and the fall-off in profitability in the advanced industrial economies, capitalist corporations began to seek profitable returns in new areas. This led to a growth in foreign investment and the idea of global production. . . . Large amounts of money looking for profitable investment could now be moved around the world much more easily (Kirby, 1996, p. 165).

Secondly, the globalisation process affects the *political sphere*. It is interesting to note that globalisation can have two consequences as far as nationalism is concerned. First, as we have said, the promotion of global capitalism may weaker national boundaries. Second, nationalism may actually be strengthened as a result of globalisation. In this case nationalism can be understood as a return to a respect for 'local' roots. Nationalism can become a form of resistance against the tide of globalisation and modernisation: 'For example, Islamic movements in the world, and the Euro-sceptics in the UK, can both be viewed as presenting forms of resistance which contain their own distinct form of anti-modernity' (Best, 1996, p. 9).

The third area we will concentrate upon is the relationship between globalisation and *culture*. This will involve us in an examination of the debate about the consequences of globalisation on local cultures and identities and the extent to which media imperialism has occurred.

It is not possible to enter into a meaningful debate about globalisation without referring to the development and impact of transnational corporations (TNCs). These are gigantic corporations such as IBM, News International, Coca Cola, Pepsi, Sony, Lever, Volkswagen and Ford which originated in the USA, Japan and Europe but their markets and operations are now world-wide. The assets and annual sales of these corporations are so substantial that they exceed the gross national product (GNP) of many countries (Sklair, 1993). The business activities and interests, corporate strategies and work forces are global rather than restricted to one nation. The economic and political power wielded by them means that capitalism is no longer simply a system where nations intract – these corporations operate beyond the boundaries of nation-states. They shape both internal relations and national divisions of labour.

The 'British' car industry is an example of transnational corporations at work. Ford and Vauxhall are both owned by US companies. Rover is owned by BMW, which is German. Ford also owns Jaguar, and the largest exporter of cars from Britain is the Japanese company Nissan.

Cultural dimensions of globalisation

In recent decades there has been a revolution in communication systems. Thirty years ago it was not envisaged that the introduction of satellite broadcasting for military use would herald satellite television broadcasting as a global entertainment medium. Other new technologies such as cable and information communication technology have transformed the scope of the mass media. Mass media industries have become global enterprises. This expansion is evident both in the scale of audiences and the concentration of global media ownership. We saw in Chapter 4 that the media is 'big business', what may have surprised you is the extent to which media industries are dominated by so few major players (for a quick revision refer to p. 22 and reexamine Murdoch's global media empire).

The globalisation of the mass media clearly raises concerns in terms of ownership and control, hegemony, and the impact of First World and Third World relationships. With the massive expansion of transnational corporations and related advertising, it is now possible to recognise and purchase products such as Coca Cola, Levi jeans, Mars bars and McDonald's burgers world-wide. Theoretically, it must now also be possible to travel round the world and never have to eat indigenous food. What Ritzer (1993) terms 'McDonaldisation' means that both the decor and the menu are immediately recognisable in whatever country we find ourselves. This can be reassuring, because it is familiar, but it may also be evidence of a decline in local cultures.

Exercise 11.3

Have you spent a holiday in a foreign country? If you have:

 1. How easy was it to find restaurants that served British or English food?

 2. What does this tell you about the impact of tourism?

As well as food, media products such as films are distributed globally. Films such as 'Jurassic Park', 'Superman', 'Independence Day' and 'Star Wars' were global box office hits. The rerelease of the latter in 1997 was tipped to go global for the second time around. However it does not necessarily follow that the availability and world-wide popularity of goods and media products from transnational corporations will lead to the globalisation of culture, as we shall see.

A global culture?

Waters (1995, p. 145) outlines what he sees as major signs of a global culture. For him these are inextricably linked to technological change.

1. Miniaturisation: this refers to a reduction in the size of media-related machines, partly in connection with Japanese design criteria. Sony became the first effective miniaturiser when it bought the patents for the transistor radio, which was actually an American invention. The trend also applies to cassette players, CD players, TVs, computers, mobile phones and so on.
2. Personalisation: historically we have seen a general reduction in the size of the audience – from theatre audiences, to families for television, and individuals for personal computers (including lap-tops) and personal 'Walkman' headsets.
3. Integration: here various technologies become integrated as they are centred on the development of the microchip.

4. Diffusion: access to mass media technologies is becoming widespread with regard to reception and transmission. As a consequence of cheaper receivers and technological advances in space and fibre-optics, increasing numbers of people have access to media products and are faced with an increasing range of choice. It is clear that it has become impossible to retain national sovereignty in terms of satellite television reception.

5. Autonomisation: concern about passive audiences has risen as more and more people gain access to cable and satellite TV. Although there is increased 'talk-back' capacity via telephones and interactive PCs and the production of home-produced media via VCRs and camcorders, there is also a fear that individuals are becoming relatively passive players seated in front of their monitor screens.

Globalisation and cultural imperialism

Almost all of this technology is the product of advanced capitalist societies, as is much of the content, and Waters (1995) argues that this is having important effects on globalisation and culture:

- It exports the ideology of consumerism. For example advertising sells an idealised Western life-style as well as sex and status, as exemplified in the song 'I'd like to buy the world a Coke'. Capitalism and consumerism are presented unquestionably as ideal systems.
- National boundaries are dissolving as we increasingly learn to look at the world through global spectacles. For example, during the Gulf War we were able to witness the unfolding events from the safety of our armchairs: 'when an American fighter pilot bombs a building in Baghdad we are there with her seeing what she sees and war becomes a spectacle' (ibid., p. 149).
- The world is becoming media-saturated and we are able to experience world events simultaneously: 'The demolition of the Berlin Wall, a major political event becomes a rock concert; the Olympic Games expands its range of sports to include artistic rather than athletic events (rhythmic gymnastics, synchronised swimming, free-style skiing) in order to reach a wider global audience; These media events are . . . deliberately constructed as stylised mass entertainments and they are, in Durkheimian terms, collective representations of global commitments to democracy, consumption, capitalism and liberal tolerance of diversity' (ibid.)
- They connect people separated by great distances into communities of interest or value-commitment, producing simulated communities.

Exercise 11.4

As part of compiling a glossary of key concepts, you will find the following terms very useful. Learn them and get a friend to test you on them.

- **Imperialism** refers to domination by one nation over another. It is often used to describe the form of rule by Western powers in the late nineteenth and early twentieth centuries over foreign countries and peoples, as, for example, in the colonial rule of the British Raj in India.
- **Cultural imperialism** is 'the aggressive promotion of Western culture, based on the assumption that its value system is superior and preferable to those of non-western cultures' (Bilton *et al.*, 1996, p. 656).
- **Media imperialism**: 'The process whereby the ownership, structure, distribution or content of the media in any one country are . . . subject to substantial external pressures from the media interests of any other country or countries without proportionate reciprocation of influence by the country so affected' (Boyd-Barrett, 1977, p. 117).

Globalisation and sport – a case study: the World Cup 1994

Sport has not been exempt from the process of globalisation. In fact many commentators consider that sport exemplifies the globalisation process. The 1994 World Cup football championship, held in the USA, demonstrated the power of transnational corporations. It seems paradoxical that the venue should have been the USA – the only major country in the world without a national football league had been awarded the accolade of hosting the World Cup championships. However, as Wagg (1995) points out, the prerequisite was not a 'thriving national association football culture', but rather a 'thriving commercial culture. . . . Its business was business, especially show business.'

ITEM A

According to Wagg (1995) Joao Havelange's position as president of FIFA from 1974 has affected the cultural history of international football:

'Havelange . . . opened the way for a massive commercialising of the game internationally. . . . Under Havelange, FIFA, like the International Olympic Committee and, indeed, all sports administrative bodies of any size, has become primarily a franchising body, licensing entrepreneurs to trade on its own activities (for example, to broadcast the matches under its jurisdiction) and commodifying its own authority – as, for instance, in designating its sponsors the "official World Cup airline", "the official World Cup soft drink", "the official World Cup chocolate bar", and so on. As a consequence, the financial power of FIFA, as stewards of the world's most popular spectator sport, is now enormous.

The interplay between these political and commercial strategies has been crucial during the time of the Havelange regime, and there is little doubt that, in determining the course that international football culture has taken, commercial factors now greatly outweigh considerations of the "passion" for the game that may be felt among the people of poorer nations.'

Exercise 11.5

i The 1996 World Cup also brought 'official' commodities to our screens, for example Coke Cola and Adidas. Examine the televising of any major international sports event, for example a golf tournament or Formula One racing, and see which products are given prominence.

To return to the debate about cultural imperialism, some writers take an optimistic view whilst others adopt a much more pessimistic position on the impact and influence of globalisation. Some writers perceive it negatively as having accentuated the unequal relationships between nations, enlarging the gulf between rich and poor nations. The central assumption for those who argue that cultural imperialism has taken place is that the Western, or specifically American, cultural value system of consumerism and individualism has been exported to other countries, especially countries in the Third World that are new to media technologies. The flow of international communication has therefore followed the contours of power created by the Western transnational corporations.

More and more people across the globe are receiving the same message from the same centres of communication power. Thus it is assumed that local and indigenous cultures are being undermined or eroded. Hamelink (1995) shares this view. He sees an 'information imbalance' between the core – rich industrialised nations such as the USA, Japan, Western Europe an countries and Australia – and the periphery, including the continents of Africa, Asia and Latin America. This imbalance is multifaceted. It may refer to access to new technology – hardware and software; it may refer to information capacity – the ability to produce, record, process and distribute information; and it may refer to different forms of information – scientific and cominercial, financial and commercial, military, political and current affairs.

His argument is supported by Massey (1993), who sees inequality in power relationships. On the one side are the 'jet-setters, the ones sending and receiving the faxes and the e-mail, holding the international conference calls, controlling the news, organizing the investments and the international currency transactions', whilst on the other side are 'the refugees from El Salvador or Guatemala and the undocumented migrant workers from Michoacan in Mexico crowding into Tijuana to make perhaps a fatal dash for it across the border into the USA to grab the chance of a new life' (ibid., pp. 61–2).

This approach prioritises the cultural over the political and the economic, it presents the existence of a global society as a possibility or indeed a reality. Sreberny-Mohammadi (1991, p. 120) rejects the views of the more pessimistic writers on globalisation and culture, even though she recognises that they allow us to see 'global dynamics and relationships, taking their cue from much older models of imperialism, and the suggested linkages between foreign policy interests, capitalist expansion and media infrastructures and contents'.

Some arguments against the existence of cultural imperialism

The global situation is constantly changing. Developing countries such as China are currently improving their manufacturing capability and are themselves producing information hardware. For example China has been rapidly catching up and is one of the largest producers of television sets, and other countries are increasingly engaged in producing information hardware. Nonetheless it is important to establish whether individual or national identities can survive in the face of a supposed global cultural onslaught.

Smith (1990) takes the position that global culture is a contradiction in terms. For him, cultures must be rooted in a sense of community, history and heritage – a 'global culture' would be universal and rootless. Globalisation actually allows for the renewal of local traditions and cultural practices.

Dowmunt (1993) also argues that 'there is no single, homogenised, global village'. For him, the factor that more than any other explodes the concept of a unified 'global village' is economic inequality: 'in Africa and other areas of the "south" the cost of a receiver [TV] is beyond the means of the average income, and television ownership in many countries in the world is confined to city-dwellers with a higher than average income' (ibid., p. 2).

Sepstrup (1989) has also warned against assuming cultural effects:

The process of global flow is shaped and modified by many factors. Differences or affinities of language and culture between partners to any exchange can either discourage or encourage flow. The media production capacity and relative wealth of national media systems are also relevant, since poorer countries are more vulnerable to foreign media reception, and vice versa.

Exercise 11.6

 Write a paragraph outlining the extent to which the arguments against cultural imperialism are justified.

Globalisation and local empowerment

Giddens (1990) has a relatively optimistic view of globalisation and its consequences. He defines globalisation as the intensification of world-wide social relations which link distant localities in such a way that local events are shaped by events occurring many miles away and vice versa. It is the addition of 'vice versa' that is so important here, because he sees the local situation as having an effect on the global one, so the process is not simply one-way.

Sreberny-Mohammadi (1991, p. 121) clearly shares this viewpoint. She maintains that the 'global culture' argument is historically dated as, in 1990, 'it is clear that the international media environment is far more complex than that suggested by the "cultural imperialism" model whose depiction of a hegemonic media pied piper leading the global mice, appears frozen in the realities of the 1970s, now a bygone era'.

We would argue that the model of cultural imperialism is also dated in terms of its implied media effects on audiences. Paradoxically, at a time when the conventional wisdom of audience research in Britain and Europe is that audiences are active negotiators of media texts, it is ironic if not a little patronising to assume that Third World audiences are passive recipients of powerful Western media messages. To us, this assumption resonates strongly with the argument expressed in earlier years about the vulnerability of children and young people to media influence (see Chapter 9 for a review of the media effects models). We have argued that media texts may have many layers of meanings, so the producers of these texts cannot possibly guarantee how they will be read by global audiences. The concept of agency is important here: viewers or consumers of the text have the ability to interpret and reinterpret messages according their specific subjectivities.

Some writers also assert that globalisation actually opens up a 'cosmopolitanism' that brings tolerance of cultural difference in its wake. We do wonder, however, what is cosmopolitan about drinking British beer and eating fish and chips in a Spanish holiday resort?

Link exercise 11.7

Using the information in this chapter and in Chapter 9 on audiences, answer the following questions and fill in the missing words:

ku

1. What does the term subjectivity mean?

i

2. Two examples of subjectivities that affect the way a person interprets a media text are . . . . and . . . .

i

3. The study of signs and symbols is called . . . .

i

4. The media effects model that sees the viewer as an independent reader is called . . . .

5. Name three strengths of the approach that you identified in question 4.

Missing words:

- semiology
- reception analysis
- gender
- age
- ethnicity

Case studies of globalisation

Various ethnographic studies have examined the impact of the global on the local. The examples below demonstrate some of the positive effects of communication technology, but it is important to remember that we have chosen only a small selection of studies and the process of globalisation is dynamic.

India

The mass media system in India has steadily expanded during the last 40 years to become the largest in the world. Radio has an almost nation-wide reach, and TV signals reach 70 per cent of the country. There are 30 million radio sets, 7.8 million TVs, half a million VCRs and 20 thousand newspapers (1334 of which are dailies) with a combined circulation of 55 million copies (1985). India produces approximately 760 films per year.

However there are marked disparities between areas. Mass media in India is urban-based and largely caters for the middle and upper classes. As stated above, television signals read 70 per cent of the population, but viewing is limited to about 12.2 per cent with 'convenient access' (Yadava and Reddi,1988, p. 123).

Neena Behl (1988) spent a year in a rural village that was in the process of urbanisation. Her study was ethnographic and she charted the introduction of television into the village and its impact on village life. She found that the mere presence of television affected the use of time by the villagers. In the traditional way of life the day was divided into four periods: predawn, sunup, dusk and night. The first involved preparing for the day, with women rising early to make tea for themselves and the men. Sunup started the work-day proper, dusk was the time to prepare for the night, while the night was the time for evaluation and preparation for the following day. However the introduction of television changed nighttime into television time, with significant implications for the lives of women in the village: 'The object of orientation of their lives has shifted from the absolute demands that men make upon them to the demands that TV makes of them. Not only are cooking habits and menus changing, but orientation to the TV set as a cultural object frees them from the control of men' (Behl, 1988).

The TV set was placed in the women's quarters not the men's, to signify its central importance in the household. This meant that men and women spent more time together than they did previously. She saw this as facilitating communication and providing the means for the villagers to get to know each other better. Some of the young women had become more aware of personal appearance and hairstyles had been copied from the TV.

Yadava and Reddi (1988) saw changes taking place in urban India too as a result of the introduction of new media. Television remained largely urban-based and restricted to middle and upper social groups. In some towns and cities the television set had become a status symbol. Often neighbours and friends would drop by to watch programmes with a family that owned a set. Yadava and Reddi found that the TV had brought changes to the urban family, but changes that in their view were positive. As one interviewee said, 'All family members get together at 7 pm and enter the home instead of going anywhere. I think this is good for the family.'

Australia and New Zealand

What of the spread of global TV on aboriginal culture? Today there are many different aboriginal TV 'styles'. Some have taken an oppositional stance, some have used the technology to strengthen their traditional culture, some want to take part-ownership shares, and others want representation. Batty (1993) relates the story of two different responses to new media by two Aboriginal communities.

Ernabella is a remote community in South Australia and home to the Pitjantjatarra tribe, who lived a relatively traditional life-style, had won land rights and ran a well-organised community. They prepared well for the arrival of satellite TV owing to their concern about what they had seen on video cassettes. They set up a media committee to monitor developments and started the Ernabella Video Project in 1983. Recording local events became very popular and it became the *de facto* video channel. It was also used to induct young people into the ways of the ancestors – with stories of the aboriginal 'Dreamtine'. The experience engendered a 'kind of local renaissance in traditional dance, performance and singing' (ibid., p. 113). EVTV also overcame funding difficulties and set up its own TV station. It purchased a satellite dish and selectively rebroadcast satellite material.

However the same success was not enjoyed by the Central Australian Aboriginal Media Association (CAAMA). When it was set up in 1985 it merely wanted to gain access to the new satellite service in order to provide 'culturally appropriate TV programming' for the aboriginal population of the Northern Territory. However it was on successful in warding off commercial pressure and the TV station became a typical commercial station that happened to be Aboriginal-owned.

The situation is different for Maoris in New Zealand, as Derek Tini Fox (1993) shows in *Honoring the Treaty*. Maoris make up 25–30 per cent of the population, but TV programmes for the Maori community take up less than 1 per cent of total air-time and the Maori language is given limited radio time.

The Maoris are pressing for a large stake in the national broadcasting system. Although there is some growth in support for local, tribal TV stations, the main demand is for greater representation.

North Africa: Egypt and Morocco

A study by Abu-Lughod (1990) examined the impact of tape recorders, radios and television on Bedouin people of the Western Desert. She found that the new media technology served to bring people together for long periods and realigned social relationships. Rather than crushing the Bedouin identity, the new media actually revitalised Bedouin culture rather than subsuming it under Egyptian culture, especially through poetry and song. However soap operas portraying Egyptian urban middle-class life revealed new options to Bedouin women, 'specially the possibility of marrying for love and living independent of the extended family, so that the dominant Egyptian mediated culture is used as a language of resistance against the authority of the tribal elders' (quoted in Sreberny-Mohammadi, 1991, p. 132).

Hannah Davis (1990) who studied a small Moroccan agricultural town, found that pictures of the king hung alongside pictures of the Beatles. According to Davies:

> public space is male space, and thus it is the women who crowd around the television and the VCR at night watching Egyptian, Indian and French films ... the transcultural mix of symbols is apparent when one young girl organises a traditional religious feast yet defiantly appears wearing a denim skirt and earrings; thus, such symbols may be used in personal struggles to define, test or transform the boundaries of local lives (quoted in Sreberny-Mohammadi, 1991, p. 133).

Exercise 11.8

 You may have come across case studies as a research method in your work on methodology. We have used some examples of media influence as case studies in this section, what do you see as the strengths and limitations of using case studies in sociological research? We have started the list for you.

Strengths	Limitations
1. They allow in-depth analysis of a micro area	1. They may be completely unrepresentative of other such areas
2. They support an interpretivist approach	2. They are unreliable and unrepeatable
3.	3.
4.	4.

Hybridity – fish and chips with curry sauce?

The mass media might be seen as helping the process of cultural growth, diffusion, invention and creativity, but there is increasing evidence of 'resistance' by receiving nations. Lull and Wallis (1992) use term 'transculturation' to describe the process of 'mediated cultural interaction' in which Vietnamese music was crossed with North American music to produce a new blend. In the UK music industry the term 'crossover hit' is used when one generic product is accepted into another genre (Branston and Stafford, 1996, p. 145).

Another term that is gaining currency is 'hybridity'. This is frequently used in the context of art and music for products that reflect different cultural influences. For example 'Salma and Sabine are Pakistani sisters who sing Abba songs in Hindi; Rasta-Cymm is a Welsh speaking reggae band and El Vez is a Latino Elvis impersonator with attitude'. These are examples used by Robins (1997) to illustrate hybridity within and between cultures.

Exercise 11.9

1. Think of examples of contemporary music styles that can be said to reflect 'hybridity'.
2. To what extent is hybridity a useful concept to describe current trends in popular music? Try to answer this question in 150 words.

Conclusions: is there a global media culture?

Globalisation may lead to a more homogenised culture. For Hamelink (1983, p. 22) the process of homogenisation 'implies that the decisions regarding the cultural development of a given country are made in accordance with the interests and needs of a powerful central nation and imposed with subtle but devastating effectiveness without regard for the adaptive necessities of the dependant nation'. We can see, then, that there are two contradictory trends at work both globally and nationally: towards cohesion or towards fragmentation. Globalisation can promote both, it depends on the context.

Media content can be understood and interpreted in many different ways by audiences, so that the fear of potential cultural damage from transnationalised media cultural products may well be exaggerated. However we do not know whether the same status is given to all readings.

A global media culture is likely to embody many Western capitalist values such as the free market, consumerism, individualism and commercialism. Discovering how these values are received and appropriated by global audiences needs systematic research. Globalisation is a dynamic process and the media world changes daily. New mergers occur, more resistance is generated. It is important for you to monitor events and to keep as up to date as possible with new developments.

Exercise 11.10

 We have divided the arguments about globalisation into those that are supportive and those that are critical of the process. What we would like you to do is find an appropriate example for each of the following statements, using material from this chapter and/or your sociology textbook. The evidence could be in the form of a theory, a study, an event or a quotation. This exercise will test your interpretation and application skills. We have done the first two for you.

Supportive arguments

- The mass media spreads 'modernity' and democracy – this was a prevalent view in the 1950s and 1960s.
  Example: this idea emerged from sociological theories of modernisation.
- Global communication may extend the shared symbolic space, helping to liberate people from the constraints of time and place.
  Example: the Internet.
- It may be culturally enriching
- It may challenge the xenophobia, ethnocentrism and nationalism of national systems.
- It may produce a 'new world order' of international peace and understanding now that the Cold War is over.

Critical arguments

- Fear has been expressed about the potential for US cultural imperialism (invasion and coercion). The main debate, then, relates to the interests of the poorer South against the developed North.
- Cultural identity – it has been suggested that European culture, and different national cultures within Europe, might be undermined by the importation of US-produced media.
- The ending of the division between East and West in Europe has produced a new division of haves and have-nots as regards the material resources upon which to build cultural identitiesl. This has also involved a more commercialised culture that is less controlled by national cultural policies.

- The ideologies of national cultures are undermined. However cultural imperialism is a complex concept and one that tends to ignore the rich diversity of Third World nations. Among this confusion, the impact of global cultural processes is unknown and unknowable.

New technologies: where do we go from here?

> Multimedia, the information superhighway and the Internet have changed our world almost beyond recognition. Electronic networks have revolutionised the human relationship to time and space, and have undermined national boundaries (Spender, 1995).

The difficulty with writing about new technology is that by its very nature it ceases to be 'new' very quickly. This raises problems for us as authors in that as soon as this book goes into print, this section will already be out of date. As students of the media you may even be using forms of media technology in your homes, schools and colleges that, as we write this final section, are not yet available.

In this section we have necessarily been selective and have chosen to examine the following 'new' technologies: satellite and cable, digital and roll-up television, multimedia the Internet. We shall also look at the social impact of these technologies, as far as can be ascertained at present.

Without question the 1980s and 1990s have witnessed a technological revolution as far as the media industries are concerned. This has affected information technology in particular and involved its production, distribution and access. For example with the arrival of the information superhighway, the buzzword of the 1990s, it was predicted that all homes would eventually be connected by fibre-optic cable. 'At the moment four separate technologies have separate electronic paths into the home: telephone, terrestrial broadcast, cable and satellite . . . in future all will travel down the same cable and have as their outlet a single computer/television' (Giddens, 1997). However we have no clear indication of when this will take place.

Satellite television: BSkyB

In 1982 News International acquired the majority shareholding in the pan-European Sky Channel and by March 1990 Sky could reach one million homes in Britain. In November 1990 it merged with British Satellite Broadcasting and became British Sky Broadcasting (BSkyB). By October 1995 the number of British homes receiving BSkyB, either by satellite dish or cable, had exceeded 4.5 million, or the equivalent of one in five homes.

How much do you know about BSkyB?

1. BSkyB is watched more by females than males: true/false.
2. More young people in the 4–15 age group watch satellite TV than ITV: true/false.
3. Fewer ABC1 homes own satellite TV than do C2 homes: true/false.
4. Homes with children are more likely to have satellite TV: true/false.

(Answers at the end of the chapter.)

Roll-up TV

One of the latest developments in media technology is flat-screen television. British military research scientists at the Defence Evaluation and Research Agency (DERA) have produced a flat TV screen that is capable of being rolled up like a map. This breakthrough may revolutionise home viewing by replacing bulky, fragile TV sets with screens that can be hung on walls.

At present the cost of such screens is very high (around £1–2000), but Canon has already unveiled a thin screen based on ferroelectric liquid crystals rather than the cathode-ray tube. It is assumed that some day soon the walls of many homes will be adorned with such screens, which will be able to display images when not receiving TV programmes.

Digital media

We are currently moving into the digital age, which is heralded by some writers as the greatest technological innovation since the introduction of the printing press. What does digital mean? To be brief, the difference between analogue (the current broad casting system) and digital is that the former relies upon 'recording and storing or displaying information in a suitable form, after first converting measurements from their original form. In this way, what is mediated by the device is an "analogy" of the real thing' (Branston and Stafford, 1996, p. 186). Digital technology relates only to numbers, so all information is translated into numerical data.

The first media technology to use the digital method was the compact disc. With the introduction of digital television, the audiences will be offered a picture of cinema quality. The analogue signal is made up of 625 scan lines – this is almost half what the digital screen can hold, so with digital broadcasting the image we see will be much sharper. Furthermore digital signals can be compressed, which means that many more channels can be broadcast than at present. The signals for digital television will be transmitted to TV aerials, satellite dishes or cable TV, but they will need to be decoded by a small computer box situated on the TV receiver. This has consequences for the debate on ownership and control because the company that controls the rights to the decoding hardware is likely to be a part of a megacorporation.

Digital data will play an extremely important role in the future. Digitisation allows for the combination of different media technologies (for example image, text, graphics, animation and sound) into a single medium – what is known as multimedia (Negroponte, 1995).

Multimedia resources

Multimedia resources store data in digitised form on either hard disk or compact disc. This makes it possible, for example, to link animations to static diagrams, to link a clip of video to a descriptive paragraph, and to link an audio recording to words or pictures.

Negroponte (1995) predicts that the personal computer will expand to become a television set as well as an 'electronic gateway' for cable, satellite and telephone. The multimedia capability of computers will be dramatically expanded, allowing a far greater degree of interactive involvement by the users.

Competition for digital television

Digitalisation is predicted to change the face of television and again will affect ownership and control. As an example of this, during the spring of 1997, two rival consortia were competing for the contract from the Independent Television Commission to bring digital television to Britain. The first, British Digital Broadcasting, is a consortium of BSkyB, Carlton, Granada and the BBC. The second, Digital Television Network, is owned by a leading cable operator, International Cable Tel, together with Turner and ITN. They proposed very different programming for the new system.

ITEM B

Channels offered by British digital broadcasting

- Sky Movies – already available on satellite and cable.
- Movie Channel – as above.
- Sky Sports – existing channel.
- Carlton Select – already available, mainly reruns.
- Granada Plus – already available, archive reruns.
- Granada Good Life – already exists, lifestyle programmes.

- Carlton films – new movie channel.
- Carlton Entertainment – new channel for light entertainment.
- Granada Sports Club – sports (but not live), features and news-based programmes.
- Granada Shopping Channel – home-shopping from TV.
- BBC Channels – a mixture of mainly archive programmes.

Channels offered by digital television network

Twenty-three channels, 19 interactive and information services. The channels include the following:

- Money channel (together with the Consumers' Association).
- Knowledge network – mainly educational channel to 'encourage learning'.

- British Sports Channel – new and unusual sports.
- Metro TV – network of local city-based stations for local communities.
- Plus natural history station, music station, Cartoon Network, pay-per-view movies, Hindi station and so on.

Exercise 11.12

Using information in Items B and C and elsewhere:

 1. On the basis of what you already know about ownership patterns in the media, which consortium was most likely to with the contract?

 2. What reasons can you give for your answer?

 3. Refer back to Chapter 3, then describe how manipulationist Marxists would use the material in Items B and C to support their arguments about ownership and control?

The internet

The birth of the Internet goes back thirty years. It was initially part of a US military project to set up communication links that, theoretically at least, would survive a large-scale war. As a response to the launching of the first Soviet satellite, Sputnik, into space in 1957, the US government set up the Advanced Research Projects Agency (ARPA). This agency was given a brief to develop new technologies. With the Cold War still affecting relation between the USA and the Soviet Union, the US government was fearful that the immense amount of data stored electronically at ARPA was vulnerable. If there were a full-scale war, then some form of information network would be less vulnerable than isolated computer units. So in 1969 the ARPAnet was set up to investigate the possibility of setting up a computer network using satellites, telephone lines and radio technology.

In the 1980s the National Science Foundation (NSF) developed the NSFnet by linking five university supercomputers. 'Between 1984 and 1988 the number of host computers on the Internet grew from 1000 to 60 000. In 1990 the US government decided that the Internet was far too important to be controlled by the military. Administration of the net passed to the NSF which now looks after the "backbone" of the Internet' (*Guardian Education*, 1 January 1996).

Today the Internet is an information resource in many schools and homes, and has important implications for the business community. It is now possible for international conferences to take place across the Internet, so that delegates are able to join in conferences without the need to travel from their home countries.

A major part of the Internet is the World Wide Web. Indeed, like a cuckoo in a nest, it threatens to take over its host. The Web is in effect a global multimedia library ... How many people are actually connected to the Internet is unknown. It is thought there are some 35 million people on line throughout the world. In terms of global population as a whole, the number is not large – but it is as big as a medium-size country. More important is its rate of expansion. It has been estimated that the Internet has grown at a rate of 200 per cent annually since 1985 (Giddens,1997, p. 394).

Exercise 11.13

Write a brief description of each of the following:

- Cyber cafe
- Internet provider
- electronic mail
- Modem
- World Wide Web

The social impact of new technology

Where discussing the social impact of new technology it is important to note that much of the technology is not that 'new'. Cable has been around since the 1930s and satellite since the 1960s. However, what is new is their availability and the speed of their take-up. Not surprisingly, social commentators have responded differently to the likely impact of new technology on society.

Raymond Williams (1974, p. 151) for instance, speculated that these new technologies might produce 'locally based yet internationally extended television systems' that would transcend national media institutions such as the BBC, but he was more guarded in his views about the power of the 'para-national corporations' that are likely to control the technology and override national democracies.

Other commenters, like Garnham, viewed the proliferation of television channels not as a response to consumer demand but as a result both of the search of multi-national hardware manufacturers for new markets, and of the industrial and financial strategies of various governments (Garnham, 1986).

Interactive TV

It seems very likely that we shall all be engaging with interactive TV early in the twenty-first century. This has important consequences for sociologists predicting future outcomes. We need to ask what these new media products will be and whether we as audiences will be divided into 'media-rich' and 'media-poor'. It is possible, in the worst case scenario, that we shall all be home-workers based in front of computer terminals – irrespective of whether we are students, teachers, shoppers religious leaders and so on our daily lives will be dominated by our homes as work-stations. This will have important social consequences for communities in towns and cities as well as the workforce as a whole.

Computers

Although the expansion of the computer industry has been extremely rapid, access to computer technology remains unequal. Information technology is still only available to a small percentage of the global population. Many homes across the world have no electricity and half the people in the world have never made a phone call. Information inequality is closely related to economic inequality. Access to computers is unequal both within and between countries. It is estimated that 43 per cent of Americans have never used a computer, and only 31 per cent of the population own one. Computer use is dominated by the middle-class.

The Internet

There is a close correlation between high income and use of the Internet. A survey of the users of the World Wide Web found that half of American Internet users have annual household incomes of more than $50 000 and 25 per cent have incomes above $80 000. It is interesting that men are twice as likely to be Web users than women. Far from reducing traditional inequalities in power and knowledge, it seems that access to the Web may provide yet more advantages for those who are already privileged holders of 'cultural capital'.

Exercise 11.14

Undertake a survey of students' use of computers and the Internet at your school or college. You may need to sample a percentage of different age groups and you could look at differences by gender as well.

 1. What method of sampling would be most appropriate for this survey?

 2. To what extent will your sample be a representative one?

3. What do you understand by the term 'second order construct'? How might it be relevant to the construction of your questionnaire?

3. Give three possible hypotheses that you could investigate in this area.

Regulation and surveillance

It seems likely that widespread broadcasting via the Internet will be with us in the early twenty-first century. This may ring alarm bells for many sociologists concerned with regulation and control. Existing legislative control is exercised over the Internet by the Independent Television Commission (ITC), but with the possibility of over 200 channels to monitor, it seems an impossible task. The Home Office has been working on a formula to control the Internet, however, as Bell (1996) argues:

> The decision to formalise rules may in any case be in vain. Unless it is possible to see who is putting up a site – which is easily disguised – it is impossible to place sanctions on them. If they are doing it from another country, it is particularly fruitless . . . A further consideration which will make broadcasters think about Internet distribution is globalisation. The global TV channel in the form of MTV or CNN already exists, but to achieve it involves negotiating carriage contracts with local cable or satellite companies, battling alongside competitors. One site on the Internet fits all.

New technology and the workforce

One of the consequences of the adoption of new technology by the media has been the impact it has had on staffing levels. Traditional typesetting crafts are no longer necessary as highly professional desk top publishing software packages have become available (you may have used some yourselves with some success). The introduction of computer software for the printing industry was the major cause of the industrial disputes during the 1980s between the print unions and proprietors Eddy Shah and Rupert Murdoch. This led to reduced staffing levels and journalists having to prepare their own copy for their newspapers. So workers became redundant, deskilled, and those who remained had to become multiskilled. The ultimate development may be automation, as has happened in some radio stations in the USA. The negative impact of new technology on staffing can be summarised as follows:

- There is a reduction in the need for specialist skills and an increase in generic computer skills.
- Redundancy and deskilling lead to loss of union power.

The following are three possible effects of new technology:

- People will be allowed greater choice. They can select the Internet a multiplicity of information and programming.
- Information will become freely available, copyright will cease.
- Control will be taken from the hands of governments as the quantity of information will become too large to control.

1. For each of the above factors, suggest at least one possible negative and one positive outcome of each effect.

2. In approximately 150 words, examine the extent to which the new media technologies have provided a greater opportunity to correct the information imbalance in societies.

Examination focus

To date there has not been a specific question on globalisation and the media. However questions have been asked about globalisation and development. We would like you to attempt the following questions using material from this chapter and Chapter 5.

1. Critically examine the contribution of theories of globalisation to the understanding of the role of the media in contemporary societies.
2. Globalisation is simply another term for cultural imperialism. (discuss with reference to sociological evidence).

Answers to exercise 11.11, p. 234

1. False: whilst terrestrial TV is skewed towards a mainly female audience, 56 per cent of Sky's audience is male.
2. True: 16 per cent compared with 13 per cent.
3. False: 46 per cent of ABC1 compared with 29 per cent of C2.
4. True: 45 per cent compared with 30 per cent of the rest.

References

Abbott, P. and C. Wallace (1996) *An Introduction to Sociology: Feminist Perspectives* (London and New York: Routledge).

Abu-Lughod, L. (1990) 'Bedouins, Cassettes and Technologies of Public Culture', *Middle East Report*, vol. 159, no. 4, pp. 7–12.

Adorno, T. (1991) *The Culture Industry* (London: Routledge).

Allan, P., J. Benyon and B. McCormick (1994) *Focus on Britain* (London: Perennial Publications).

Althusser, L. (1971) *Lenin and Philosphy and Other Essays* (London: New Left Books).

Alvarado, M., R. Gutch and T. Wollen (1987) *Learning the Media* (London: Macmillan).

Ang, I. (1985) *Watching Dallas* (London: Methuen).

Ang, I. (1991) *Desperately Seeking the Audience* (London: Routledge).

Axford, B. (1992) 'Leaders, Elections and Television', *Politics Review*, vol. 1 no. 3.

Back, L. and V. Quaade (1993) 'Dream Utopias, Nightmare Realities: Imaging Race and Culture within the World of Benetton Advertising', *Third Text*, no. 22 (Spring).

Baehr, H. and G. Dyer (eds) (1987) *Boxed In: Women and television* (London: Pandora).

Bandura, A. (1965) 'Vicarious Processes: A Case of No-Trial Learning' in L. Berkovitz (ed.), *Advances in Experimental Social Psychology*, vol. 2 (New York: Academic Press).

Bandura, A. and R. Walters (1963) *Social learning and Personality Development* (New York: Holt, Rinehart and Winston).

Barker, M. (1983) 'How Nasty are the Video Nasties?', *New Society*, 10 November.

Barker, M. (1997) 'The Newson Report: A Case-Study in "Common-Sense"', in M. Barker and J. Petley (eds), *Ill Effects: The Media/Violence Debate* (London and New York: Routledge).

Barnard, S. (1989) *On the Radio* (London and New York: Routledge).

Barratt, D. (1986) *Media Sociology* (London: Tavistock).

Batty, P. (1993) 'Singing the Electric: Aboriginal Television in Australia', in Dowmunt, 1993.

Baudrillard, J. (1983) *Simulations* (New York: Semiotext).

Behl, N. (1988) 'Equalizing Status: Television and Tradition in an Indian village', in J. Lull (ed.), *World Families Watch Television* (California, London and New York: Sage).

Bell, E. (1996) 'Media Coming Soon: Nightmare on the Net', *Observer*, 28 July.

Bellos, A. (1996) 'Dieting children choose wrong role models', *Guardian*, 28 March.

Belsey, A. (1992) 'Privacy, publicity and politics', in A. Belsey and R.

Chadwick (eds), *Ethical Issues in Journalism and the Media* (London and New York: Routledge).

Belson, W. (1978) *Television Violence and the Adolescent Boy* (Farnborough: Saxon House).

Ben-Yehuda, N. (1980) 'The European witch craze of the 14th to 17th centuries: a sociologist's perspective', *American Journal of Sociology*, vol. 86, no. 1.

Ben-Yehuda, N. (1985) *Deviance and Moral Boundaries: Witchcraft, the Occult, Science Fiction, Deviant Sciences and Scientists* (Chicago: University of Chicago Press).

Berelson, B. (1948) 'Communication and Public Opinion', in W. Schramm (ed.), *Communications in Modern Society* (Urbana, IL.: University of Illinois Press).

Berger, J. (1972) *Ways of Seeing* (London: BBC Pelican).

Berkowitz, L. (1962) *Aggression: A Social Psychological Analysis* (New York: McGraw-Hill).

Bilton, T. *et al.* (1996) *Introductory Sociology*, 3rd edn (Basingstoke and London: Macmillan).

Blumler, J. (1977) *The Political Effects of Mass Communications*, Open University course DE 353, Unit 8 (Milton Keynes: Open University).

Blumler, J. G. and D. McQuail (1968) *Television and Politics: Its Uses and Influence* (London: Faber and Faber).

Boyd-Barrett, O. (1977) 'Media Imperialism', in J. Curran (ed.), *Mass Communication and Society* (London: Edward Arnold).

Boyd-Barrett, O. and C. Newbold (eds) (1995) *Approaches to Media: A Reader* (London and New York: Arnold).

Branston, G. and R. Stafford (1996) *The Media Student's Book* (London: Routledge).

Bretl, D. and J. Cantor (1988) 'The portrayal of men and women in US television commercials', *Sex Roles*, vol. 18 (9/10).

Brown, J. D. and K. Campbell (1986) 'Race and Gender in Music Videos: The Same Beat but a Different Drummer', *Journal of Communication*, vol. 26.

Browne, K. (1994) *An Introduction to Sociology* (Cambridge: Polity Press).

Bruch, H. (1978) *The Golden Cage: the Enigma of Anorexia Nervosa* (Cambridge, Mass.: Harvard University Press).

Brunsdon, C. (1982) 'Crossroads: notes on soap opera', *Screen*, vol. 22, no. 4 (Society for Education Film Limited).

Brunsdon, C. (1984) 'Writing about soap opera', in L. Masterman (ed.), *Television Mythologies* (London: Comedia/MK Press).

Buckingham, D. (1987) *Public Secrets: EastEnders and its Audience* (London: BFI).

Buckingham, D. (1990) *Children Talking Television: The Making of Television Literacy* (London: Falmer Press).

Buckingham, D. (ed.) (1993) *Reading Audiences: Young People and the Media* (Manchester: Manchester University Press).

Butler, D. and D. Kavanagh (1988) *The British General Election 1987* (London: Macmillan).

Cantril, H. (1940) 'The Invasion from Mars' in T. O'Sullivan and Y. Jewkes (eds), *The Media Studies Reader* (London and New York: Arnold, 1997).

Cashmore, E. and B. Troyna (1990) *Introduction to Race Relations*, 2nd edn (London: The Falmer Press).

Cathcart, B. (1995) 'Sleaze: Nolan as Dirt Buster', *Independent on Sunday*, 23 July.

Chibnall, S. (1981) 'The production of knowledge by crime reporters', in S. Cohen and J. Young (eds), *The Manufacture of News* (London: Constable).

'ChildWise' (forthcoming) *The Lost Boys: Boys Retreat into Private Fantasy World*, report of a survey conducted by the SMRC ChildWise Monitor 1997.

Clarke, J. (1996) 'Gender and Education Revisited', *Sociology Review*, vol. 5, no. 4.

Clarke, J. (1997) 'Domestic Violence Revisited', *Sociology Review*, vol. 6, no. 4.

Cohen, S. (1972) *Folk Devils and Moral Panics: The Creation of the Mods and Rockers* (London: MacGibbon & Kee).

Connell, R. W. (1971) *The Child's Construction of Politics* (Melbourne: Melbourne University Press).

Coward, R. (1984) *Female Desire: Women's Sexuality Today* (London: Paladin).

Coward, R. (1987) 'Sexual Violence and Sexuality', Feminist Review (ed.), *Sexuality: A Reader* (London: Feminist Review/Virago).

Crace, J. (1996) *The Guardian*, Resources Section, 17 September.

Cumberbatch, G. (1989) 'Violence and the Mass Media: The Research Evidence', in G. Cumberbatch and D. Howitt, *A Measure of Uncertainty: The Effects of the Mass Media*, Broadcasting Standards Council Research Monograph (London: John Libbey).

Cumberbatch, G. (1997) 'Media Violence: Science and Common Sense', *Psychology Review*, April.

Cumberbatch, G. *et al.* (1990) *Television Advertising and Sex Role Stereotyping* (London: Broadcasting Standards Council).

Curran, J. (1996) 'Rethinking Mass Communications', in J. Curran, D. Morley and V. Walkerdine (eds), *Cultural Studies and Communications* (London and New York: Arnold).

Curran, J. and J. Seaton (1991) *Power Without Responsibility: The Press and Broadcasting in Britain*, 4th edn (London: Routledge).

Davis, H. (1990) 'American Magic in a Moroccan Town', *Middle East Report*, 159:19,4, pp. 12–18.

Deem, R. (1978) *Women and Schooling* (London: Routledge & Kegan Paul).

Dennis, N. and G. Erdos (1992) *Families without Fatherhood* (London: IEA Health and Welfare Unit).

Denscombe, M. (1993) *Sociology Update* (Leicester: Olympus Books).

Denscombe, M. (1996) *Sociology Update* (Leicester: Olympus Books).

Dominick J. and G. Rauch (1972) 'The Image of Women in Network TV Commercials', *Journal of Broadcasting*, vol. 16.

Dowmunt, T. (1993) 'Channels of Resistance', BFI/Ch 4, UK.

Dworkin, A (1980) 'Pornography and Grief', in L. Lederer (ed.), *Take Back the Night* (New York: William Morrow).

Dyer, R. (1993) *The Matter of Images: essays on representations* (London: Routledge).

Edwards, S. E. (1991) 'Photography and the Representation of the Other', *Third Text*, nos 16/17 (Autumn/Winter).

Elliott, P. (1977) 'Media organizations and occupations: an overview', in J. Curran *et al.* (eds), *Mass Communication and Society* (London: Edward Arnold).

Elliott, P. (1980) 'Press performance as political ritual', in H. Christian (ed.), *The Sociology of Journalism and the Press, Sociological Review* Monograph no. 29 (University of Keels).

Evans, H. (1984) quoted in Curran and Seaton (1991), p. 88.

Ferguson, M. (1983) *Forever Feminine: Women's Magazines and the Cult of Femininity* (London: Heinemann).

Feshbach, S. (1961) 'The stimulating vs. cathartic effects of a vicarious aggressive experience', *Journal of Abnormal and Social Psychology*, vol. 63, pp. 381–5.

Feshbach, S. and R. D. Singer (1971) *Television and Aggression: An Experimental Field Study* (San Francisco: Jossey-Bass).

Fiske, J. (1987) *Television Culture* (London: Methuen).

Franklin, R. (1994) *Packaging Politics. Political Communications in Britain's Media Democracy* (London: Edward Arnold).

Gallagher, M. (1980) *Unequal Opportunities* (Paris: UNESCO).

Galtung, J. and M. Ruge (1981) 'Structuring and selecting news', in S. Cohen and J. Young (eds), *The Manufacture of News* (London: Constable).

Garnham, N. (1986) 'The Media and the Public Sphere', in P. Golding and G. Murdock (eds), *Communicating Politics* (Leicester: Leicester University Press).

Gauntlett, D. (1995) *A Profile of Complainants and their Complaints* (London: Broadcasting Standards Council).

Gauntlett, D. (1995) *Moving Experiences: Understanding television's influences and effects*, Academia Research monograph 13 (London: J. Libbey).

Geraghty, C. (1983) '*Brookside* – No Common Ground', *Screen*, vol. 24.

Geraghty, C. (1991) *Women and Soap Opera* (Cambridge: Polity Press).

Gerbner, G. (1973) 'Cultural Indicators: The Third Voice', in G. Gerbner, L. Gross and W. Melody (eds), *Communications Technology and Social Policy* (New York: Wiley).

Gerbner, G. and L. Gross (1980) 'The Violent Face of Television and its Lessons', in E. Palmer and A. Dorr (eds), *Children and the Faces of Television: Teaching, Violence, Selling* (New York: Academic Press).

Giddens, A. (1990) *The Consequences of Modernity* (Cambridge: Polity).

Giddens, A. (1994) 'Living in a Post-Traditional Society', in Ulrich Beck, Anthony Giddens and Scott Lash, *Reflexive Modernity* (Cambridge: Polity).

Giddens, A. (1995) 'The far side of modernity', *Social Science Teacher*, vol. 25, no. 3.

Giddens, A. (1997) *Sociology*, 3rd edn (Cambridge: Polity Press).

Gill, R. (1988) 'Altered Images', *Social Studies Review*, vol. 4, no. 1.

Golding, P. (1974) *The Mass Media* (London: Longman).

Golding, P. (1993) Inaugural Lecture, Loughborough University.

Golding, P. and G. Murdock (1991) 'Culture, Communication and Political Economy', in J. Curran and M. Gurevitch (eds), *Mass Media and Society* (London: Edward Arnold).

Goode, E. and N. Ben-Yehuda (1994) *Moral Panics: The Social Construction of Deviance* (Oxford: Blackwell).

Gramsci, A. (1971) *Selections from the Prison Notebooks* (London: Lawrence & Wishart).

Gray, A. (1987) 'Women and Video', in H. Baehr and G. Dyer (eds), *Boxed In: Women On and In Television* (London: Routledge and Kegan Paul).

Gray, A. (1992) *Video Playtime: The Gendering of a Leisure Technology* (London: Routledge).

Grice, A. (1996) 'The Election: Runners and Riders', *Campaign*, 15 November.

GUMG (1976) *Bad News* (London: Routledge).

GUMG (1980) *More Bad News* (London: Routledge).

GUMG (1982) *Really Bad News* (London: Writers and Readers).

GUMG (1985) *War and Peace News* (Milton Keynes: Open University Press).

Gunter, B. (1995) *Television and Gender Representation* (London: John Libbey).

Hagell, A. and T. Newburn (1994) *Young Offenders and the Media: Viewing habits and preferences* (London: PSI).

Hall, S. (1975) 'The "structured communication" of events', in UNESCO, *Getting the Message Across* (Paris: UNESCO).

Hall, S. (1980) 'Encoding and decoding', (revised extract) in S. Hall *et al.*, *Culture, Media and Language* (London: Hutchinson).

Hall, S. (1981) 'The Whites of their Eyes: Racist Ideologies and the Media', in G. Bridges and R. Brunt, *Silver Linings: Some Strategies for the Eighties* (London: Lawrence & Wishart).

Hall, S. (1982) 'The Rediscovery of Ideology: Return of the Repressed in Media Studies', in M. Gurevitch, T. Bennett, J. Curran and J. Woollacott (eds), *Culture, Society and the Media* (London and New York: Routledge).

Hall, S. and C. Critcher, T. Jefferson, J. Clarke, B. Roberts (1978) *Policing the Crisis: Mugging, the State, and Law and Order* (London: Macmillan).

Halloran, J. D. (1964) 'The Effects of Mass Communication, with Special Reference to Television, Television Research Committee', Working Paper no. 1 (Leicester: Leicester University Press).

Halloran, J. D. (1970) *Mass Media in Society: The Need for research*, reports and papers on mass communication, no. 59 (Paris: UNESCO).

Halloran, J. D. (1990) 'Mass Media and Violence', in R. Bluglass and P. Bowden (eds), *Principles and Practice of Forensic Psychiatry* (New York: Churchill-Livingstone).

Halloran, J. D. (1995) 'The Context of Mass Communication Research', in Boyd-Barrett and Newbold.

Hamelink, C. (1983) *Cultural Autonomy in Global Communications* (New York: Longman).

Hamelink, C. J. (1995) 'Information Imbalance Across the Globe', in J. Downing, A. Mohammadi and A. Sreberny-Mohammadi, *Questioning The Media: A Critical Introduction*, 2nd edn (London: Sage).

Haralambos, M. and M. Holborn (1995) *Sociology: Themes and Perspectives*, 4th edn (London: Collins Educational).

Haraway, D. (1980) 'A Manifesto for Cyborgs: Science, Technology and Socialist Feminism in the 1980s', *Socialist Review*, vol. 15.

Hartmann, P. and C. Husband (1974) *Racism and the Mass Media* (London: Davis-Poynter).

Harvey, D. (1989) *The Condition of Postmodernity* (Oxford: Basil Blackwell).

Hearn, J. and D. H. J. Morgan (1990) 'Men, Masculinities and Social Theory', in J. Hearn and D. H. J. Morgan (eds), *Men, Masculinities and Social Theory* (London: Unwin Hyman).

Herman, E. S. and N. Chomsky (1988) *Manufacturing Consent: The Political Economy of the Mass Media* (New York: Pantheon).

Himmelweit, H., P. Humphreys and M. Jaeger (1985) *How Voters Decide* (Milton Keynes: Open University Press).

Hobson, D. (1982) *Crossroads: The Drama of a Soap Opera* (London: Methuen).

Hodge, R. and D. Tripp (1986) *Children and Television: A Semiotic Approach* (Cambridge: Polity).

Hoggart, R. (1958) *The Uses of Literacy* (Harmondsworth: Penguin).

Horkheimer, M. and T. Adorno (1973) *Dialectic of Enlightenment* (London: Allen Lane).

IBA Yearbook (1987).

Jameson, F. (1991) *Postmodernism* (London and New York: Verso).

Jenkins, P. (1992) *Intimate Enemies: Moral Panics in Contemporary Britain* (New York: Aldine de Gruyter).

Johnson, P. (1964) 'The Menace of Beatleism', *New Statesman*, 28 February.

Johnston, P. (1994) 'MPs want a ban on horror for hire', *Daily Telegraph*, 1 April.

Jones, A. (1993) 'Defending the Border: Men's Bodies and Vulnerability', *Cultural Studies from Birmingham*, no 2.

Jones, A. (1997) 'Special agents: Gender, Rationality and Visual Pleasure in the X-Files', *Sociology Review*, vol. 7, no. 1.

Jones, M. (1997) 'Masculinity Revisited', *Sociology Review*, vol. 7, no. 3.

Jones, M. and J. Dungey (1983) *Ethnic Minorities and Television* (Leicester: Centre for Mass Communication Research, University of Leicester).

Jones, M. and M. Jones (1996) 'Techno-Primitives: British television science fiction and the "grammar of race"', *Sociology Review*, vol. 5, no. 3.

Jones, P. (1993) *Studying Society: Sociological Theories and Research Practices* (London: Collins Educational).

Katz, E. and P. Lazarsfeld (1955) *Personal Influence* (New York: Free Press).

Kelly, A. (1987) *Science for Girls* (Milton Keynes: Open University Press).

Kershaw, J. (1980) Lecture to UK Association Conference for the International Year of the Child.

Kirby, M. (1996) *Investigating Political Sociology* (London: Collins Educational).

Kitzinger, C. and P. Skidmore (1994) 'Playing safe: media coverage of child sexual abuse prevention strategies', *Child Abuse Review*, vol. 3, no. 4.

Klapper, J. (1960) *The Effects of Mass Communication* (New York: Free Press).

La Fontaine, J. (1994) *The Extent and Nature of Organised Ritual Abuse: Research Findings* (London: HMSO).

Lawson, T. and J. Garrod (1996) *The Complete A-Z Sociology Handbook* (Sevenoaks: Hodder and Stoughton).

Lang, K. and G. E. Lang (1966) 'The Mass Media and Voting', in B. Berelson and M. Janovitch (eds), *Reader in Public Opinion and Communication*, 2nd edn (New York: Free Press).

Lazarsfeld, P., B. Berelson and H. Gaudet (1948) *The People's Choice* (New York: Columbia University Press).

Lazier, L. and A. Gagnard Kendrick (1993) 'Women in Advertisements: Sizing up the Images, Roles and Functions', in P. J. Creedon, *Women in Mass Communication*, 2nd edn (London: Sage).

Lea, J. and J. Young (1993) *What is to be Done about Law and Order?* (London and Boulder, Colorado: Pluto Press).

Leavis, F. R. and D. Thompson (1933) *Culture and Environment* (London: Chatto and Windus).

Leman, J. (1991) 'Wise scientists and female androids: class and gender in science fiction', in J. Cerner (ed.), *Popular Television in Britain: Studies in Cultural History* (London: DFI).

Lewis, J. (1991) *The Ideological Octopus: An Exploration of Television and its Audience* (New York and London: Routledge).

Linné, O. (1995) 'Media Violence Research in Scandinavia', *Nordicom-Information*, nos. 3–4.

Linné, O. and M. Jones (1998) 'The Single Parent as Folk Devil' (work in progress).

Lippmann, W. (1956) *Public Opinion* (New York: Methuen).

Lobban, G. (1974) 'Data report on British reading schemes', *The Times Educational Supplement*, 1 March.

Lowery, S. A. and M. L. De Fleur (1988) *Milestones in Mass Communication Research*, 2nd edn (Harlow: Longman).

Lull, J. (ed.) (1988) *World Families Watch Television* (Newbury Park and London: Sage).

Lull, J. and R. Wallis (1992) 'The Beat of Vietnam', in J. Lull (ed.), *Popular Music and Communication* (Newbury Park, CA, and London: Sage).

Lyotard, J.-F. (1984) *The Postmodern Condition: A Report on Knowledge* (University of Minnesota Press).

MacDonald, D. (1957) 'A Theory of Mass Culture', in B. Rosenberg and D. White (eds), *Mass Culture* (Glencoe, Ill.: Free Press).

Marsh, D. (1985) 'Politics', *Developments in Sociology*, vol. 1.

Marshall, G. (1987) 'Whatever happened to the working class?', *Social Studies Review*, vol. 2, no. 3.

Massey, D. (1993) 'Power-geometry and a progressive sense of place', in J. Bird *et al.* (eds), *Mapping the Future: Local Cultures, Global Change* (London: Routledge).

McCombs, M. E. and D. L. Shaw (1973) 'The Evolution of Agenda-Setting Theory: 25 Years in the Market Place of Ideas', *Journal of Communication*, vol. 43, no. 2.

McQuail, D. (1994) *Mass Communication Theory, an introduction*, 3rd edn (London: Sage).

McLuhan, M. (1964) *Understanding Media* (London: First Sphere Books).

McRobbie, A. (1991) *Feminism and Youth Culture: From Jackie to Just Seventeen* (London: Macmillan).

McRobbie, A. (1996) 'More!: New sexualities in Girls' and Women's Magazines', in J. Curran, D. Morley and V. Walkerdine (eds), *Cultural Studies and Communications* (London and New York: Arnold).

Meehan, D. M. (1983) *Ladies of the Evening* (New York: Scarecrow Press).

Mercer, K. (1994) *Welcome to the Jungle: New Positions in Black Cultural Studies* (London: Routledge).

Miliband, R. (1973) *The State in Capitalist Society* (London: Quartet Books).

Miller, D. L. (1985) *An Introduction to Collective Behavior* (Belmont, California: Wadsworth).

Miller, D. and G. Philo (1996) 'Against Orthodoxy: The Media Do Influence Us', *Sight and Sound*, vol. 12.

Miller, D. L. (1985) *An Introduction to Collective Behaviour* (Belmont, CA: Wadsworth).

Mitchell, A. (1990/91) 'Televising the House', *Talking Politics*, vol. 3, no. 2 (Winter).

Modleski, T. (1982) 'The Search for Tomorrow in Today's Soap Operas', in *Loving with a Vengeance* (New York: Methuen).

Morgan, D. H. J. (1994) *Developments in Sociology* vol. 10 (Ormskirk: Causeway Press).

Morley, D. (1980) *The 'Nationwide' Audience* (London: British Film Institute).

Morley, D. (1986) *Family Television: Cultural Power and Domestic Leisure* (London: Comedia)

Mosca, G. (1939) *The Ruling Class* (New York: McGraw-Hill).

Mulvey, L. (1975) 'Visual Pleasure and Narrative Cinema', *Screen*, vol. 16, no. 3.

Muncie, J. (1987) 'Much Ado About Nothing?: The Sociology of Moral Panics', *Social Studies Review*, vol. 3, no. 2.

Murdock, G. (1990) 'Large corporations and the control of the communications industries', in M. Gurevitch, T. Bennett, J. Curran and J. Woollacott (eds), *Culture, Society and the Media* (London and New York: Routledge).

Murdock, G. and R. McCron (1979) 'The Television and Delinquency Debate', *Screen Education*, vol. 30 (Spring).

National Viewers and Listeners Association (1994) *A Culture of Cruelty and Violence* (London: NVLA).

Negrine, R. (1989) *Politics and the Mass Media in Britain* (London: Routledge).

Negrine, R. (1996) *The Communication of Politics* (London: Sage).

Negroponte, N. (1995) *Being Digital* (London: Hodder and Stoughton).

Neuman, W. R., M. Just and A. Crigler (1992) *Common Knowledge* (Chicago, Ill.: University of Chicago Press).

Newburn, T. and A. Hagell (1995) 'Violence on Screen', *Sociology Review*, vol. 4, no. 3.

Newson, E. (1994) 'Video violence and the protection of children', *Psychology Review*, vol. 1, no. 2.

Newton, K. (1990) 'Making news: The Mass Media in Britain', *Social Studies Review*, vol. 6, no. 1.

Nixon, S. (1996) *Hard Looks: Masculinities, Spectatorship and Contemporary Consumption* (London: UCL).

Noble, G. (1975) *Children in Front of the Small Screen* (London: Constable).

Oakley, A. (1982) *Subject Woman* (London: Fontana).

Ohmae, K. (1991) 'Global Consumers Want Sony, Not Soil', *New Perspectives*, Autumn (USA).

O'Sullivan, T., B. Dutton and P. Rayner (1994) *Studying the Media: an introduction* (London: Edward Arnold).

O'Sullivan, T., J. Hartley, D. Saunders and J. Fiske (1995) *Key Concepts in Communication* (London: Methuen).

Pahl, R. and J. Winkler (1974) 'The Economic Elite: Theory and Practice', in P. Stanworth and A. Giddens (eds), *Elites and Power in British Society* (Cambridge: Cambridge University Press).

Pareto, V. (1963) *A Treatise on General Sociology*, ed A. Livingstone (New York: Dover Publications).

Parsons, T. (1992) 'The Tattooed Jungle', ITV.

Peak, S. and P. Fisher (1996) *The Media Guide 1997* (London: Fourth Estate).

Perkins, T. (1979) 'Rethinking Stereotypes', in M. Barrett, P. Corrigan, A. Kuhn and V. Wolff (eds), *Ideology and Cultural Production* (London: Croom Helm).

Philo, G. (1990) *Seeing and Believing* (London: Routledge).

Pines, J. (ed.) (1992) *Black and White in Colour: Black People in British Television since 1936* (London: BFI).

Postman, N. (1985) *The Disappearance of Childhood: How TV is Changing Children's Lives* (London: Comet).

Price, S. (1993) *Media Studies* (London: Pitman Publishing).

Probyn, E. (1992) 'Theorizing Through the Body', in L. F. Rakow (ed.), *Women Making Meaning: New Feminist Directions in Communication* (New York: Routledge).

Ritzer, G. (1993) *The McDonaldization of Society* (Thousand Oaks: Pine Forge).

Robins, K. (1997) 'What is Globalisation?', *Sociology Review*, vol. 6, no. 3.

Rock, P. (1981) 'News as eternal recurrence', in S. Cohen and J. Young (eds), *The Manufacture of News* (London: Constable).

Root, J. (1986) *Open the Box* (London: Comedia).

Rutherford, J. (1988) 'Who's that Man?', in R. Chapman and J. Rutherford (eds), *Male Order: Unwrapping Masculinity* (London: Lawrence and Wishart).

Sanderson, T. (1995) 'Out and about', *Guardian*, 12 June.

Schlesinger, P. (1987) *Putting 'Reality' Together* (London: Methuen).

Seidman, S. (1994) *Contested Knowledge: Social Theory in the Postmodern Era* (Cambridge, Mass.: Blackwell).

Sepstrup, P. (1989) 'Research into International TV Flows', *European Journal of Communication*, vol. 4, no. 4, pp. 393–408.

Seymour-Ure, C. (1974) *The Political Impact of Mass Media* (London: Constable).

Seymour-Ure, C. (1991) *The British Press and Broadcasting since 1945* (Oxford: Basil Blackwell).

Sherman, B. L. and J. R. Dominick (1986) 'Violence and sex in music videos: TV and rock in roll', *Journal of Communication*, vol. 36.

Shulman, M. (1973) *The Ravenous Eye* (London: Cassell).

Signorelli, N. and M. Morgan (eds) (1990) *Cultivation Analysis* (California and London: Sage).

Silverstein, B., L. Perdue, B. Peterson and E. Kelly (1986) 'The Role of the Mass Media in Promoting a Thin Standard of Bodily Attractiveness for Women', *Sex Roles*, vol. 14 (9/10).

Simpson, A. (1985) 'Charity begins at Home', *Ten-8*, no. 19 (Birmingham).

Skeggs, B. and J. Mundy (1992) *Mass Media Issues in Sociology* (London: Macmillan).

Skidmore, P. (1995) 'Just another moral panic? Media reporting of child sexual abuse', *Sociology Review*, vol. 4, no. 4.

Sklair, L. (1993) 'Going Global: Competing Models of Globalisation', *Sociology Review*, vol. 3, no. 2.

Smith, A. D. (1990) 'Towards a Global Culture', *Theory, Culture and Society*, vol. 7, nos 2/3, pp. 171–91.

Spender, D. (1983) *Invisible Women: Schooling Scandal* (London: Women's Press).

Spender, D. (1995) *Nattering on the Net: Women, Power and Cyberspace* (London: Spinifex).

Sreberny-Mohammadi, A. (1991) 'The Global and the Local in International Communications', in J. Curran and M. Gurevitch, *Mass Media and Society* (London: Edward Arnold).

Stableford, B. (1987) *The Sociology of Science Fiction* (London: Borgo Press).

Stanworth, M. (1983) *Gender and Schooling* (London: Hutchinson).

Stolz, B. A. (1990) 'Congress and the War on Drugs: An Exercise in Symbolic Politics', paper presented to the at American Society of Criminology, Baltimore, 9 November.

Strinati, D. (1992) 'Postmodernism and popular culture', *Sociology Review*, vol. 1, no. 4.

Strinati, D. (1995) *An Introduction to Theories of Popular Culture* (London and New York: Routledge).

Sugrue, B. and C. Taylor (1996) 'Cultures and Identities', *Sociology Review*, vol. 5, no. 3.

Sugrue, B. and C. Taylor (1996) 'From Marx to Man. City: Sociology and popular culture', *Sociology Review*, vol. 6, no. 1.

Tellenbach, M. (1992) *Cable and Satellite Europe*, no. 106.

Thomsen, C. W. (ed.) (1989) *Cultural Transfer or Electronic Imperialism* (Heidelberg: Carl Winter Universitatsverlag).

Thoveron, G. (1986) 'European Televised Women', *European Journal of Communication*, vol. 1, no. 3.

Tini Fox, D. (1993) 'Honouring the Treaty', in Dowmunt (1993).

Trowler, P. (1996) *Investigating Mass Media*, 2nd edn (London: Collins Educational).

Troyna, B. (1981) *Public Awareness and the Media: A Study of Reporting on Race* (London: Commission for Racial Equality).

Tuchman, G. and A. Kaplan Daniels, J. Benét (eds) (1978) *Hearth and Home: Images of Women in the Mass Media* (New York: Oxford University Press).

Tunstall, J. and M. Palmer (1991) *Media Moguls* (London: Routledge).

Turkle, S. (1988) 'Computational reticence', in C. Kramarae (ed.), *Technology and Women's Voices* (London: Routledge).

van Djik, T. A. (1991) *Racism in the Press* (London: Routledge).

van Zoonen, L. (1991) 'Feminist Perspectives on the Media', in J. Curran and M. Gurevitch (eds), *Mass Media And Society* (London and New York: Edward Arnold).

Vernon, J. A., J. A. Williams Jr, T. Phillips and J. Wilson (1990) 'Media stereotyping: a comparison of the way elderly women and men are portrayed on prime-time television', *Journal of Women and Ageing*, vol. 2, no. 4, pp. 55–68.

Vincent, R. C. (1989) 'Clio's Consciousness Raised? Portrayal of Women in Rock Videos Re-examined', *Journalism Quarterly*, vol. 66.

Vincent, R. C., K. Davis and L. Boruszkowski (1987) 'Sexism on MTV: The Portrayal of Women in Rock Videos', *Journalism Quarterly*, vol. 64.

von Feilitzen, C. (1994) 'Media Violence – Research Perspectives in the 1980s', in O. Linné and C. J. Hamelink (eds), *Mass Communication Research: On Problems and Policies: The Art of Asking the Right Questions* (Norwood, NJ: Ablex Publishing).

Wagg, S. (1992) 'I Blame the Parents: Childhood and Politics in Modern Britain, *Sociology Review*, vol. 1, no. 4.

Wagg, S. (1994) *Developments in Politics*, vol. 5 (Ormskirk: Causeway Press).

Wagg, S. (1995) 'The Business of America: Reflections on the World Cup', in S. Wagg (ed.), *Giving The Game Away: Football Politics and Culture on Five Continents* (London: Leicester University Press).

Walker, J. A. (1994) *Art in the Age of Mass Media* (London: Pluto).

Waters, M. (1995) *Globalisation: Key Idea* (London and New York: Routledge).

Welsh, I. (1997) 'Power and Globalisation', *Developments in Sociology*, vol. 13.

Whale, J. (1997) *The Politics of the Media* (London: Fontana).

Whannel, G. and J. Williams (1993) 'The Rise of Satellite Television', *Sociology Review*, vol. 2, no. 3.

Williams, R. (1963) *Culture and Society 1780–1950* (Harmondsworth: Penguin).

Williams, R. (1974) *Television, Technology and Cultural Form* (London: Collins).

Williamson, J. (1978) *Decoding Advertisements: Ideology and Meaning in Advertising* (London: Marion Boyars).

Winn, M. (1985) *The Plug-In Drug* (Harmondsworth: Penguin).

Winship, J. (1987) *Inside Women's Magazines* (London and New York: Pandora).

Wober, M. (1978) 'Televised Violence and Paranoid Perception: The View from Great Britain', *Public Opinion Quarterly*, vol. 42, no. 3, pp. 315–21.

Wober, M. and B. Gunter (1982) 'Television and Personal Threat: Fact or Artifact? A British View', *British Journal of Social Psychology*, vol. 21, pp. 43–51.

Wolf, N. (1990) *The Beauty Myth* (London: Vintage).

Wood, J. (1993) 'Repeatable Pleasures: Notes on Young People's Use of Video', in D. Buckingham (ed.), *Reading Audiences: Young People and the Media* (Manchester: Manchester University Press).

Woodford, S. (1982) 'Race on TV-switching channels?', in P. Cohen and C. Gardner (eds), *It ain't Half Racist, Mum: Fighting racism in the Media* (London: Comedia Publishing Group and Campaign Against Racism in the Media).

Woodhams, S. (1993) 'Signs of the Times? An Introduction to Semiology', *Sociology Review*, vol. 2, no. 4.

Yadava, J. S. and U. V. Reddi (1988) 'In the Midst of Diversity: Television in urban Indian Homes', in J. Lull.

Young, J. (1971) 'The role of the police as amplifiers of deviance, negotiators of drug control, as seen in Notting Hill', in S. Cohen (ed.), *Images of Deviance* (Harmondsworth: Penguin).

Author Index

Abbott, P. 115
Abu-Lughod, L. 230
Adorno, T. 78–80
Allan, P. 213
Althusser, Louis 37–8, 44, 62
Alvarado, M. 122, 125, 129, 132, 136–8
Ang, I. 118, 168
Axford, B. 197–8

Back, L. 127–8
Bandura, A. 159–60, 179
Barker, M. 173, 185
Barnard, Steve 28–9
Barratt, D. 105
Batty, P. 229
Baudrillard, J. 73
Behl, Neena 228–9
Bell, E. 239
Bellos, A. 113
Belsey, A. 215
Belson, W. 181, 183
Ben-Yehuda, N. 142–4, 148, 153–4
Berelson, B. 157
Berger, J. 110
Berkowitz, L. 179
Bevan, Aneurin 206
Bilton, T. 218
Blumler, J. 193
Boyd-Barrett, O. 93, 224
Branston, G. 21, 57, 104, 172, 174, 231, 234
Bretl, D. 111
Brown, J. D. 112
Browne, Jackson 87
Browne, K. 189
Bruch, H. 114
Brundson, C. 118
Buckingham, D. 119, 168, 174, 182–3, 185, 187

Campbell, K. 112
Cantor, J. 111
Cantril, H. 159
Cashmore, E. 121, 123
Centre for Contemporary Cultural Studies 107
Chibnall, S. 99
Clarke, J. 147

Cohen, Stanley 142
Connell, R. W. 201
Cottle, Simon 100
Coward, Rosalind 69, 114
Crace, J. 89, 94
Cumberpatch, G. 111–12, 179
Curran, J. 17, 25, 131

Davis, Hannah 230
De Fleur, M. L. 158–9, 192
Dennis, N. 149
Denscombe, M. 33, 48, 56, 195
Dominick, J. R. 111, 112
Dowmunt, T. 226
Dungey, J. 121
Dworkin, A. 67
Dyer, R. 133–5

Edwards, S. E. 128
Elliott, P. 98, 100
Evans, H. 52

Ferguson, Marjorie 69
Feshbach, S. 179
Fisher, P. 11, 12, 35
Fiske, John 41, 84
Franklin, R. 208, 210–11
Freeth, Tony 121, 131

Gallagher, Margaret 110
Galtung, J. 90–1, 99
Garnham, N. 237
Garrod, J. 135, 145, 176, 189, 202
Gauntlett, David 175, 215
Geraghty, C. 118–19
Gerbner, G. 164, 167, 180
Giddens, A. 218, 220, 227, 233, 237
Gill, Ros 107
Glasgow University Media Group 44–5, 62, 94, 99, 101, 122, 186
Golding, P. 17, 25, 51, 189
Goode, E. 142–3, 148, 153–4
Gramsci, Antonio 42–4, 54, 62, 67
Gray, A. 118–19, 169
Greenslade, Roy 52
Grice, A. 197

Gunter, B.   181

Hagell, A.   184, 186
Hall, S.   55, 62, 94–5, 98, 122–6,
    131, 146, 153, 155, 168
Halloran, J. D.   163, 180
Hamelink, C.   225, 231
Hammersley, Martin   170
Haralambos, M.   83
Haraway, D.   68
Hartmann, Paul   129
Harvey, D.   75–6
Hearn, J.   116
Hebdige, D.   171
Himmelweit, H.   201
Hobson, D.   168
Hodge, R.   185
Hoggart, Richard   82
Horkheimer, M.   78
Husband, Charles   129

Jameson, F.   73
Jenkins, P.   154
Jones, Andy   116, 118
Jones, Marsha   120, 121, 126, 151
Jones, Matthew   126
Jones, P.   77

Katz, E.   161
Kelly, E.   115
Kendrick, A. Gagnard   112
Kershaw, J.   148
Kirby, M.   220
Kitzinger, C.   94, 147
Klapper, J.   180

La Fontaine, Jean   148
Lang, J. E.   93
Lang, K.   93
Lawson, T.   135, 145, 176, 189,
    202
Lazarsfeld, P.   161, 192
Lazier, L.   112
Lea, J.   165
Leavis, F. R.   82
Leman, J.   124
Lewis, J.   168
Linné, O.   151, 185
Lippmann, Walter   106
Lowery, S. A.   158–9, 192
Lull, J.   231
Lyotard, F.   73

MacDonald, D.   81
Marcuse, H.   78–80
Massey, D.   225
McCombs, M. E.   93
McCron. R.   174
McLuhan, Marshall   4, 76
McQuail, D.   51, 55, 82, 84, 93,
    100, 162, 193
McRobbie, A.   69–72
Meehan, D. M.   109
Miliband, Ralph   37–8, 47
Miller, D.   146, 186
Mitchell, A.   206
Modleski, T.   119
Morgan, D. H. J.   116, 150
Morgan, M.   165
Morley, D.   120, 168–9, 187
Mosca, Gaetano   83
Mulvey, L.   110
Muncie, J.   145–6
Mundy, J.   174
Murdock, G.   17, 40, 51, 52, 97,
    174

Negrine, R.   54,193–4, 200–1
Negroponte, N.   235
Neuman, W. R.   200–1
Newbold, C.   93
Newburn, T.   184, 186
Newson, Elizabeth   184–5
Newton, K.   189–90, 209
Noble, G.   160

Oakley, A.   116
Ohmae, K.   218
O'Sullivan, T.   27, 32, 105, 116

Pahl, R.   51
Palmer, M.   19
Pareto, Vilfredo   83
Parsons, Tony   83–4
Peak, S. and Fisher, P.   11, 12, 35
Peirce, Charles   170
Perdue, L.   115
Perkins, T.   105
Peterson, B.   115
Philo, Greg   122, 186
Postman, N.   177
Price, S.   171
Probyn, E.   114

Quaade, V.   127–8

Rauch, G.   111
Reddi, U. V.   228–9
Ritzer, G.   222
Robins, K.   231
Rock, P.   98
Root, J.   114
Ruge, M.   90–1, 99
Rutherford, J.   116–17

Sanderson, T.   133
Saussure, Ferdinand de   170
Schlesinger, P.   98
Seaton, J.   17, 25
Seidman, S.   68, 73

Sepstrup, P.   226
Seymore-Ure, C.   18, 20, 25, 26,
     207–8, 212
Shaw, D. L.   93
Sherman, B. L.   112
Shulman, M.   175
Signorelli, N.   165
Silverstein, B. L.   114–15
Simpson, A.   132
Singer, R. D.   179
Skeggs, B.   174
Skidmore, P.   94, 147, 154
Sklair, L.   221
Smith, A. D.   226
Spender, D.   233
Sreberny-Mohammadi, A.   226–7,
     230
Stableford, B.   126
Stafford, R.   21, 57, 104, 172, 174,
     231, 234
Stolz, B. A.   153
Strinati, D.   73–4, 79–81
Sugrue, B.   74, 81

Taylor, C.   74, 81
Thompson, D.   82
Thoveron, G.   111
Tini Fox, Derek   230
Tripp, D.   185
Trowler, P.   95, 13, 45
Troyna, B.   121, 123, 129
Tuchman, G.   65, 109, 133,
     137

Tunstall, J.   19
Turkle, S.   119

van Dijk, T. A.   129–31
van Zoonen, L.   65–6
Vernon, J. A.   136
Vincent, R. C.   112
von Feilitzen, C.   184–5

Wagg, S.   49, 150, 174, 189, 208,
     224
Walker, J. A.   74
Wallace, C.   68, 115
Wallis, R.   231
Walters, R.   179
Waters, M.   222–3
Welsh, I.   220
Whale, J.   46–7
Whannel, G.   34
Williams, J.   34
Williams, Raymond   82, 237
Williamson, Judith   69
Winkler, J.   51
Winn, M.   177
Winner, Michael   174
Winship, Janice   69
Wober, M.   181
Wood, Julian   183, 187
Woodford, Sue   121
Woodhams, S.   170–1

Yadava, J. S.   228–9
Young, Jock   142, 165

Subject Index

aboriginal culture 229
Advanced Research Projects
Agency 236
Advertising Standards
Authority 197
advertising 3, 10, 38, 197, 65, 70,
75, 110–11, 114, 137, 172, 222,
223
budgets 210
and racism 127–8
revenue from 11, 47
age 8
representation of 135–8
ageism 135
agenda setting 2, 55, 87, 93, 144,
196
allocative control 51
Althusser, Louis 38, 44, 62
'Americanisation' 219
amplification of deviance 142–56
Annan Report (on television)
(1977) 30
apartheid, in South Africa 43
Arena magazine 118
audiences 2, 5, 47, 55, 59, 69, 77,
84, 88–9, 132–3, 157–87, 165,
167
and gender 118
autonomisation 223

Back to Basics campaign 149
Back to the Future (film) 76
Baldwin, Stanley 18
BBC Home Service 26
BBC Light Programme 26
BBC Third Programme 26
Beaverbrook, Lord 17, 190
behaviourist psychology 159
Benetton 127–8
bias, in the news media 77, 87,
91–2, 189
Bill, The (TV programme) 167
Blade Runner (film) 76
Blair, Tony 20, 43, 195, 199
Blake's Seven (TV
programme) 125
Bliss magazine 70
Blue Peter (TV programme) 132
Bobo doll 159

Border TV 25
Breakfast Television 31
breakfast radio 28
British Broadcasting Company 25
British Broadcasting
Corporation 25, 29–30, 56
British Satellite Broadcasting (TV
company) 33
Broadcasting Act (1990) 27, 214
Broadcasting Act (1996) 35
Broadcasting Bill (1990) 31, 56
Broadcasting Complaints
Commission 31, 215
Broadcasting Standards
Council 31, 215
broadcasting 25–35
BSE, in the press 203
BSkyB (satellite TV company) 21,
33–4, 211, 233
Bulger, James 159, 175–6, 178, 185

Cable Authority 31
Cable News Network (CNN) 239
cable TV 18
camcorders 223
Campbell, Naomi 122
catharsis effect 179
CD Roms 114, 151,185, 195, 210,
219
Central Australian Aboriginal Media
Association 229
Central TV 25
Centre for Contemporary Cultural
Studies 44
child sexual abuse 147–8
Child's Play 3 (horror video) 2,
76, 178, 185
children and politics 200–2
cinema 14
Citizen Kane (film) 19
class dealignment 191
commercial radio 26–9, 38
commodity capitalism 45
commodity fetishism 79
competitive tendering 30
computers 238
and gender 12, 13
consumer sovereignty 30, 49, 55,
59

consumerism 223
Contempt of Court Act 213
content analysis 26, 65,107–8, 118,
    130, 136, 152, 165–7
copycat violence 177, 184
Crawford Report (on radio)
    (1922) 25
crime on television 166–7
Crimewatch UK (TV
    programme) 166–7
cultivation analysis 164–5, 180–1,
    197
cultural capital 41, 77, 80, 84, 170
cultural imperialism 219, 223–7
cultural studies 170
culturalist approaches 99

D Notices 214
Daily Express, The 10, 17, 20,
    52–3, 89, 190, 196
Daily Herald, The 190
Daily Mail, The 10, 17, 89, 196
Daily Mirror, The 10, 17, 18, 19, 89
Daily News, The 190
Daily Record, The 17
Daily Star, The 89
Daily Telegraph, The 10, 18, 21,
    189
Defence Evaluation and Research
    Agency 234
desensitisation 177
desk-top publishing 11
Diana, Princess of Wales 46, 215
'digital corporatism' 13
'digital liberation' 13
digital media 234–6
digital television 34–5, 235
Doctor Who (TV programme) 125
dominant ideology 42, 53, 55
Douglas, Sue 52

eating disorders 113
elderly on television 137–8
electoral stability 191
Ernabella Video Project 229
Esquire magazine 118
ethnic minorities 2
ethnicity and representation 121–3
ethnocentricity 4
ethnography/ethnographic
    approach 168–70, 182–3, 228
European, The 25
Eurosport 39
Everywoman magazine 12, 47, 67

Family Television (book) 168
femininity 69–70
feminism 2, 111
feminist perspectives on the
    media 64–73

feminist theory 107
FHM magazine 118
film 14
'folk devils' 142, 151
franchises (for commercial
    broadcasting) 30–1
Frankfurt School of cultural
    analysis 78–82

gatekeeping 2, 55, 87, 93–4
gay politics 72
gender 168
    and the mass media 64–73
    and media use 14
    and newspapers 11
    and representation 107–8
    and television 108
Glasgow Evening News 17
Glasgow University Media
    Group 44–5, 62
'global village' 4, 76
globalisation 2, 218–40
    and sport 224–5
GQ magazine 118
Gramsci, Antonio 42–4, 54, 62, 67
Guardian, The 10, 21, 195, 196,
    199, 213, 219

Hall, Stuart 62
Harmsworth, Sir Lester 17
Hartmann, Paul 59
Hearst, William Randolph 19
hegemony 41–5, 48, 54–5 ,92, 95,
    131, 138, 203, 222, 227
Hersant, Robert 19
Hollick. Lord 52
Home and Away (TV
    programme) 184
homogenisation 231
homosexuality 133–5
Husband, Charles 59
hybridity 231
hypodermic syringe model 158–61

identity/identities 68, 70, 74, 77,
    84, 221
ideological state apparatus 38, 44
ideology 59, 62, 67
imperialism 224
Independent Broadcasting
    Authority 31
Independent on Sunday 20, 209
Independent Television
    Authority 30
Independent Television
    Commission 31, 235, 239
Independent, The 20, 21
inferential structures 87, 94–6, 123,
    203

information technology   12, 220
instrumentalist analysis of the
    media   40, 45, 48–54, 58–9,
    196
integration, of technologies   222
interactive PCs   223
interactive television   238
Internet, The   12, 13, 114, 128, 174,
    185, 211, 233, 236–8   •

Jackie magazine   69
journalism   47, 49, 54, 59, 89–90,
    96, 212
Juke Box Jury (TV programme)   83

Lawrence, Philip   159
legitimation   53
lesbian feminism   134
libel   213–14
liberal feminism and the mass
    media   65–8, 69
Loaded magazine   118
London Daily News   25
London Evening News   17

Mackenzie, Kelvin   35
magazines   5, 38, 172
  and feminism   12
  men's   12, 115, 118
  women's   113–15
Major, John   20, 149, 209
male bodies   117–18
male gaze   110, 123
Manchester Guardian, The   189
manipulationist view of the
    media   46, 95, 203
marginalisation   55
Marie Claire magazine   70, 71, 72
Martinez, Nathan   178
Marxism   77–8
Marxist theories of the media   21,
    36–45, 56, 62, 92, 203, 219
masculinity   116–18
mass culture debate   63, 78–84
mass media
  in Australia and New
    Zealand   229–30
  and bias   202–6
  and children   172–86
  debate over ownership and
    control   48–59, 91–2, 222
  and democracy   189–91
  diffusion of   223
  diversification of   16–17, 19, 20,
    48–9
  effects of   2, 77, 132, 157–87,
    172–86
  in Egypt and Morocco   230
  and elections   190–6
  feminist perspectives on   64–73

horizontal integration of   16, 18
  in India   228–9
  integration of   16–17, 20
  internationalisation of   16–18, 20,
    48
  ownership of   47, 13, 25, 36–63,
    170, 190, 202
  and political parties   211
  and politics   188–96
  and representation   104–41
  and the state   212–13
  and stereotyping   105–7, 110
  and surveillance
  vertical integration of   16
  and violence   172–86
Maxim magazine   118
Maxwell, Robert   18–19, 25
McDonaldisation   222
media conglomerates   18–19
media imperialism   221, 224
'media moguls'   19–25
'media saturation'   5
mediacentric approach   157–8, 161,
    180
Men's Health magazine   118
metanarratives   73–4
  decline of   76–8
miniaturisation   222
Mirror Group (IPC)   19, 25
modernism   74
moral panics   2, 142–56, 176
  characteristics of   143–6
  theories of   153–4
More! magazine   70, 71, 116
Morning Post   190
MTV   25, 39, 112, 239
Murdoch, Rupert   18–20, 21, 35,
    43, 46, 47, 190, 239
music   5
music videos   112–13

National Science Foundation   236
National Viewers and Listeners
    Association   174
nationalism   221
Natural Born Killers (film)   178
'New Labour'   20, 43, 195, 198–9
New Right   147–8
New Socialist magazine   47
New Society magazine   47
New Statesman magazine   47
'new laddism'   120
new technologies   2, 12, 218–40
news agencies   19, 40
News Corporation   21–3
News International   21, 33–4, 233
news, production of   87–103
News on Sunday   25
News of the World   20, 25
news values   2, 55, 89–90

newspapers 3, 5, 10, 59
  circulation figures 24
  and gender differences 88
  owners/ownership of 3, 24, 202
  political bias of 203
  quality/broadsheet 10, 47, 204
  readership of 10–11, 46, 88–9
  tabloid 10, 47, 159, 196, 213
  and voting 195–200
Newsround (TV programme) 132
Nolan Committee (on standards in
  public life) 210
Northcliffe, Lord 17

observational learning effect 179
Official Secrets Act 212–13
one-parent families 148–50
operational control 51
opinion leaders 161–2, 192
opinion polls 199–200
ownership of mass media 16–19

'Pacific Rim' countries 4
partisan alignment 191
party political broadcasts 193–4,
  196
patriarchy 66
Peacock Report (on the BBC)
  (1986) 30
Penny Dreadfuls 173
People's Choice, The (book) 192
Personal Influence (book) 161
personal computers 18–19
personalisation 222
Pilkington Report (on commercial
  television) (1960) 30
pluralist theories of the media 21,
  25, 34, 45–48, 56, 58–9, 62, 92,
  95, 131, 203
political economy 51, 97, 100
politics and the mass media 188–96
popular culture 75, 84
pornography 66, 174
Post, The 20, 25
postmodern feminism and the mass
  media 68–73
postmodernism 2, 73–8, 84, 128
press barons 17, 19
Press Council 214
Prevention of Terrorism Act 212
privacy laws 215
proprietorial control 53
public service broadcasting 26
Pulp Fiction (film) 76

quiz programmes 41

race, grammar of 124
racism, 123, 129
  and advertising 127

radical feminism and the mass
  media 66–8
Radio Authority 31
Radio Caroline 27
Radio Times 9
radio 5, 26–9
  audiences 27
reception analysis 118, 158, 162,
  167, 182–3, 200
Reed International Group 19
reinforcement effect 180
reinforcement theory 107, 163, 169
Reith, John 25
relativism 77
representation 2, 172
  age 135–8
  ethnicity 121–3
  men 115–18
  sexuality 133–5
research methods 8
Rothermere, Lord 17, 190

satellite broadcasting 18, 19, 221
satellite television 33–4, 201, 223
Scott Inquiry 213
selective exposure 56
selective perception 56
selective retention 56
semiology 67, 108, 170–2
sex, sexuality 70–3
  representations of 133–5
Shah, Eddie 20, 25, 239
simulacra 73
situation comedies 131, 138
Sky (satellite broadcasting
  company) 20
Sky Channel (satellite TV) 233
sleaze 209
soap operas 65, 109, 118, 138, 184
social class 10, 11
socialist feminism and the mass
  media 68, 69
Spare Rib magazine 12, 47, 67
Spice Girls, The 113
spin doctors 208
sponsorship 39
Springer, Axel 19
Spycatcher incident 213
stereotypes 132
stimulation effect 179
structuralist Marxist analysis of the
  media 42–5, 54–5, 58
Sugar magazine 116
Sun, The 10, 18, 20, 46, 88, 96,
  190, 195, 196, 198
Sunday Correspondent, The 20,
  25
Sunday Express, The 52
Sunday Mail 17

Sunday Pictorial 17
Sunday Sport 20
Sunday Times, The 20, 196
superwaifs 114
symbolic annihilation 109, 133, 137

Tattooed Jungle, The (TV documentary) 83
techno primitives 124
television 3, 5
  crime on 166–7
  gender 108
  news 92–4
  ownership of 7
  in parliament 206–7
  and political bias 204–6
  viewing figures 9
Terminator 2 (film) 184
Thatcher, Margaret 20, 43, 52, 149, 220
Times, The 10, 17, 20–1, 52, 189, 195, 219
Tisdall, Sarah 212
Today (newspaper) 20, 25
transculturation 231
transnational corporations 222, 225
TV zombies 177
Twelve Monkeys (film) 76
Twentieth Century Fox 20
two-step flow hypothesis 161–2, 192

uses and gratifications approach 162–4

V-chip 174
video 169
  cassette recorders 223, 230
  games 119
  'nasties' 2, 174
  ownership of 7
  recording 18
videos 201
Virago Press 67
Viva (radio station) 67

Wapping dispute 20
War of Jennifer's Ear (news story) 194, 196
War of the Worlds (film) 146, 154
Weekly Dispatch 17
Whitehouse, Mary 174
women and technology 119–10
Women's Press 67
women's magazines 66, 68–73
women, body image of in the media 113
women, portrayal of in the media 3
World Wide Web 238
Wright, Peter 213

youth groups 171
youth market 26